Other Books by
ROBERT GITTINGS

Biography and Criticism

Young Thomas Hardy
John Keats
John Keats: The Living Year
The Odes of Keats
The Mask of Keats
The Keats Inheritance
Shakespeare's Rival
The Living Shakespeare (editor)

Plays and Poems

Collected Poems
The Makers of Violence
Out of this Wood
Wentworth Place
Famous Meeting
The Tower my Prison
Matters of Love and Death
Conflict at Canterbury

Thomas Hardy's
Later Years

Thomas Hardy in old age, sketch by Augustus John

Thomas Hardy's Later Years

by ROBERT GITTINGS

MECHANICS' INSTITUTE

An Atlantic Monthly Press Book

LITTLE, BROWN AND COMPANY · BOSTON · TORONTO

FIRST AMERICAN EDITION

T 04/78

LIBRARY OF CONGRESS CATALOGING IN PUBLICATION DATA

Gittings, Robert.
  Thomas Hardy's later years.

  "An Atlantic Monthly Press book."
  Bibliography: p.
  Includes index.
  1. Hardy, Thomas, 1840–1928—Biography. 2. Authors,
English—20th century—Biography. I. Title.
PR4753.G49   823'.8 [B]   77-19236
ISBN 0-316-31454-4

ATLANTIC–LITTLE, BROWN BOOKS
ARE PUBLISHED BY
LITTLE, BROWN AND COMPANY
IN ASSOCIATION WITH
THE ATLANTIC MONTHLY PRESS

Contents

Illustrations

Frontispiece

Thomas Hardy in old age, sketch by Augustus John

Following Page 84

Following Page 100

Following Page 148

Reproduced by permission of the Dorset County Museum, except for the frontispiece, 1 and 2, 3a, 3c, 3d, 4d, 7, 13, 15, which are by permission of James Gibson, Victoria and Albert Museum (Theatre Museum), Radio Times Hulton Picture Post Library, Macmillan, Desmond Hawkins, Miss K. M. E. Murray, Tate Gallery, Mrs. Gertrude Bugler, and Norman Atkins respectively.

To my wife

Acknowledgements

THOMAS HARDY seems to have spent scarcely a single day when he did not have a pen in hand, whether to compose a novel or a story, draft or polish a poem, copy and comment on a passage from his reading, make notes in his commonplace book on every conceivable topic, undertake countless revisions for fresh editions of his work, and, all the time, to write tens of thousands of letters, personal, practical, or purely business. No one can claim to have read all that his meticulous classical script committed to paper. That I have been able to tackle even a portion of it has been due, in the first place, to the generous award of a Research Fellowship from the Leverhulme Trust Fund. The expenses of travel and transcription could not possibly have been faced without this grant.

Secondly, I could not have hoped to handle such material without a willing, skilful and informed helper. My research assistant has been my wife, Jo Manton, a biographer in her own right. Her accurate appreciation of sources and her historical acumen have led to many of the new and better insights into Hardy's life that this book may possess. Her enthusiasm has been unabated. It is a literal fact that this book would never have been finished without her help, which has extended to providing the first accurate translation from the French of the essay on Thomas Hardy in *Mes Modèles* by J.-E. Blanche.

I have been lucky in finding helpful specialist enthusiasts throughout. Among many, I should single out Jennifer Aylmer of the Theatre Museum, the Victoria and Albert Museum, Laurence Irving and his sister Lady Brunner, all for theatrical information; Graham Handley, Principal Lecturer in Education at the College of All Saints, Tottenham, for exhaustive enquiries in Enfield, and, in the same area, D. O. Pam, Local History and Museum Officer, London Borough of Enfield, P. A. Glennie, Headmaster of St. Andrew's C. of E. Primary School, Enfield, and J. D. Westaway, M.B.E., Correspondent to the School Managers. Finally, Michael Meredith, the Librarian, School Library, Eton College, gave me lively encouragement and generous access to his fine Hardy collection there.

Among libraries and archives, I have to thank primarily, as always, the staff of my local West Sussex County Reference Library at Chichester, who have solved my innumerable problems with charming efficiency. The same must be said of the staff of the Dorset County

Reference Library, the Dorset County Archivist and her staff, and, of course, the inimitable R. N. R. Peers, and the facilities which he provides so generously at the Dorset County Museum, with such considerable expense of his own often hard-pressed time. I must thank the librarians, and archivists, and staff of the Berkshire County Record Office, the Bodleian Library, the British Library Reading Room and Department of Manuscripts, the Brotherton Library of the University of Leeds, the General Registry, the Portsmouth City Library, the Public Record Office, the Warneford Hospital, and the Wiltshire County Record Office. Particular mention must be made of the Director and Staff of the Special Collections, Colby College Library, Waterville, Maine, for their prompt and efficient provision of material to keep pace with my work. Another special set of acknowledgements and thanks must go to the Trustees of the late E. A. Dugdale: in particular for permission to print large extracts from the letter of Emma Hardy to Mrs. Kenneth Grahame, and in general for their helpful acquiescence in my use of non-substantial quotation throughout the book from the letters of Thomas, Emma, and Florence Hardy.

I am most grateful to authorities already in the Hardy field: J. O. Bailey, Frank Giordano Jr., Evelyn Hardy and Desmond Hawkins (these last two authors of outstanding single-volume biographies of Hardy), Denys Kay-Robinson, John Laird, Michael Millgate, Harold Orel, Norman Page, F. B. Pinion, and R. L. Purdy, the authoritative bibliographer of Hardy, who will forgive some differences of inter-pretation in my general debt to his scholarship. Among all these, I must single out James Gibson, editor of the definitive *The Complete Poems of Thomas Hardy*. As with my first volume, he has not only given me the benefit of his extensive knowledge of Hardy texts, but has provided countless points of reference from his own collection of Hardiana, and has extended his many good offices to reading and commenting on the draft typescript of the present volume.

Help has notably come from interested individuals, whose names I can do no more than list, with apologies for any omissions: Gertrude S. Antell, John Antell, Norman Atkins, Melvyn Bragg, Daniel Farson, Dr. Roger Fiske, Violet Hilling, Dr. Richard Hunter, Mr. and Mrs. Jesty, Margaret E. Lane, Mrs. L. Largent, Mrs. Ann MacCaw, Mrs. K. Needham-Hurst, Lady Nihill, Kenneth Phelps, Elizabeth Potts, Profes-sor Edward Sampson, Mrs. R. P. Voremberg, Terence de Vere White; with a special word of gratitude to Gertrude Bugler for giving me such full and accurate information, allowing me to see letters, and for reading and correcting those sections of my book in which she plays a part.

The following acknowledgements are made to the owners of these sets of letters: the Brotherton Library, the University of Leeds, for

letters from Florence Hardy to Edward Clodd; the Director, Special
Collections, Colby College, Waterville, Maine, for letters from Emma
Hardy to the Revd. Richard Bartelot and to Rebekah Owen and also
for letters from Florence Hardy to Paul Lemperly and to Rebekah
Owen; the Trustees of the Thomas Hardy Collection and the Curator of
the Dorset County Museum for various letters in the collection to and
from Thomas Hardy; the Provost and Fellows of Eton College for
letters from Florence Hardy to Siegfried Sassoon and to Louisa Yearsley
in the School Library, Eton College; Mr. H. P. R. Hoare and the
National Trust for a letter from Emma Hardy and letters from Florence
Hardy to Alda, Lady Hoare, in the Wiltshire County Record Office.
The sources of these sets of letters are not further indicated in the Notes.
My best thanks are due to Evelyn Hardy and F. B. Pinion for their
transcriptions from other named sources.

Copyright in illustrations belongs to the Thomas Hardy Collection,
Dorset County Museum, with the following exceptions: 1 and 2, the
Gabrielle Enthoven Collection, Theatre Museum, Victoria and Albert
Museum; 3a, the Radio Times Hulton Picture Post Library; 3c,
Macmillan; 3d, Desmond Hawkins; 4d, Miss K. M. E. Murray; 7, the
Tate Gallery; 13, Mrs. Gertrude Bugler; 15, Norman Atkins.

Foreword

MY FIRST volume, *Young Thomas Hardy*, covered the first three-dozen years of Hardy's life, his origins in an obscure Dorset hamlet, his determined self-education, his vision of himself as a seer and prophet to his generation, his attempt to deny the rural past that had nurtured him, his hard-won achievement with his first successful novel, and a middle-class marriage. It also showed the damage these strenuous efforts had inflicted on an abnormally sensitive and secretive personality, always wistfully looking back across the gulf that success had created between his "simple self that was" and his carefully cultivated appearance as an English man of letters.

The remaining fifty years, summarized in a brief epilogue to the previous book, are the subject of the present volume, its sequel. To some degree, its story is an extension of these former events. Hardy remained a man torn between two worlds. His need to renew his Dorset roots brought him back to live and work near his birthplace. Yet the position he had reached in the world's eyes, and the heady effect of admirers—particularly women—dragged him only half-protesting into fashionable and aristocratic society, and the routines of the late Victorian and Edwardian London season. His obsession with the women of this world, especially with its amateurs of literature, added to the already formidable conflicts of his inner life. More obviously, it helped to bring about disaster in his first marriage to the erratic and not untalented Emma Gifford, the subject of so many ill-founded legends.

The strains of this double life marked him as a sad and worn man. His greatest inspiration came from his family and the dark rural history of his race. That story is intimately woven into the superb and dramatic artistry of his most mature novels. It permeates the poems he was to write in their hundreds up to the very end of his long life. Yet his unceasing search for love and understanding in a sophisticated world he never really managed to enter left him subject to continual disappointment and sometimes bitter revulsion.

In the last twenty years of his life, he seemed to have found an answer in a young woman who came from the same social background as himself, and had experienced much the same emergent and disillusioning struggles. Yet the accepted picture of an autumnal calm, enshrined in second marriage, proves as false as the other personal images he so sedulously projected. Stresses prevailed literally to his death-bed. What these were, and their intimate connection with his novels and poems, form the story this sequel attempts to tell.

Thomas Hardy's
Later Years

1

The Idyll

In the spring of 1876, Thomas and Emma Hardy, both then thirty-five years old, were living in furnished lodgings at Yeovil in Somerset. A year earlier, his fourth novel, *Far From the Madding Crowd*, had brought him the general acclaim and recognition his first three published works had lacked. Thomas Hardy's fifth novel, *The Hand of Ethelberta*, appeared on 5 April 1876. The reviews which emerged in that month, and early in the next, threw doubts on its quality. The *Athenaeum* found it carelessly written, the *Spectator* entertaining as a fable, but no more. The *Saturday Review* named it as frankly unworthy of the author of *Far From the Madding Crowd*, and George Saintsbury in *Academy*, though more favourable, noticed "a scrappiness which is the frequent drawback of novels written for periodicals".[1] Perhaps more ominously, for an author who had been married less than two years, Hardy's wife did not like it.

Emma's faith in their marriage, in spite of his peasant background and her middle-class family, had been justified by the triumphal progress of *Far From the Madding Crowd* in their first wedded year. Her unconcealed irritation that her only sister had been the first to marry was soothed when she found herself the wife of a successful novelist. It delighted her that the first long general review of her husband's work had come from Paris,[2] a city which held for her the happiest memories of their honeymoon. There are signs that she already saw Hardy as an international figure, like her beloved Balzac, and herself in the role of a great writer's intellectual helpmeet.

Biographers have always cast Emma Hardy as a thoroughly commonplace middle-class woman with no taste, whose attempts at literature were ridiculous. This was not how she appeared to herself, nor does it correspond with her modest but quite real achievements. She wrote in a vivid, well-observed, and even poetic style. The poor education given to middle-class Victorian girls may have left her shaky over spelling and grammar; but it had not damaged a lively turn of phrase and unusual imagery. Two magazine articles, "The Egyptian Pet" and "In Praise of Calais", show really excellent, sustained descriptive powers.[3] The latter is pictorial, in the manner of Hardy's favourite Bonington, with bright spots of significant colour picking out details of a bustling sea-port. Both won approval from literary friends, the first from Edmund Gosse,[4] the latter from Mrs. Watts-Dunton. Emma's four surviving travel diaries[5] are packed with equally delightful touches, both of character and colour. In the first year of their marriage, she had completed a story, *The Maid on the Shore*, whose Cornish setting at least bears comparison with Hardy's more mature *A Pair of Blue Eyes*. Critics have made an Aunt Sally of the deplorable poetry she tried to write in her sixties, and failed to realize the genuine talent latent in her prose. Finally, far from trying to adapt Hardy to a middle-class life, she was trying to live what she believed to be a bohemian existence with him, and to have a hand in his literary and creative life by her active partnership.

Under Hardy's direction, she had set herself to copy into a stout ruled notebook the extracts from books and newspapers he had made in previous years, and to bring them up to date with quotations from his recent reading. The raw material for a self-taught and self-improving novelist was laid out neatly in her still-schoolgirl hand, and by the beginning of April 1876, she had provided him with over 200 entries. The three largest categories were his historical reading in Macaulay, his weekly contemporary reading in the *Saturday Review*, and, apparently in the early months of 1876, laconic extracts from lives of the artists Raphael and Michelangelo. These, with a key word or two underlined, were just the kind of references Hardy loved to insert, somewhat self-consciously, into descriptive passages of his novels. Emma's labour was clearly designed to provide fodder for his future productions.[6] Whether, or not such self-improving interpretations were happy for the reader, they were a necessity for the writer.

The carping reviews of April brought a sudden urgency into the process. Hardy took over the notes himself,[7] and plunged into a bout of self-education. This was nothing new. At every turning point in his creative life, he had resorted to intensive study, in the belief that everything, poetry, prose, history, style, philosophy, was to be learnt by hard application and methodical treatment. There was concentration on the Greeks, including Plato and Aeschylus, but equally on such widely-spaced sources as the Greville Memoirs and J. G. Wood's *Insects at Home*.

By the end of May, with perhaps about 450 entries, old and new, copied, the process was broken for a fortnight by a short second honeymoon tour in Europe. It is not known whether this fulfilled some educational need in Hardy, or whether Emma felt it her due. It was probably paid for by the publication in the U.S.A. during that month of *The Hand of Ethelberta* in book form. At all events, the Hardys set off for Holland and the Rhine, their journey charted by Emma at the other end of the tiny notebook she had used as the diary of their original honeymoon in Rouen and Paris. On their way back, whether by chance or more likely by Hardy's deliberate design, they diverted through Belgium, and visited the field of Waterloo not many days before the anniversary of the battle on 18 June. Obsessed as always by this event, so much a part of his own folk and family history, Hardy spent the whole of a very long hot day dragging Emma all over the battlefield, until she felt faint and ill. He was also so obsessed by details, such as the exact location of the Duchess of Richmond's ball, that he could not restrain himself from investigating that too, and writing a letter to the papers about it. Emma's diary contains the pathetic little note—her first sign of any criticism of her single-minded and some-times intolerant husband—"Today I am still fatigued & Tom is cross about it."[8] A miserable passage back to Harwich, on a windy night with cattle aboard, can hardly have improved matters.[9]

The quarrel at Waterloo anticipated a strained situation when they returned home. The last entry in Emma's diary of their tour reads, "Going back to England where we have no home and no chosen county." A life of furnished lodgings was beginning to lose its glamour for her, in spite of the belief she was sharing it with an author who would redeem by some new classic work the comparative failure of his last book. It is possible that some members of her family shared her doubts. Hardy records "hints from relatives that he and his wife 'appeared to be wandering about like two tramps'", although in fact they had simply returned to their old address at Yeovil in Somerset which, as Emma had said, was not "chosen county" for either. Yet the plethora of note-book entries suggests hours of solid work rather than an aimless existence. The wounding phrase probably came from Emma's unsatisfactory but supercilious brothers, Walter and Willie Gifford. Living out of packing-cases was beginning to irk even Hardy. A diary entry on 25 June about "the irritating necessity of conforming to rules which themselves have no virtue" was probably aimed at his brothers-in-law with their mystical regard for unfurnished rather than furnished rental. Yet he needed a more settled background for a deliberate campaign of self-improvement before he felt ripe for another major novel. Early in July, he and Emma went to Bristol, the Gifford family city, and bought £100 worth of furniture in two hours. On 3 July, they moved it into their first real home.

This was a small semi-detached house called Riverside Villa, looking over the willowy reaches of the Stour, in the little market-town of Sturminster Newton in north-east Dorset. The villa was rendered in dusky grey, and in the garden Hardy planted a monkey-puzzle, token of Victorian middle-class respectability. It was a friendly place, and in it Emma had her first taste of provincial Dorset society. Callers included the Dashwoods, members of the firm of local solicitors which had given the poet, William Barnes, his first job. Emma was able to pick up the neighbourhood's history and anecdotes, which she hoped to weave into novels, for she still regarded herself as a novelist too. It was a very real part of the Hardys' marriage that they had a shared appreciation of literature and especially of poetry. One of Hardy's many poems which look back on this time shows them reading together in their idyllic riverside setting, as the swallows swooped over the sunset water-meadows outside.

> A dwelling appears by a slow sweet stream
> Where two sit happy and half in the dark:
> They read, helped out by a frail-wicked gleam,
> Some rhythmic text . . .

Keats was one of the "rhythmic texts" they shared in this romantic mood. His poetry had been a continuing presence in the novel which Hardy always regarded as *their* story, *A Pair of Blue Eyes*.[10] Now another shared delight, Emma's singing to the piano in the dusk, may have brought back to his mind Keats' s great love-narrative, *The Eve of St. Agnes,* for he copied into his notebook the line

> The music yearning like a god in pain . . .

and when he eventually came to write his next novel, he took the Song of the Indian Maiden, from Keats's *Endymion, as* its epigraph.

Yet the main purpose of their reading and copying was not to make an anthology of enjoyed literature. The hundreds of notes and quotations, with which they filled the pages of the notebook this idyllic summer and autumn, had a strictly practical purpose; they were to be ammunition in Hardy's new campaign to capture the heights of a really great novel.

Hardy's plan was not merely to copy extracts, but to select them as illustrations of some particular point of character, which could thus be reinforced and driven home in the pages of a narrative, providing a kind of home-made dictionary of learned and useful allusions. This involved selecting and heading each note with the characteristic to be illustrated, each carefully underlined, and then quoting from the source he was reading some pithy phrase or parallel allusion. For example, Note 345 reads:[11]

> Prominent mediocrity: conspicuous by the very intensity of his medi-
> ocrity—the late Bishop Sumner.

This illustration is annotated S.R., showing that Hardy had read it in his favourite *Saturday Review*. The allusion is exactly used to bolster a general comment on human nature in his next novel:

> Was Yeobright's mind well-proportioned? No. A well-proportioned
> mind is one which shows no particular bias . . . Its usual blessings are

happiness and mediocrity. It produces the poetry of Rogers, the paintings of West, the statecraft of North, the spiritual guidance of Sumner;

The interchangeable nature of such comments is shown by the fact that in later editions of *The Return of the Native*, Hardy substituted for Sumner's name that of his predecessor as Bishop of Winchester, Dr. Tomline. Such notes were simply used as fill-ups, to be slotted into a story wherever Hardy felt a strengthening allusion was needed. Two entries, numbers 611 and 613, based on Charles MacKay's *Memoirs of Extraordinary Popular Delusions and the Madness of Crowds*, an extremely popular work, whose first edition of 5000 copies had sold in three days, illustrate this purely practical novelistic purpose exactly. They read:

611 *Miraculous animation*. It is said that Albertus Magnus & Thos. Aquinas between them animated a brass statue, wh. chattered, & was their servant.

613 "Coup de Jarnac" a sly & unexpected blow so called from duel.

They then appear duly in *The Return of the Native* as

He seemed a mere automaton . . . He might have been the brass statue which Albertus Magnus is said to have animated just so far as to make it chatter and move, and be his servant.

. . . this species of *coup-de-Jarnac* from one he knew too well troubled the mind of Wildeve.

Only a few entries earlier, a note on the Pitt diamond, "carried in a hole cut in the heel of a shoe, for greater security", is repeated almost word for word in the novel, to reinforce the idea of Christian Cantle putting the guineas in his boots for safety. No less than seventy-five maxims or aphorisms from the Jesuit Balthasar Gracian, taken from an article in the *Fortnightly Review*,[12] are copied in Emma's hand, to be saved up by Hardy for extensive use a few years later in *A Laodicean*.

Apart however from a few entries which are possibly in Emma's hand, Hardy took care to copy himself the extracts from the largest single source in the whole notebook. This is the work of the founder of the system of Positive Philosophy, Auguste Comte, Hardy had read Comte intently in the years between 1870 and 1873, using mostly *A General View of Positivism*, translated by the English Positivist, J. H. Bridges, which he was given by his tragic friend and mentor, Horace Moule, some time before the latter's suicide in 1873. In 1875, he had discussed Positive Philosophy, encouraged by the man who succeeded Moule as his guiding intellectual influence, Leslie Stephen. Now, in 1876, he made a close study of one particular section of Comte's philosophic writing, *Social Dynamics, or the General Theory of Human*

Progress, from Comte's *System of Positive Polity*, just issued in a translation by another English Positivist, Edward Spencer Beesly. In the
summer and autumn of 1876, Hardy copied over 130 remarks, definitions, and comments from Comte's *Social Dynamics*, a harvest which he
stored up for use in nearly all the novels he wrote for the next twenty
years. In the 1890s, *Tess of the d'Urbervilles* was hailed by English
Positivists as reading "like a Positivist allegory or sermon", while in
Jude Hardy actually provided a Positivist heroine, Sue.[13] This is not
to say that Hardy was ever a Positivist. He seems to have had doubts,
even during this time, especially about Comte's assumption of inevitable rational progress by mankind. However, he was sufficiently
immersed in the Comtian world to attempt a pen-and-ink illustration
of social progress as "a looped orbit", an idea which he had discussed
at length the previous summer with Leslie Stephen,[14] and to which he
returned several times in his own later writings.

Comte is not easy reading, and this all must have taken some highly
concentrated study, especially with the summer delights of the Stour
at his doorstep, and a boat always ready for excursions with Emma
among the reedy islands, with their rushes "standing like a palisade
against the bright sky". Yet Hardy not only mastered this philosophic
task, but found time for favourite passages from Carlyle's *French
Revolution*, which he seems to have read at various times in his life
both for the history and for its vivid phrases. This continued unbroken
until the end of October, when a change took place. On the last day of
this month, Tuesday the 31st, Emma's egregious brothers, Willie and
Walter, arrived for a two-day stay, leaving early on the morning of
the Thursday.[15] It was apparently the only time that any relatives of
either Hardy or Emma came to see how they were doing at Sturminster. The remark often attributed to them, that the Hardys were
living in a place so remote that a new species of bird on the lawn was
an event, is not perhaps true,[16] though it sounds like Walter Gifford's
captious style. What is more to the point, the brothers' stay marks a
complete change in Hardy's notebook habits. From this exact date, he
ceases to make extracts from full-length volumes, like Comte's *Social
Dynamics*. His notes now are taken almost entirely from articles in
magazines, the *Saturday Review, Fortnightly Review, Edinburgh Review,
Cornhill, Nineteenth Century, Blackwood's*, and even the *Daily News*,
which provided some lighter and more homely items such as one on
pigeons—"The best breed of homing pigeons is that known as Belgian
Voyageurs: will beat an express train." Even the highly provincial
Dorset County Chronicle was allowed its say among the more learned
notes with "*A Shorthorn Cow*—the highest price ever given was for the
'Duchess of Geneva'—7000 guineas."

Evidently the brothers' visit, or something said by them during it, had brought home to Hardy that he was not getting on with writing another book: now, as a result, his preparations did not allow time for more than periodical reading, sometimes much more trivial than during his lengthy period of pure learning. Now he must put his accumulation of information and philosophy to creative use. His relatives-in-law and even Emma herself may have reminded him that he had not even a contract for any money-earning book. He must have something to offer. A visit to London in December was probably for book purposes, though Hardy only mentions his attendance at a conference at St. James's Hall on the Eastern Question; there he heard Mr. Gladstone speak, and witnessed Anthony Trollope's refusal to sit down when the Duke of Westminster, in the chair, tried to stop him exceeding the time-limit for speakers.[17] A more important excursion, both for the book, and for his private life with Emma, was to Bockhampton, to spend Christmas with his parents.

Although Emma had been on expeditions with Hardy's sisters, during her stay the year before at Swanage, this seems to have been her first meeting with her mother-in-law. There is a complete silence by Hardy on this point, and to the end of his life he never commented on the relationship between the two women. Family tradition has it that Emma was not well received, and with Jemima Hardy's strong character and possessive attitude this seems likely enough. A woman who, in Hardy's childhood, had stood up to the powerful wife of the local landowner, Mrs. Martin, was not to be overawed by the daughter of a failed solicitor. Hardy himself only describes his father's anecdotes of village bands and Christmas entertainments. The real importance of the visit was that he once more renewed acquaintance with his greatest creative inspiration, the homestead and the Heath beyond it. Many critics, including Hardy himself, have expressed surprise that he lived at Sturminster, but made his homeland heath the setting of *The Return of the Native*. This is to ignore—as Hardy did for his own reasons—the tremendous impact this Christmas visit made. To take only one instance, the most powerful visual scene in the book, the gambling at night by the light of glow-worms, was derived from an anecdote about Hardy's grandfather, doubtless told him by his father on this occasion.[18] Nearly all critics of *The Return of the Native* have recognized that the major character in the story is the Heath itself. Hardy himself began the novel with a full-length chapter devoted to the Heath, its appearance, its history (with characteristic historical notes from the Domesday Book and Leland's *Itinerary*), and the relation of huge and "haggard Egdon" to the processes of human life. What nearly always surprises those who form a picture from the novel of this giant waste is how small it is in actual geographical fact, and how little it seems to contain, even in bad weather, of the brooding menace with which

Hardy invests it. The simple reason is that Hardy, returning to it this Christmas after an interval of very different experience, and in the company once more of his powerful mother, saw the place, in his novelist's imagination, as it had appeared to him as a child. The huge stature of Bhompton Heath, Duddle Heath, and Puddletown Heath, in the composite guise of the fictional Egdon Heath, is seen from the eye-level of a very small boy. It is not often noticed that *The Return of the Native* is the one novel by Hardy where a child plays a large part, and in which a completely convincing picture of a child is given. One has only to contrast Johnny Nunsuch in this novel with the weird, symbolic non-child Little Father Time in *Jude the Obscure*. Hardy's "sad little boy" and his adventures on Egdon are some of the most moving scenes of the novel, and the most important in the plot, from his unconscious part in the rendezvous of Eustacia and Wildeve on the evening of 5th November to his fateful meeting on the Heath with Mrs. Yeobright, and his gradual revelation to Clym Yeobright of her last hours.

There is little doubt that this realistic figure of a child, unique in all Hardy's work, embodies his own childhood experiences on and about the Heath. Later in life he confessed to Hermann Lea "the childish fears he had felt in crossing that lonely stretch of heathland by himself when it was dusk or even at times quite dark". He told Lea how "he had often run fast to escape his fears produced by the sudden movement of a pony or deer, or a form that loomed in the half-light before being recognizable as a mere bush".[19] Similarly, Johnny in the novel

> ran until he was out of breath . . . The thorn-bushes which arose in his path from time to time . . . whistled gloomily, and had a ghastly habit after dark of putting on the shapes of jumping madmen, sprawling giants, and hideous cripples.

In addition, the year and a day that the story occupies seems to fall some time during the decade 1840–50, that is, the exact years of Hardy's own childhood before he went to school in Dorchester; transportation to Australia, which was officially ended in 1850, is still invoked as a current fact by one of the characters in the novel· Hardy also uses other scenes, not connected with the boy Johnny, which appear to embody actual events known to have made a deep impression on his own childish mind. One is the "raffle" or competition decided by dice-throwing, where the childlike Christian Cantle wins an unwanted prize, just as the child Hardy had done. The Christmas Mummers scene, with its emotional prominence, and its strongly-felt sexual undercurrent, seems likely to be a transmuted memory of that Mummers' show at Puddletown, where the adolescent Hardy had made advances to his older cousin, Rebecca Sparks; for Rebecca's young brother, Jim

Sparks, appears in this scene of the novel, scarcely disguised, by the alteration of one letter, as Jim Starks, a character not used anywhere else in the book. He shows the nature of Rebecca's impulsive and forthright brother by acting his part as the Valiant Soldier so vigorously that he feigns death in the play by "coming down like a log upon the stone floor with force enough to dislocate his shoulder". In an exactly similar way their father, the carpenter James Sparks senior, had appeared in Hardy's first published novel, *Desperate Remedies*, as James Sparkman, a joiner.

These associations with his childhood, aided by renewed contact with his mother's fund of folklore and legend, were what Hardy took away to Sturminster from his Christmas visit to the Bockhampton home; he seems to have started writing the novel immediately. Many critics have suggested that the "return" of the hero is literally the return of Hardy, and that Clym Yeobright should be identified in some way as Hardy, while Mrs. Yeobright is a picture of Jemima Hardy. It is claimed that Hardy himself said Mrs. Yeobright was based on his own mother, though the witness for this, Sir Sydney Cockerell, is not always reliable on other matters.[20] If this really were so, it seems strange that Hardy himself placed Mrs. Yeobright as the least important of all the main characters in the book, though here, admittedly, he was providing hints for the illustrator of the serial version of the novel,[21] and not necessarily passing judgement based on his own preferences. Yet, as he wrote, a far more potent basis was provided by his deliberate notes of the past summer. Nearly all the main themes which critics have discovered in *The Return of the Native* have their origins in his notebook entries. Clym Yeobright, that over-thoughtful man, who tries to apply his philosophy of improvement by reason to rough Egdon, has come back from Paris "acquainted with ethical systems popular at the time". Within a year of the volume publication of the novel, he was recognized by a reviewer as "in fact a humanitarian, touched with the asceticism of a certain positivistic school". Though Hardy shows, much as his mentor Leslie Stephen had done in his philosophical essays, how Comte's positivist optimism is defeated by the nature of actual life, Clym ends as he had begun, as an ethical teacher upon Egdon, taking his texts from a much wider selection than the first book of Kings which he quotes in the closing paragraphs. The battle which some have seen between paganism and Christianity in the story, repeats many of the ideas from Comte which Hardy had noted. "Fetichism"—defined in note 641 from Comte as "universal adoration of matter"—is found by many on Egdon; the precise word is used by Hardy to describe the mood of the listener to the subtle sound of the dried heath-bells of the past summer. The notes on Greek literature and tragedy bore fruit in the strict classical unity of time, to a year and a day, the Oedipus

theme of Clym's partial blindness,[22] and the five-act structure, which
many critics see in the five first books, marred only by the additional
"Aftercourses" book to compensate the serial readers for so much
unrelieved tragedy. Even such a minor source of notebook entries as
J. G. Wood's *Insects at Home* played its part. From two notebook
entries which Hardy had entitled *Beauty* and *The nearer the lovelier*, he
extracted Wood's descriptions of the tiger-beetle, and applied them,
almost word for word, to the impression created at various times by
the beauty of Eustacia. Though he needed no book-source to tell him
about the behaviour of ants on the Heath, Hardy also undoubtedly
used Wood's comment that colonies of ants appear, year after year, at
the same place, to strengthen Mrs. Yeobright's dying meditations as
she lies on the Heath near one of these ant-processions.[23] There are
many other minor transferences, such as the comparison of Egdon with
"the ancient world of the carboniferous period", which Hardy had
noted from a book-article in the *Saturday Review*, early in 1877, when
he began to write the novel.[24]

For the urgent matter, directly he returned to Sturminster after
Christmas, was to get his new-found impressions of boyhood down on
paper, and provide something to tempt serial-publishers. Though he
wrote quickly, drawing on the deep and well-stocked recess of early
memory, it proved unexpectedly difficult to interest the magazines.
Considering the brilliant popular success of *Far From the Madding
Crowd* only three years before, this seems surprising. It may show
that the disappointment felt by readers of *The Hand of Ethelberta*
had been more serious for Hardy's reputation than has generally been
reckoned. Feeling he could not try *Cornhill* again, since its editor,
Leslie Stephen, had been doubtful about the propriety of the story for
his readers, Hardy wrote to *Blackwood's Edinburgh Magazine* on 13
February 1877, offering them what he described as a pastoral story on
the lines of *Far From the Madding Crowd*, hardly an accurate parallel,
but one which, he hoped, would sell the novel for serial publication.
Blackwood's were interested, but when he sent them the first fifteen
chapters on 12 April, they rejected his offer within a fortnight.[25] This
was a crisis. He was committed to writing with no assurance of money
coming in. In these straits he made two moves. He suggested that
Smith, Elder, who had published his last two novels in volume form,
might like to reprint *A Pair of Blue Eyes*, in which the original publisher, Tinsley, had no further interest. Though negotiations broke
down, the novel was in fact reprinted later that year, thanks to the
interest of a fellow Dorset man, Charles Kegan Paul, literary adviser
to the publishing house of S. King & Co., and founder, under his own
name, of the firm that succeeded them.[26] He was to prove a needed
standby. Hardy's second move was to submit the new story so far as it

had gone to Stephen and the *Cornhill*, but the expected rejection soon came, and on 16 June Hardy offered the novel to yet another magazine, *Temple Bar*, with the same result. He was running through the recognized literary magazines which offered serialization, and it must have been with relief that he eventually placed the novel, sometime that autumn, with the magazine *Belgravia* for serial publication to begin in the January of 1878.[27] He also managed, on a visit to London, to sell the Americal serial rights to Henry Harper, who claimed to have picked the title from Hardy's list.[28]

By all signs, in spite of the delights of Sturminster, 1877 was a year of financial anxiety, ending as it did with yet one more attempt to raise money, a correspondence with Baron Tauchnitz about continental editions of Hardy's books.[29] Also, Hardy resorted this Christmas to selling a short story to a children's annual. As a further source of anxiety and expense, Hardy's father, now in his middle sixties, was suffering badly from rheumatism, and his son had to take him to Bath that autumn to undergo the cure. Serialization in *Belgravia* was accompanied, a month later in February 1878, by a serial publication in one of the magazines controlled by Harper, who was to be his principal American publisher, yet the strain of managing negotiations from such a remote place as Sturminster must have been considerable. There is no reason to doubt, therefore, that it was, as he himself says, on Hardy's own initiative that he and Emma went up to London early in February to look for a house, and signed a three-year agreement for one in the middle of the month. On 18 March their kindly neighbour Mrs. Dashwood gave them a bed while their furniture was being packed, and a few days later they moved into "The Larches", 1 Arundel Terrace, Trinity Road, Upper Tooting, close to Wandsworth Common, and the convenient transport of Wandworth Common Station. The Sturminster Newton idyll was over—"Our happiest time", as Hardy afterwards nostalgically noted.[30]

Many aspects of the stay had certainly been idyllic, the spring birdsong in the Blackmore Vale, the summer dancing on the green to celebrate Queen Victoria's fortieth Coronation anniversary, the lush cottage gardens where "the gooseberries that were ripening on the twigs at noon are in the tart an hour later". Yet it had been a year of professional setbacks and disappointments, and perhaps of personal ones too. One incident, soon after midsummer, disturbed Hardy. He and Emma found that their maid, Jane, whom they liked very much, had kept the bolts of the back door oiled, so that her young man could slip in silently, and frequently spend the night with her. When they discovered this, she crept out early next morning, and never came back, either to them or to her own cottage home. Six weeks later, on 13 August, Hardy made the pathetic and often-quoted note, "We hear that Jane, our late servant, is soon to have a baby. Yet never a sign of one is there for us." Exactly a month earlier, on 13 July, he had made another note, which may well be connected with this better-known one—"The sudden disappointment of a hope leaves a scar which the ultimate fulfilment of that hope never entirely removes."[31] For the Hardys, there was no ultimate fulfilment. Their marriage remained childless to the end. It is difficult and perhaps dangerous to come to any definite judgement about this. One can only say that it was this fact, as much as any, which made Hardy describe these Sturminster months in a much-later poem as

> A preface without any book,
> A trumpet uplipped, but no call;
> That seems it now.

Yet, like so much that Hardy wrote about his earlier years, this is not the final verdict. This poem, and many others of sad reminiscence, were conceived some forty years later, when he was full of remorse for his own imperceptions, for a happiness that was within his reach, but which he somehow did not grasp: of the good things at hand, which he was too self-absorbed to see. For Hardy, more than most creative artists, was deeply self-centred. He regarded himself as one of the chosen few who had a mission to his age; his obsessive markings in his Bible show a belief not in the message of that book—like so many Victorian thinkers, he lost his faith in the 1860s—but in himself as a kind of latter-day seer and prophet, an Isaiah or an Ezekiel. Human contact, especially domestic love once the initial excitement had worn off, meant little to him. Life was largely important as the material for his art. Morbid, brooding, an avid collector of oddity and irony, the term happiness is difficult ever to apply to him. Yet he was happy during what he called the Sturminster Newton idyll, even if his enjoyment showed itself in such form as his endless interest in sinister stories. He attended inquests, collected tales of gruesome country superstitions, accumulating them for use in *The Return of the Native*. He paid little attention to laying any sort of foundation for a real and mutually satisfying marriage. He was wedded to the overwhelming idea of himself as an author and seeker for truth. It was in furtherance of this search that he turned his back on this twenty-month idyll. Anne Thackeray, the novelist's daughter, had told him London was essential for authorship. For his career he would leave the native county to which he already owed so much. He was putting Clym Yeobright's experiment in reverse, and returning to London.

2

The Theatre of Life

TRINITY ROAD is a long, straight avenue, running north to south from Wandsworth High Street to Tooting Bec Station. About two-thirds of the way along, on the east side, just beyond the last straggling outskirts of Wandsworth Common, is Arundel Terrace, which forms a short stretch of the main road. The terrace consists of eight three-storey yellow brick villas of a standard design—half-basement and area, bow-windowed first-floor front parlour. No. 1, into which the Hardys moved, was the northernmost corner house of the row; its situation, by any standards, was bleak. The entire north wall of the house was exposed, there was no south aspect whatsoever, and only a very small garden at the back. Wandsworth Common itself had been saved from builders and placed under public control in 1871; but it remained largely as it was described at that date, bare, muddy, and sloppy after a little rain, undrained, and almost devoid of any trees.[1] This did not, however, deter the builders in Trinity Road, and two large villas, afterwards a Girls' School, were going up opposite Arundel Terrace when the Hardys arrived in March 1878.[2]

Almost every biographer makes great play with Hardy's own words, written in old age, about this area and this house "at Tooting, where they seemed to feel that 'there had passed away a glory from the earth' ", to which he added, "And it was in this house that their troubles began." There is no need to imagine, however, a sudden and lasting disenchantment and marital disillusion directly Hardy and Emma set foot in Arundel Terrace. To do so is to ignore completely Hardy's next sentence—"This, however, is anticipating unduly." The difficulties of the next three years were at least partly due to the house itself. Whenever the wind was north-east there were bound to be "troubles". In the wet January of 1879, rain poured in through the exposed and badly-hung door.[3] In the cold January of 1881, snow drifted in thickly, covering the inside passages, and even forcing its way through the windows, so that Emma's cherished window-plants were as white as if they were growing out of doors.[4] Moreover, throughout their three-year lease, Hardy was clearly suffering from growing physical malaise, with lassitude and nervous fears, confirmed in autumn 1880 by a severe internal haemorrhage.

Yet these three years began as a time of real enjoyment. Hardy had renewed friendship with the elderly Alexander Macmillan, who had shown such sympathetic understanding over his first, unpublished novel. Macmillan, who now left much of the publishing business to his nephew Frederick, had lost his wife in 1871; he quickly remarried a younger woman, a school-friend of his children's governess, and of Italian extraction. They too had settled in South London. The two old Commons of Tooting Graveney and Tooting Bec had recently been acquired as open spaces for the public. Unlike Wandsworth Common they were charming and countrified, especially Tooting Graveney, with its small round pond and gypsy settlements. Splendid new houses, with very large tree-filled gardens, had sprung up on the north side,[5] and Macmillan bought one of these, which he rechristened Knapdale, after the home of his clan in Argyll.[6] This house, with its broad croquet lawns and beautiful view over the pond, was a constant port of call for the Hardys. Indeed, Hardy was guilty of innocent aggrandisement when he wrote of "their neighbours, the Macmillans" and "Knapdale, near our house". Macmillan's spacious detached mansion was at least a mile away from Hardy's little terrace-row, at the far end of Tooting Bec Road, then called Streatham Lane. This lane was the scene of Hardy's later, moving poem, *Beyond the Last Lamp*. The visit of some hours, which the poet pays, and during which two lovers continue sadly to pace the unlit lane, was clearly one which Hardy paid to the Macmillans; Hardy inscribed an autograph copy of the poem to Macmillan's son, George.[7]

Many of Hardy's fruitful London contacts were made or renewed at Knapdale. It was there that summer that he and Emma met Thomas Huxley, for whom Hardy already had a great admiration. The following summer, he was to meet again at Knapdale John Morley, whom he had not seen since the latter had advised him on his earliest attempt, *The Poor Man and the Lady*. Hardy, perhaps a little irked by the final débâcle of his first manuscript, represents Morley as talking in embarrassingly conventional platitudes—"Well, since we met, you have . . .", and so on. Emma enjoyed the successful garden-parties of the lively Mrs. Macmillan, and the friendship of her eldest step-daughter, Maggie. Further afield, in Kensington, they visited Hardy's Dorset admirer, Kegan Paul, himself now a publisher. Emma was also introduced to the household of yet another publisher, George Murray Smith, and Hardy justified his return to London by negotiating with Smith, on 20 September, the book publication of *The Return of the Native*. Besides these occasions where the Hardys visited together, there were many masculine gatherings when Hardy, in his own somewhat quaint phrase, "fell into line as a London man again". On 18 June he was elected a member of the Savile Club and visited the West End in hearty company. On 3 August, he and William Minto, critic and editor of the *Examiner*, who had proposed him for membership, were joined at the Club by Walter Herries Pollock, a dramatic collaborator. The evening ended in Henry Irving's dressing-room at the Lyceum, with Irving stripped to the waist, and all drinking champagne in tumblers.[8]

This was a very different life from the homely, quiet evenings with Emma at Sturminster Newton, the patient copying of hundreds of notes to fit Hardy for the task of becoming a great light in English literature. Though she loyally continued to take down nice things that other people said about her husband's work,[9] Emma was now left much alone. Hardy was out, dining at clubs, visiting the theatre, and, with a man friend, going to the Derby. Silent and shy, his small features disguised by a large, soft beard, he walked the streets observing men and women, especially the latter. He had a horror of attracting attention; sitting in a stage-box, he was seen hiding his face behind his hand.[10] At the same time, he listened and peered about him wherever he went, a confirmed eavesdropper and voyeur, recalling word-for-word conversations heard in John Steven's Holywell Street bookshop off the Strand, while himself appearing to be absorbed in a book.[11] Capitalizing on his return to London, he swiftly wrote and sold magazine stories. The most notable and longest was adapted and selected from his first rejected novel, *The Poor Man and the Lady*. Under the title, "An Indiscretion in the Life of an Heiress", it appeared in July in the *New Quarterly Magazine*, and in the U.S.A. in *Harper*'s. Over and above these immediate money-making tasks, there was the need to prepare a new novel. Hardy returned to the theme, learnt from his grandmother, of the war against Napoleon, and the rumoured threat to the Dorset coast in 1804-1805. He ransacked newpapers and books in the British Museum, copying into his notebook every detail of these invasion years. Army regulations, local Dorset news, the King's visit to Weymouth, military drill, and meticulous drawings of ladies' fashions and hair-styles, all were neatly chronicled in his small, classical script. Nor did he neglect eye-witness memory. On Sunday 27 October 1878, he met at Chelsea Hospital an old pensioner who had actually been in the terrible retreat of Sir John Moore to Corunna. If not the "grand drama of the wars with Napoleon" he had planned in 1877, this was going to be a miniature rehearsal in a realistic Dorset background, on his own cottage doorstep.

The need to make this new book a success was emphasized by a brutal shock. On 4 November, *The Return of the Native* was published in book form, embellished by a map of its Dorset setting, drawn in Hardy's own hand. On 23 November came the first review. It was in the *Athenaeum*, and it was as devastating as the first lethal review of Hardy's youth in the *Spectator*. The novel, over which Hardy had spent so many months of loving care and learned preparation at Sturminster Newton, was judged "a book distinctly inferior to anything of his which we have yet read". The old charges of immorality were raised; Eustacia and Wildeve "know no other law than the gratification of their own passion". Most wounding, his style was criticized, especially his handling of dialect. Hardy replied to this last charge with dignity and sense, in a letter which was printed the following week:[12]

> ... An author may be said to fairly convey the spirit of intelligent peasant talk if he retains the idiom, compass and characteristic expressions, although he may not encumber the page with obsolete pronunciations of the purely English words and with mispronunciations of those derived from Latin and Greek. In the printing of standard speech hardly any phonetic principle at all is observed: and if a writer attempts to exhibit on paper the precise accents of a rustic speaker he disturbs the proper balance of a true representation by unduly insisting upon the grotesque element; thus directing attention to a point of inferior interest, and diverting it from the speaker's meaning, which is by far the chief concern where the aim is to depict the men and their natures rather than their dialect forms.

His hurt feelings show through the measured prose. The popular idea of rustic speech was to stress "the grotesque". Yet the men Hardy wished to portray were those whose speech was, as he stresses, "*intelligent* peasant talk", not uncouth ignorant yokels. Nearer home than that, they were Hardy's own relatives, including his closest. Years later, Hardy's sister Mary, overhearing a Dorset man say, "Where's the coal-box to?", was reminded of the way their father spoke.[13]

Criticism, as usual, prostrated Hardy. In this week, between review and letter, he entered in his diary, "*November* 28. Woke before it was light. Felt that I had not enough staying power to hold my own in the world,"[14] a measure of the psychological shock he had just received. Although two days later, W. E. Henley in the *Academy* said the book "excites both interest and imagination, and takes a first place among the novels of the season", he also condemned most of the comic, rural dialogue as unnatural, while *The Times* on 5 December roundly remarked that Hardy's peculiarity of language was carried too far, though it grudgingly praised the descriptive scenes. Yet Hardy's other habitual reaction to attack was to fight back. The New Year saw him starting the new novel; it was, at any rate, sketched for Leslie Stephen's consideration by mid-February[15] 1879. With firm persistence, he retained its entirely Dorset setting, and its historical nature, even though Stephen himself demurred at his introducing actual historical characters; however, he admitted, "I like to have a bit of history in the background, so to speak", and cited Thackeray's skilful handling of the Waterloo scenes in *Vanity Fair*.[16]

Though precise dates are uncertain, the writing of the book, *The Trumpet Major*, went ahead fast in 1879. By mid-September half the book was finished, and the magazine *Good Words* had agreed to serialize it during 1880. Hardy's life all through the year 1879 was composed of three strands, which may be seen in the texture of the work itself. The first, of course, was his historical reading and study. More visits to the British Museum, more copying of exact period detail, including carica- tures by Gillray, gave him the accurate flavour of the years 1804-1805. He even attended the funeral of Louis Napoleon at Chislehurst to study the features of Prince Napoleon, the Emperor's nephew. Secondly, he explored his own Dorset roots. Taking as excuse a New Year's Eve note from his father, saying his mother was ill and hoping to see him, he paid two visits of a fortnight each, one in the first half of February in icy cold and snow, and the other for the middle weeks of August, also unluckily in appalling wet. Yet the weather counted for little beside the memories and the cherished, familiar atmosphere he found there. His father, delighted to see him, told him innumerable tales of bygone days, with their usual gruesome quota of hangings and whippings, but also of exact details, such as the habits of the old Puddletown choir, and the location of the old Dorchester post office.[17] A story, probably told by his mother, spoke of a dumb woman in her original part of Dorset near the Somerset border, who suddenly uttered the rhyme

> A cold winter, a forward spring,
> A bloody summer, a dead King.

The French Revolution immediately followed. During his August visit, he also found staying with relatives his cousin, Jim Sparks, the Windsor carpenter, and discussed with him their common ancestors in faraway times.[18] Jim's builder employer in Windsor was himself also a Puddle- town man, whose sister, true to his Dorset origins, Jim Sparks had married.[19]

These two strands, historical study and family reminiscence, are firmly woven into the construction of the novel, and give it remarkable unity and a steady sense of reality. Hardy was determined that the charges of unreality, brought against *The Return of the Native*, should not be repeated.[20] At the same time, there was a third factor, never noticed before. Without it, the characters would perhaps seem trivial: the girl who cannot make up her mind between suitors, familiar in so many Hardy novels, the stock elders, the comic chorus folk. What gives the work its solidity, in spite of its relatively small compass, is that these rest on universal figures from the traditional rituals of the theatre. The novel draws on Hardy's extreme, personal interest in the stage during the year 1879, when he was actually trying his hand at dramatic adaptation.

It is easy to see how the idea that he might adapt one of his own novels for the stage came into Hardy's mind just at this time. During the evening at the Lyceum on 3 August 1878, ending with the champagne party in Irving's dressing-room, Hardy had seen the actor perform in *Jingle*. This was a play adapted from *Pickwick Papers* by James Albery. Albery, like Hardy, had been trained as an architect. Like Hardy, he had deserted his profession, and after a number of unsuccessful plays, had at last found fame with *Two Roses;* this was the forerunner of much modern domestic comedy, in which Irving made his first notable mark in 1870 in the part of Digby Grant. If Albery could leave architecture for drama, Hardy, with the advantage of his own books to dramatize, might do so too. The obvious choice for stage-adaptation was *Far From the Madding Crowd*, both from its popularity as a novel, and its strong plot. It was an inspired time to begin dramatic work. Ellen Terry had joined Irving as his leading lady in 1878, and in 1879 she was playing Portia to his Shylock, both performances of great power and originality. Nor would Hardy lack advice on the difficult art of writing for the theatre. One of his companions in the *Jingle* evening had been Walter Herries Pollock, the play-adaptor, though Hardy claimed that his own first draft, which he called "*The Mistress of the Farm*—A pastoral drama", had been adapted "alone and unassisted".

The fate of this adaption was not vastly important, as it proved; yet Hardy's concentration in 1879 on theatrical matters held great importance for the novel he was also writing, *The Trumpet-Major*. Briefly, the pattern of the book, embracing nearly every major character, derives from the old Italian Comedy of Masks, whose debased form, the harlequinade, was showing in nearly every Victorian theatre, burlesque, and ballet. To take character by character, Anne Garland, the heroine who dances tantalizingly between the brothers John and Bob Loveday, is the typical Columbine,[21] demure, coquettish, but susceptible enough to prefer in the end the flashy, spangled Harlequin. This, in the novel, is Bob Loveday, who has all the attributes of a stage harlequin, down to the merest detail. He dresses in startling finery, which he shows off in Chapter 30. When he wishes to make a special effort to win Anne, he deliberately "struts", as Hardy wrote, in his naval lieutenant's new uniform (Chapter 39). The scene where he escapes from the press-gang (Chapter 31) is very closely based on the theatrical rituals of the Italian comedy. It was traditional for Columbine and her lover to be hotly pursued by authority; it was known in stage terms as "The Chase". This happens in the novel when Anne and Bob are both pursued by the press-gang. Stronger even in tradition was the great "Leap" or "Jump" of Harlequin. One nineteenth-century harlequin made such a feature of this that the theatre where he performed was actually known as "the Jump".[22] Bob's huge jump out of the press-gang's hands into the apple-tree, his "figure flying like a raven's across the sky", is Harlequin's giant "Leap". Immediately after, he executes Harlequin's traditional trick-scenery routine, a sequence perfected by the great theatre family of Lupino, of diving through a set of trap-doors and collapsible stage-flats. Bob flies up on the hoist, through the trap-doors of the mill, with the skill of a stage-acrobat, "whirled up by the machinery", as if into the flies of a theatre.

There are even more striking resemblances in other characters. Old miser Derriman is the traditional Pantaloon, foolish-cunning, nervous, shrunk, wizened, at his death "little more than a light, empty husk". His odd fondness for Anne—"I believe the old gentleman is in love with you", says her mother—is the exact counterpart of Pantaloon's traditional feeling for Columbine. She was often his ward, just as Anne finds herself old Derriman's heiress. Next, in precise detail, is the Boasting Captain of the Italian masks—Shakespeare's Captains Pistol and Parolles—here represented by Festus Derriman. In the earliest draft of the novel, he was *Captain* Delaylynde, a Dorset family name which Hardy also used in his review of William Barnes' poems.[23] In every way Festus is the boasting soldier of the masks, cowardly when in danger, vainglorious when there is none, drunken, incompetent even in military matters (Chapter 7). There remains Anne's unsuccessful suitor, John Loveday, the trumpet-major himself. Here Hardy deserts the nineteenth-century English usage, common since Grimaldi, of the jovial Clown; he gives us, as many contemporary harlequin ballets did, the French creation of the sad, pensive, white-faced Pierrot. John's pallor is often remarked on; so is his thoughtfulness and simple-heartedness. "When he was a boy he was the simplest fellow alive," says his brother in Chapter 33. His tragic end, foreshadowed in the last sentence of the novel, is Pierrot's melancholy final exit. In fact, much of the novel is conceived theatrically in terms of entrances and exits, accompanied by stage-lighting effects. In Chapter 31, Bob is suddenly discovered by the light of the lantern when he enters "still radiant in the full dress he had worn with such effect at the Theatre Royal". John's exit on the last page is even more dramatic and stage-lit.

> The candle held by his father shed its waving light upon John's face and uniform as with a farewell smile he turned on the door-stone, backed by the black night;

His footsteps die away, off-stage, as the curtain falls on him for ever.

Was Hardy conscious of building his two other novelistic elements, those of historical event and Dorset local colour, upon this third structure of universal theatrical tradition? One can only say that his interest in the theatre at this time was personal in a very particular sense. In the novel, Festus, the boastful soldier, marries the comedy actress, Matilda—Captain marrying Soubrette, again in mask tradition. A real comedy actress was certainly in Hardy's mind at this time. In his diary for 4 December 1879, he entered this note.[24]

> Helen M—th—s's face. A profile not too Greek for an English fireside, yet Greek enough for an artist's eye: arch, saucy style of countenance, dark eyes, brows & hair, the last low on forehead.

The play-going Hardy had spotted an actress just beginning to make an impression on the London stage. This was Miss Helen Mathews. She did not attract "an artist's eye", in the theatrical journals of the time, until two years after she had attracted Hardy's; but the picture of her then playing a leading role is certainly "Greek enough", with its classical features.[25] She had also, by the time Hardy made his note, played some "saucy" roles, and won praise for her comedy. One of her characterizations was Lady Sneerwell in *The School for Scandal*, which she played on tour, and which pleased the critics when she gave it at the Olympic Theatre a year or so later.[26] As this suggests, Helen Mathews was no ingénue. She was now thirty years old, though Hardy, like his own Bob Loveday with Matilda, may have imagined her younger. She had already several years' theatrical experience in the provinces, with parts in contemporary plays by James Albery, and in Shakespeare with Emily Fowler's touring company.

Helen Mathews had, too, the brunette looks and the "arch" expression, which had always attracted Hardy, both in his own cousin, Tryphena Sparks, and in another actress of his earlier London days, Mrs. Scott-Siddons, whose Rosalind had set him off writing sonnets. Besides, it is clear from other entries in his diary that the eye of the impressionable Hardy was beginning to rove at this precise time, and to settle on chance-met young women. The train journey from Tooting gave him plenty of opportunities. On one such journey to Town, on 27 June 1879, he saw in the railway carriage, "a statuesque girl" with "absolutely perfect" features and a face "not unlike that of a nymph". On the homeward journey, by happy chance, he sat opposite "a contrasting girl of sly humour—the pupil of her eye being mostly under the eyelid".

The fact is, after five years of marriage, his thoughts were on the wing. Emma was nearly forty. Her heavy beauty had run to fat, her figure to dumpiness.[27] Her lameness and consequent lack of exercise in Town, where she missed the country horse-riding, contributed. The imaginative Hardy required nymphs and sylphs, of past memory or present discovery. It is likely Emma guessed. In August he took her on an appallingly wet holiday to Weymouth, the scene of this poem.

> She charged me with having said this and that
> To another woman long years before,
> In the very parlour where we sat,—

Sat on a night when the endless pour
Of rain on the roof and the road below
Bent the spring of the spirit more and more . . .

"Long years before" was the time of Hardy's Weymouth jaunts with Tryphena. Now, ten years later, Emma seems to have found him out.

Whatever difficulties may have begun to occur in private life, Hardy's novel, *The Trumpet-Major*, was a triumphant success with the critics. The historical setting, the realistic Dorset background, were both accepted as Hardy at his best. His careful study of the two water-mills at Sutton Poyntz, on the outskirts of Weymouth, had resulted in a convincing yet romantic setting for his story. Hardy himself was so involved in this that he actually designed the pictorial cover. The whole book shows his distinctive gift of making places and people at one. The mill itself is as much a leading personage in the story as the two families of Loveday and Garland. The substructure of theatre ritual gave a continuous dramatic interest to the plot. Though miniature in scale, it is thoroughly satisfying in achievement. It was serialized all through 1880 in *Good Words* with notable success, in spite of some minor bowdlerizing by Dr. Macleod, the Scottish clergyman editor. Its publication in volume form, in October of that year, was greeted with universal praise. The *Spectator*, relieved that Hardy did not attempt another high tragedy like *The Return*, found it "observant, truthful, humorous". The pontifical *Athenaeum* thought John Loveday the best character Hardy had yet drawn, and the *Westminster Review* "decidedly the best story which Mr. Hardy has yet written". Gosse, in a private letter, considered it to rank with the "cream" of Hardy's work. George Saintsbury congratulated him on abandoning the pretentious diction of previous books, and the *Saturday* praised the group scenes.

There was only one drawback to this success: but it was a daunting one. The book in volume form simply did not sell. Smith, Elder, had the same dismal response for it that *The Return of the Native* had received. Need for money forced Hardy to keep writing, though signs of distress and pressure had already begun to appear, even in *The Trumpet-Major*. Not only did he reproduce practically verbatim a chapter-opening from *Desperate Remedies*; in order to cut corners and meet serial demands, he had reproduced also almost word for word in Chapter 23 a humorous description of a militia drilling scene from one of his historical authorities, C. H. Gifford's *History of the Wars Occasioned by the French Revolution*. Unfortunately, it seems, he did not notice that Gifford himself had lifted the scene from an earlier fictional source.[29] His own silent plagiarism, when it was found out, caused him endless trouble and irritating controversy; here it is a witness to haste and stress. His remedy for small sales was now the American, Henry Harper. Harper's *Weekly* had published Hardy's two short stories in 1878, and Hardy gave him a smuggling tale, *The Distracted Preacher, in* spring 1870. Now he placed another with him, *Fellow-Townsmen*, which Harper serialized, immediately after it appeared in the English *New Quarterly*, in April/May 1880. Then Harper came forward with a new proposal. He was launching a European Edition of his *Weekly*; would Hardy provide a full-length serial? He offered excellent terms. It was a bait that Hardy could not refuse.

Yet, by a number of small but significant incidents, the illness, forewarned by his feeling of utter lassitude as long ago as November 1878, was beginning to gain on him. All through 1880, he suffered increasingly morbid and nervous fears. On 19 May, he felt oppressed by the horror of waking at three in the morning on the outskirts of crowded London, which he imagined as "a monster whose body had four million heads and eight million eyes". By 27 July, with nearly eight chapters of the new book written, the Hardys tried a holiday abroad. They toured Normandy, but the morbid horrors persisted. In Le Havre, he was terrified by a hotel room whose floor "was painted a bloody red . . . as if struggles had taken place there", and barricaded the door. At Honfleur, the figure of the Christ on a wayside Calvary "seemed to writhe and cry in the twilight".[30] A visit to Dorset after their return brought no respite, for Hardy was pushing on with the novel in haste to provide material for the illustrator, George Du Maurier. By 16 October he had practically finished the first book, but, during a stay in Cambridge, he felt "an indescribable physical weariness", coupled with weird fancies about the wax on the candles in King's Chapel, with their reminders of the last time he saw his friend Horace Moule before the latter's tragic suicide in 1873. Returning to London on 23 October, just before *The Trumpet-Major* came out, Hardy felt worse than ever, and on Sunday 28 October he sent for a doctor.

Dr. Henry Edward Beck, who lived exactly opposite in Trinity Road, had nothing but proximity to recommend him. It was forty years since he had acquired the minimum medical qualifications of L.S.A. and M.R.C.S. He came each day, diagnosed internal bleeding, but had no suggestions. Emma, in alarm, asked the Macmillans, who sent their own doctor, Arthur Shears, M.D.[31] He put Hardy, who was in considerable pain, firmly to bed and after a few days made the suggestion that Hardy, to minimize the haemorrhage, should lie with the foot of the bed raised, so that his feet were higher than his head. He had inflammation of the bladder, caused by calculus or stone, which might need a dangerous operation; in fact, this condition recurred for the rest of his life.[32] Stress, worry, fatigue, a very damp house, prolonged bathing in Normandy—which Hardy believed, in this instance, to have been the cause—and subsequent chill would all predispose him to it. In February 1880, he called in Sir Henry Thompson, the internationally famous surgeon, who practised exclusively in diseases of the bladder, and had operated on Napoleon III for stone. Thompson, who had been recommended by Kegan Paul,[33] evidently decided against operation, but advised continued rest.

Yet work must go on. He could not let Harper and the golden opportunity slip. He would dictate the novel to Emma, to whom he afterwards paid a tribute for working "bravely at both writing and nursing".[34] Yet, not unnaturally, the last five of the six books of *A Laodicean* show a terrible decline. The first book ended with a garden-party, based on one at the Macmillans, where the delicate relationships between hero and heroine are shown, combining the impact of a summer thunderstorm with the flickering emotions of the two. It recalls the great storm scene in *Far From the Madding Crowd*. From then onward, though, Hardy fell back on every sort of borrowed literary short-cut, to meet the numbers of the serial on time. Already, he had drawn heavily on the maxims of Balthasar Gracian the Jesuit, copied so faithfully into his notebook by Emma in their Sturminster days.[35] In describing old De Stancy, who uses these aphorisms, he also lifted about two hundred words from a sketch of a notable racing man in an article, "The Turf", from an old *Quarterly Review*.[36] Now, and as always under literary pressure, he drew on his boyhood reading of the tawdry historical romances of Harrison Ainsworth. Dare, the baby-faced villain of *A Laodicean*, is an Ainsworth villain like the evil Earl of Rochester in *Old St. Pauls*, who combines a spurious innocence with the blackest villainy.[37] Not only literature but topography was pressed into service, as the novel dragged to a close. Books five and six are a travelogue of the Hardys' journeys up the Rhine and to the Low Countries in 1876 and the recent visit to Normandy. Hardy's recent theatre experience is seen in the telegrams to and from the actress's agent (Book 3). Hardy afterwards told the American William Lyon Phelps that he feared he would die, and therefore perhaps put more of the facts of his own life into the book than anything he had then written.[38] Yet, unless one counts the lengthy travelogue, all the personal incidents from Hardy's early life, the dispute about infant baptism, the discussions on the architecture, had been written before he fell ill. There is obsessive use of coincidence, and what can only be called voyeuristic incidents, which are certainly typical of Hardy himself. Captain de Stancy, inflamed by unaccustomed drink, sees through a hole in a wall the heroine exercising in a pink gymnastic dress.

Though occasional London friends such as Edmund Gosse visited him, he was largely alone with Emma. His wife's devoted care through the appallingly cold winter of 1880–81 bore fruit; a letter to her from his sister Mary pays tribute, and incidentally shows how close the two women were at this time.[39] On 10 April 1881, Hardy went out of doors in a carriage, on 1 May he finished *A Laodicean* himself in pencil, and on 3 May was given a clean bill of health by Sir Henry Thompson. A few days later he walked out alone for the first time for six months on Wandsworth Common, and repeated happily to himself in the sunshine some lines from Gray's *Ode on the Pleasure Arising from Vicissitude.* He was well again; but the illness had convinced him of two things. One was that London was bad for his health; he may well have remembered his near-breakdown in 1867. The other was that, contrary to the advice he had believed, and which had caused him to come to London, living in or near a big city harmed his work. Perhaps the larger stage, crowded with characters, confused a mind formed in a solitary Dorset hamlet. The smaller provincial setting might, after all, profit him more. At all events, he and Emma decided to live again in Dorset, with visits of only a few months a year to London.

3

Wimborne

"LANHERNE", The Avenue, Wimborne, where the Hardys moved on 25 June 1881, provided a setting, though in the town, which reminded them of their idyllic surroundings at Sturminster Newton. The road had a row of newly-planted lime trees, and, as Hardy wrote after a few days,

> Our garden has all sorts of old-fashioned flowers in full bloom: Canterbury bells, blue and white, and Sweet Williams of every variety, strawberries and cherries that are ripe, currants and gooseberries that are nearly ripe, peaches that are green, and apples that are decidedly immature.

Not only was there an orchard, a conservatory, and a vine on the wall, but they found the local society rewarding, and not at all unintelligent. There were musical evenings at the home of a County Court judge, Tindal Atkinson, and regular Shakespeare readings, in which the Hardys took part, though Dr. George Batterbury, who organized these, found Hardy very reticent.[1] Still, in such company and atmosphere, he began to feel himself again, both as a man and a writer.[2] Even the fact that *A Laodicean*, when published later in the year, was quickly remaindered, did not seem to disturb him unduly. Nor did the insult that *Harper's Magazine*, after having commissioned and serialized the work, attacked the book, when it appeared in volume form, in one of the most discouraging reviews that Hardy had ever received.[3] He may well have been compensated by a eulogistic survey of his works in the *British Quarterly Review*, a nonconformist paper which praised him to the skies.[4] By all signs, Hardy was at peace and in health again, and already exploring new plans for work.

The best evidence that Hardy found renewed health and enjoyment of life at Wimborne is that he composed a humorous poem, perhaps his first since *The Bride Night Fire*, printed half-a-dozen years before. He noticed that the churchyard of Wimborne Minster had been levelled, and all the tombstones redistributed. The architect Sir Arthur Blomfield, whom he had just met after fifteen years, reminded Hardy of the 1860s, when they had supervised the removal of hundreds of jumbled coffins from Old St. Pancras Churchyard, with strange results. "Do you remember," were Blomfield's first words, "how we found the man with two heads at St. Pancras?"[5] Hardy exploited this idea in a poem about

25

Wimborne Minster, *The Levelled Churchyard*, and invested it with an earthy humour suitable to its rural setting. Two of its verses read, in his manuscript,

> Where we are huddled none can trace,
> And if our names remain
> They pave some path or p—ing place
> Where we have never lain!

> There's not a modest maiden elf
> But dreads the final Trumpet,
> Lest half of her should rise herself,
> And half some local strumpet!

He clearly delighted in this fancy; for when much later he published the poem, the adjective "p—ing" for "pissing" was allowed to stand through several editions, and when finally changed to "porch or" in his *Collected Poems*, the alteration was made in an errata slip, which must have drawn even more attention to the word.

Even before launching into such light relief, Hardy had found inspiration for a new novel. By an astonishing chance this grew out of his recent illness. Hardy's final consultation had been with the specialist, Sir Henry Thompson. Handsome and slim, with dark penetrating eyes, Thompson was a man of myriad enthusiasms, quite outside medicine. Those who knew him well said that he hurled himself into each new subject, only to give it up after some years when he had exhausted its interest.[6] At the time Hardy met him in 1881, the ruling passion was astronomy. Thompson had made in his house at East Molesey a private observatory; he equipped it with the finest instruments, and employed a qualified assistant.[7] He was incapable of remaining quiet about whatever happened to be the reigning enthusiasm,[8] and the interview with Hardy at this time cannot have passed without a detailed description of his personal observatory. Hardy was primed for a novel set in an amateur observatory before he left for Wimborne: his first night in the new home confirmed it by the appearance of Tebbutt's Comet, which he and Emma saw from their little conservatory at "Lanherne".[9]

Hardy forged ahead with plans for his new astronomical novel. By another happy chance, on 23 July 1881, he, Emma, and his sister Kate, now a teacher at Sandford Orcas, just over the Somerset border, went from Wimborne on a wagonette drive past the estate of Charborough with its hilltop tower, a late Georgian folly, rebuilt in 1839 after being struck by lightning. Hardy seized on this for his hero's home-made observatory, though he later mixed it with features from other Dorset towers, notably the column near Milborne St. Andrew, which provided most of the setting as distinct from the architecture.[10] Moreover the old driver of the wagonette told them local stories of Miss

Drax, who once owned Charborough, and who had married a hand-some man much younger than herself.[11] From such hints came Viviette and Swithin, the heroine and hero of *Two on a Tower*, though Hardy invested them not only with age-difference but also with class-difference, on his old obsessive pattern of *The Poor Man and the Lady*.

Hardy was quick to use these ideas, in spite of spending the last week of August and the first fortnight of September touring Scotland, and the rest of September sitting under his garden-vine, correcting proofs of the volume-form *A Laodicean*.[12] At the beginning of October, *Atlantic Monthly* asked him for a serial. He clearly had the new story in preparation, since on 26 November he wrote to the Astronomer Royal for permission to see Greenwich Observatory, pretending to be asking "if it would be possible for him [Hardy] to adapt an old tower, built in a plantation in the West of England for other objects, to the requirements of a telescopic study of the stars by a young man very ardent in that pursuit". Evidently the shy Hardy had not sufficiently impressed Sir Henry Thompson, a connoisseur of conversation, to get an invitation to Molesey. However, this fictional ruse got him a pass to Greenwich, and proves that he had already fixed the details of tower and surrounding landscape by that date; in December he was writing to William Cawthorne Unwin, the engineer, for information on lens-grinding and telescopes. He also consulted books on astronomy by Richard A. Proctor, founder of the recent scientific weekly, *Knowledge*.

This, and the speed at which Hardy was obviously working—he also completed two new short stories in these autumn months—show that he was finding no handicap in living once more in Dorset. Perhaps the three years just spent in London for literary purposes had been an unnecessary mistake. It has even been suggested that his difficulties as a writer in London—the hasty plagiarism in *The Trumpet-Major*, the lack of inspiration in *A Laodicean*—"may conceivably have derived, directly or indirectly, from the bad literary company he tended to keep" during those years.[13] There may be something in this, though the statement is a sweeping one. On analysis, Hardy's literary contacts in that period fall into two distinct groups. First, there were his encounters with Tennyson, Browning, Arnold, and Henry James, whose first major novels appeared in these years. Hardy recorded them in wry, thumbnail sketches—Tennyson's wife lying on the sofa "as if in a coffin", Matthew Arnold, with a young and inexperienced hostess, not letting the ladies retire after dinner, an action which must have inconvenienced them, but of whose results that high-minded thinker seemed happily unaware. Yet these, and his continued visits to the ancient literary widow of Barry Cornwall, were brief meetings. Hardy was too shy to follow them up, and, for instance, greatly regretted that, although invited, he never again went to see the Tennysons. A soirée musicale, to meet members

of the 1878 International Literary Congress and of the Comédie Fran-
çaise, bewildered him.[14]

The second class of literary friends had been quite different. Perhaps
the most reputable was Edmund Gosse; the rest were bookish, but
without special spark, editors, translators, collaborators, part-time
writers. W. H. Pollock and the heavily-bearded J. W. Comyns Carr
were play-adaptors, Joseph Knight a dramatic critic, William Minto a
minor novelist and editor of Scott. Frederick Locker was a minor poet,
Charles Godfrey Leland, the craggy-faced American, a writer of light
verse and translator of Heine, Sir Patrick Maccombaich Colquhoun was
better known as an oarsman, secretary of Leander, than for his legal
essays; Reginald Bosworth Smith, fellow Dorset man and Harrow
schoolmaster, wrote books on North African history. Sir George Douglas,
whose brother Frank was a neighbour of Hardy at Wimborne, tried to
write romantic novels.

Perhaps the most congenial to Hardy was his exact contemporary,
Edward Henry Palmer, the orientalist, a self-taught counterpart of the
Dorchester boy Tolbort, whom Hardy had known in youth. While a
poor clerk, Palmer had learnt languages from foreign waiters in London
cafés. A Cambridge teacher of Hindustani had taken him up, as Horace
Moule had Tolbort, and he became Fellow of a College and author of a
book of Eastern travels. Sent on a secret mission to Egypt by Gladstone's government, Palmer, like Tolbort, died in his early forties, in his
instance the victim of murder by Arabs. The moving spirit in the circle
was Walter Besant, bearded like a sailor, jovial founder of the Rabelais
Club, for writers who had shown "virility"—that is, sexual frankness—
in their work, to which Hardy was flatteringly elected as an original
member. Besant was the co-author with James Rice of robust historical
romances, the Besant and Rice novels, natural successors to those of
Hardy's youthful favourite, Harrison Ainsworth, though slightly more
distinguished. With a finger in every pie, he helped in 1884 to start the
Society of Authors, where, Hardy said, "he gloats over the villainies of
publishers";[15] but he was hardly a great literary figure.

Nor had Hardy, in his three London years, encountered high society,
though he had been introduced to Sir Percy Shelley, the poet's son, and
the Russells had been present when he met Tennyson. By an irony, the
middle-class Emma now became his passport into the circles which
meant so much to him in his later London seasons.[16] Emma's uncle,
Canon Edwin Hamilton Gifford, married as his second wife a daughter
of Bishop Jeune of Peterborough. In summer 1881, just when the Hardys
were settled at Wimborne, came the social step crucial to them. On
16 August, Francis Jeune, Canon Gifford's brother-in-law, married
Susan Mary Elizabeth, the relatively young widow of Colonel the Hon.
John Constantine Stanley. Stanley had been heir presumptive to his

brother, the third Lord Stanley of Alderley, and his widow's remarriage in the Savoy Chapel was an excessively fashionable event, with royalty present. Emma was now connected, however remotely, with the highest society, including the powerful tribe of Stanley. Hardy soon became a favourite of the lively Mrs. Jeune, whose own background was aristocratic in its own right. It is ironical to think of Hardy, the son of a cook, beside this lady whose ancestors had owned half the Highlands "from sea to sea", and who complained of "the difficulty of getting a decent cook" for her lavish entertainment.[17] He at once noted a weird legend from her family history in Scotland,[18] and adopted for the name of his highborn heroine in *Two on a Tower*, Lady Constantine, the middle name of her first husband, John Constantine Stanley. He also adopted his nature for the unpleasant husband, Sir Blount Constantine; for "Johnnie" Stanley was as unreasonable and violent as the fictional Sir Blount.[19] Moreover, he took a chapter from her second husband's professional career. Francis Jeune had, as one of his first assignments in the law, the task of investigating the notorious Tichborne claimant. With a special commission, he actually visited Wagga Wagga in Australia, and came back with the impression—or so his wife afterwards asserted[20]—that the man who claimed to be the lost Sir Roger Tichborne, and who had been living in that town as a butcher, was an imposter named Arthur Orton. Jeune actually appeared *for* Orton, as a junior, and must have been relieved when his leader threw the case up. It has never been noticed before how echoes of the Tichborne case occur throughout one of the sub-plots of *Two on a Tower*. Sir Blount Constantine is reported in London when he should be hunting big game in Africa. Investigation by Hardy's young hero proves it to be a case of mistaken identity. Then again, the two reports at two different times of Sir Blount's death in Africa, on which the sub-plot hinges, at once suggest the actual death abroad of Sir Roger Tichborne, and the claimant's contention that he did not die. It may not be accidental that the Christian name of the credulous Lady Tichborne, Henriette, reminds one of Lady Constantine's name, Viviette, while her brother in the novel reappears from Rio, the last known habitation of the real Sir Roger. It is a fact, too, that Jeune used to regale guests, including Hardy, with details of the case.[21]

Hardy's portrayal of his passionate heroine, Viviette, owed less to real life than to a contemporary dramatic poem. In April 1882, when Hardy was writing the novel, Swinburne, whose work Hardy had adored in the 1860s, brought out his *Tristram of Lyonesse*. Hardy, deeply stirred by the setting where he himself had met and wooed Emma, read the new poem avidly. Physical descriptions of Hardy's heroine echo those of Iseult in the poem. He even quoted three lines of it in the novel, just before she yields to fatal passion.

He turn'd and saw the terror in her eyes,
That yearn'd upon him shining in such wise
As a star midway in the midnight fix'd.

Hardy also copied two passages from the Prologue into his notebooks, and it is clear he saw in it a parallel to his own story. He had already used the poetry of Tennyson for some of his own astronomical descriptions in the novel.[22] Here, in Swinburne's poem, he found the famous women in love all through history, from Helen to Guinevere, compared by Swinburne individually to various kinds of star. In Hardy's mind the passionate nature of his heroine was at one with these great lovers of history, and his prose when dealing with Viviette takes on the sensuous intensity of Swinburne's verse.

Aside from details of plot and sub-plots, the main design of *Two on a Tower* was, in Hardy's own words, "to set the emotional history of two infinitesimal lives against the stupendous background of the stellar universe, and to impart to readers the sentiment that of these contrasting magnitudes the smaller might be the greater to them as men".[23] This theme had been stated by Hardy fifteen years before, in two very early sonnets, *At a Lunar Eclipse* and *In Vision I Roamed*.[24] The novel shows how modern scientific discovery, by probing deeper into the universe, seems to intensify purely human problems. In this, it continues the process of *A Laodicean*, where innovations such as railway construction, the electric telegraph, technical improvement in architecture, and even revolutionary bomb-making, form the material background to a human love-story. The critics found in *Two on a Tower* not only the usual traces of immorality they expected to deplore in a Hardy plot, but also a satire on the Established Church. The editor of the *Atlantic Monthly*, which serialized the work from May to December 1882, was perturbed, and when it appeared, practically unrevised, in volume form at the end of October, public and critics were offended too. Hardy's own reply to the *St. James's Gazette* early in 1883, and his later defence,[25] are surely disingenuous, or even possibly satirical in themselves. Hardy's "studied insult to the Church", which critics found, was not confined to his plot-device by which the pregnant heroine marries a Bishop solely in order to pass off her illegitimate child as the seven months' offspring of the Bishop himself. For all that Hardy might say, broad satire of the established clergy runs right through the book, in which the Bishop does not even make an appearance until over half-way. The hero's father is a clergyman who marries beneath him, is snubbed by the gentry, drops "a cuss or two", becomes a farmer, and falls dead, "it being said . . . Master God was in tantrums wi'en for leaving his service". When the hero and heroine get married—illegally, as the report of her former husband's death is at that time false—the proceedings are described farcically. The clergyman is a locum tenens, "apt to be rather wandering in his wits"; the clerk apologetically explains, "The best men goes into the brewing; or into the shipping now-a-days." When the parson actually appears, Hardy describes him as a "somewhat sorry clerical specimen", who has been found shambling about in the cemetery, under the impression it was a funeral and not a wedding. As for Mr. Torkingham, vicar of the heroine's own parish, he is largely a figure of fun, as his punning name suggests. His clerical accent produces a distressingly comic effect when he makes the church choir adopt it; when, "expecting a question on some local business", he finds Lady Constantine wishing to consult him on a point of conscience, he "altered his face to the higher branch of his profession". When he wishes to impress the Bishop at dinner, he prepares and delivers elaborate con-versation-pieces about the last Diocesan Synod, in which he quotes back at length the Bishop's own remarks on that occasion. As for the Bishop himself, he has, according to the heroine, "very pronounced views about his own position, and some other undesirable qualities." He "had personal weaknesses that were fatal to sympathy for more than a moment" and "a mind whose sensitive fear of danger to its own dignity hindered it from criticism elsewhere". He has "the air of a man too good for his destiny", and uses what he calls "the force of trained, logical reasoning" to persuade her that, as a husband, he is "Heaven's gift". Even the cautious Mr. Torkingham, after the Bishop's death, admits he had faults, "of which arrogance was not the least". Hardy was surely indulging in further satire, when in 1895 he claimed "that the Bishop is every inch a gentleman, and that the parish priest who figures in the narrative is one of the most estimable characters".[26]

Hardy, of course, had plenty of good precedent for satirizing the clergy, notably in his much-admired Trollope. Two things, however, seem new in *Two on a Tower*. One is the generalized satire on several types of clergy, which had never occurred before in a Hardy novel—indeed, clerical satire had hardly occurred at all. Only Mr. Swancourt in *A Pair of Blue Eyes* had been portrayed as a social snob throughout that novel. The other is the almost farcical tone of his description of the habits of these satirized clerics, a cause of offence. Yet Hardy had a particular professional motive for making this farcical treatment of the clergy such a part of his new novel. In 1879 he had adapted *Far From the Madding Crowd* as a stage play.[27] A re-adaptation then took place at the hands of J. W. Comyns Carr, who in the summer of 1880 submitted the play to the management of Hare and Kendal. It was accepted provisionally by Hare, but rejected on 11 November, to add to Hardy's depression as he lay ill in bed. Mrs. Kendal afterwards claimed that she never saw it and the rejection was Hare's. Either Hare or she, however, gave the plot to their rising young actor-dramatist Arthur Pinero, without telling him where it came from. Pinero wrote a romantic farce called *The Squire*, in which the leading lady's part was a woman farm-owner. The play was produced at the St. James's on 29 December 1881, and critics at once saw some likeness to *Far From the Madding Crowd*, especially when Hardy and Carr revealed that their play had been submitted to the same management over a year before. In the first week of January 1882, Hardy, up from Wimborne, took a box to see Pinero's play, together with Comyns Carr and the monocled lawyer George Lewis, having been advised by his Wimborne friend, Judge Tindal Atkinson, of a case "on all fours with yours".[28] No writ ensued, and indeed the plays had little in common, though Lewis said unofficially, according to Hardy, that similarity of situation might make a case.[29] There was, however, great newspaper controversy, annoying to Hardy. The *Illustrated Sporting and Dramatic News* suggested a solution

> which could really be best managed by immediately producing Messrs. Hardy and Comyns Carr's play. Surely a genial manager would, in the spirit of gentle rivalry, put the other in rehearsal.

This hint was taken. Comyns Carr drastically revised their play, and after a provincial try-out at Liverpool, which the Hardys attended, and in other towns, it opened at the Globe Theatre on 29 April 1882. However, it ran barely sixty performances in London, whereas Pinero's play had a triumph of 170 nights, followed by an immensely long and successful provincial tour.[30]

The great success of *The Squire* was galling to Hardy; but he doubt-less noticed, from his stage-box, that it depended largely on the part specially written into the play for John Hare himself. This was the character of a self-styled "mad parson", the Reverend Paul Dormer. It had, of course, nothing to do with *Far From the Madding Crowd*, and might not seem particularly funny to a modern audience. It certainly bore no relation to anything in the Hardy and Comyns Carr adaptation of the novel, but a farcical clergyman, with Hare's skilled playing, kept the St. James's audiences continuously amused. In search of a wider public than his recent books had achieved, Hardy tried the theme of comic clergy in the novel he was now writing. Unfortunately, he overdid the satire. It is another irony that when in 1888 the St. James's also pilloried clergy too savagely in *The Dean's Daughter*, that play received just the same sort of shocked notices as Hardy's novel, *Two on a Tower*.[31]

Hardy's visit to London in January 1882 imported yet another theatrical element into his novels and stories. He cannot have failed to go to the big current theatrical success, the very recent revival at the Lyceum of Albery's *Two Roses*, starring his favourite Helen Mathews.[32] She had been engaged, as her first appearance at the Lyceum, to play the part of Katryn in the curtain-raiser, Planché's old-fashioned comedietta, *The Captain of the Watch*. The "Two Roses" of the main play's title, Ida and Lottie, were to be played by two very popular actresses, Fanny Josephs and Winifred Emery. At the last moment, Miss Josephs was taken seriously ill. Helen Mathews had not played Ida before, but she had played Lottie with another company in the provinces, and so was familiar with the sister-part. In these difficult circumstances, she had a startling triumph in taking over the part of Ida; by contrast the pretty Miss Emery was said to be "inoffensive but colourless". In fact, Ida, though the smaller part, is by far the better-written, as clever Miss Mathews clearly had the wit to see. Her tall, dark, slender beauty also suited the stage-directions, which require exactly that. The reviews praised her animated style, her sympathetic voice, her "earnestness and intelligence" which was "deserving of the highest praise" and her "very natural and womanly feeling". Moreover, she scored a triumph in the curtain-raiser too, playing "with great spirit". A promising future was prophesied for her. Unhappily, for some reason, this did not materialize. A very few small parts were all that came her way in the next half-dozen years, and she died in January 1890 at the early age of forty: perhaps a tragedy of poor health.

This is not to say, of course, that Hardy ever met Helen Mathews, any more than he appears to have met Mrs. Scott-Siddons who had affected him so profoundly some years before. His appreciation of her beauty and intelligence was probably entirely from the stalls or the stage-box. The situation is described in his novel of the 1890s, *The Well-Beloved*, whose hero's temperament, by many signs, was exactly that of Hardy himself. In a chapter significantly entitled "Familiar Phenomena in the Distance", Hardy wrote of his hero's pursuit of his womanly transient ideal.

> For months he would find her on the stage of a theatre: then she would flit away, leaving the poor, empty carcase that had lodged her to mumm on as best it could without her—a sorry lay figure to his eyes, heaped with imperfections and sullied with commonplace. . . . Once she was a dancing-girl at the Royal Moorish Palace of Varieties, though during her whole continuance at that establishment he never once exchanged a word with her, nor did she first or last ever dream of his existence.

So though Hardy may have allowed himself, as was his habit, some wistful domestic daydreams, in which slender Miss Mathews took the place of his stout Emma—"a profile not too Greek for an English fireside"—it is unlikely he got any further than a "sweeping glance" from his opera-glass. His admiration, however, is indirectly connected with a grotesque incident later in this year of 1882. A trivial monthly publication, *London Society*, describing itself as "an illustrated magazine of light and amusing literature for the hours of relaxation", received a poem signed "Thomas Hardy", which was duly printed above that signature in August. Entitled *Two Roses*, it played banally with the comparison between a girl and a rose—

> Thou art a rose and so is she;
> Each blossoms in the bright today.

Challenged by Hardy, the editor lamely replied that there must be two Thomas Hardys.[33] The poem had, in fact, been written, probably quite cynically, by a rascally former colleague of Hardy's at Blomfield's London office, who received and pocketed the cheque for it, and forged Hardy's signature, familiar to him, as an endorsement.[34] Hardy's indignation was immense, and justified. Not only were the verses bad, but they were clearly based, as their title and treatment suggests, on the play he had recently been watching with such a deep personal interest, *Two Roses*. In the play, the two girls, acted by Miss Mathews and Miss Emery, appear with bunches of roses, give their lovers the roses, and are frequently compared with roses. For Hardy the hoax was uncomfortably near a home-truth—and moreover a truth he could not acknowledge to anyone, least of all to Emma.

All the same, contact with the theatre, especially if he had a personal interest such as this, always had an influence on Hardy's work. His theatrical enthusiasm can be seen in two short stories published early in 1883. These are *The Three Strangers* and *The Romantic Adventures of a Milkmaid*. The first of these, a grimly humorous little tale with almost perfect unity of setting and action, is so obviously dramatic, that Hardy himself "used to think I w^d. arrange that little story for the stage: and began doing it". He did not finish; but in 1893 James Barrie wrote to ask Hardy for a one-act play, to be produced in London with some others. Hardy took up the task again, adapting it as *The Three Wayfarers*, described by *The Times* as "unquestionably the best piece of the evening".[35] As for *The Romantic Adventures of a Milkmaid*, this hastily-written piece is almost a pantomime, with innocent Cinderella-like heroine, demon-king of a Baron offering a ball-dress, a mysterious ball, a carriage and team of black horses, and a stagey happy ending. Even his novel, *Two on a Tower*, published in volume form late in October 1882, has a melodramatic ending—"Viviette was dead. The Bishop was avenged." Though some critics have approved, this comes perilously near the curtain lines of current melodramas such as *East Lynne* or *Lady Audley's Secret*.

To balance the poor reviews of this novel, there appeared a long survey praising Hardy's work. The writer of this anonymous article in the *Westminster Review*[36] was in fact the young Havelock Ellis. Following his own preferences, this advocate of free love analysed all Hardy's women, and summed up the novels in the words, "what one observes about them first is that they are all love-stories". Ellis coined a vivid general phrase for Hardy's women as "Undines of the earth", and claimed that Hardy's attitude to all these "not too good" women was "in a great degree, new". He praised Hardy as a poet in prose, compared such writing favourably with the actual Dorset poetry of William Barnes, and his descriptive passages with the verse of Emily Brontë. After commending *The Return of the Native* as "above all, the life-history of a woman in all its relations", Ellis made a surprising judgement on Hardy's more recent and future novels. He foresaw, he wrote, that Hardy would develop along the lines of *Ethelberta*, *A Laodicean*, and *Two on a Tower*, or, as he defined it, in delicate, ironic comedy. Nothing could be farther from the course that Hardy's personal and professional life was now to take. He was about to write a tragic novel in which men played the chief part, a book in which the comic irony of such previous novels, with their would-be upper-class setting, was so lacking that a publisher's reader complained it had no gentry in it.[37] Above all, he was about to move, for his own and the book's background, to his native Dorchester.

4

Dorset Home

HARDY wrote an immediate and enthusiastic letter to Havelock Ellis, complimenting him on his charming style, and speaking of his own "unmethodical books".[1] This self-depreciation was not false modesty. Hardy had realized the light-weight quality of his last three novels, and was in the grip of one of his periodic wishes to improve his work, and to surpass himself as a writer. This, as usual, was allied with his desire, since youth, to be a prophet and a leader for his generation. Looking back on this time, a few years later, he set down these feelings:[2] "Ever since I began to write—certainly ever since I wrote *Two on a Tower* . . . I have felt that the doll of English fiction must be demolished, if England is to have a school of English fiction at all." The prophet was about to break the false idols of literary worship.

As usual, he went systematically to work. At Wimborne, only a few miles from the Hampshire border, he was living on the periphery of Dorset. For fulfilment as an artist, he needed the Dorset of his childhood; all through the two Wimborne years, there were signs that he wished to return to his natural centre. Even before going to Wimborne, he had told his brother that he was looking for a plot of building land in Dorchester. Early in 1882, he wrote to the Earl of Ilchester's agent about the possibility of a building site on Stinsford Hill, near his own family home. In the same year, he said Wimborne, with its mud and damp, was too low-lying for health, and he convinced himself that Dorchester would be healthier. Intellectually as well as physically, he wished to identify himself with the county town and the county. Also in 1882, he joined the Dorset Field Club, whose headquarters were in Dorchester.[3] In August 1881, when he had only been in Wimborne a few weeks, he was visited by H. J. Moule, the watercolourist, probably the earliest acquaintance of his youth among the Moule brothers. There was for a time a scheme, suggested by Emma, of a joint book on Dorset, text by Hardy, illustrations by Moule. It came to nothing, but in the last few months at Wimborne Hardy belatedly wrote, in response to an earlier request from *Longman's Magazine,* a long article on "The Dorsetshire Labourer".

The stage was therefore set for a return to the Dorchester district. In point of fact, Emma and Hardy had not spent a great deal of time at Wimborne, though they made some attempt to join in local gatherings, and even attended some first-aid lectures, where Hardy typically noted the odd effect of a dangling skeleton, beyond which, through the window, he could see small children dancing to an outdoor band.[4] They had toured Scotland in August and September 1881, visited London and Liverpool for Hardy's theatrical ventures in 1882, and taken a trip round neighbouring West of England counties later that year. Then, in autumn, Hardy and Emma left home to spend several weeks in a little Paris apartment of two bedrooms and a sitting-room on the Left Bank. This Bohemian expedition was the way Emma thought authors ought to live. She never lost this romantic picture of herself and Hardy as two carefree vagabonds, blown by the wind of artistic impulse. Seventeen years later, she explained with evident pride, "we are erratically-minded and *actioned*! rushing off when it occurs to be easy and nice, every way".[5] However sardonically Hardy viewed her breathless and ungrammatical programmes, he obviously enjoyed his part now, "studying the pictures in the Louvre and Luxembourg, practising housekeeping in the Parisian bourgeois manner, buying their own groceries and vegetables, dining at restaurants", though being Hardy he added, "and catching bad colds owing to the uncertain weather".[6]

The Hardys, it seems, in spite of early difficulties, and perhaps jealousies, still enjoyed married happiness on this light-hearted, informal holiday. One cannot live a picnic life except with a person one likes. Yet Hardy had not quite counted the risks to this happiness of taking Emma to live in Dorchester. His work blinded him to the obvious dangers. For one thing, Emma would be in the close and critical neighbourhood of his immediate family, for whom she had virtually given up her own relatives. Her only real contact was a favourite cousin, Edith Gifford of Launceston, who in 1882 had had an experience like some woman in a Hardy short story; finding her fiancé had made a local dressmaker pregnant, she broke off her engagement, and made the young man marry the girl.[7] Emma does not seem at this time to have visited her own parents, now living at Compton Gifford near Plymouth, and within comparatively easy reach. Nor does she seem to have gone to the funeral, which they attended, of her brother-in-law at the end of November 1882, though she still kept in touch with her widowed sister, who wrote in September 1883, on hearing of the move to Dorchester, "I suppose it will be a pretty cottage quite picturesque that you will choose for yourself."[8] Nothing could be farther from reality. Back in Hardy's home town, Emma had no choice. Thomas did the choosing. Not finding a house for sale in Dorchester, he rented, as a temporary measure, a gloomy, dark building in the narrow Shirehall Lane. "He have only one window and she do look into Gaol Lane" was the local description. For a permanent home, he decided to buy land

and build. By October he had negotiated with the Duchy of Cornwall, who owned the Fordington area of Dorchester, for a plot beside the Wareham road, near an old toll-gate. Hardy was his own architect, and his brother Henry, who had taken over from their rheumatic father, was the builder.

The work of design and building all through the winter months, naturally threw Hardy back into the centre of his family. Emma tried to adapt to the new environment. She got out her watercolours, and sketched the scenes of his boyhood, sometimes on the spot, sometimes from earlier paintings by their friend H. J. Moule;[9] but there are signs that she was never really taken into the family circle. Dr. F. B. Fisher, who now looked after Hardy's father and mother, remembered how, in the Bockhampton cottage, "the whole family [of Hardys], two sons and daughters, could tell stories, and did so during the long winter evenings round the big fireplace, criticizing one another's efforts very freely".[10] He does not suggest that Emma took part in these fireside evenings, when Hardy visited the others. Strong family tradition has it that she was not welcome in Jemima Hardy's household, and there is even stronger evidence in her own words. Some years later, Emma wrote an often-quoted letter[11] on the causes of estrangement between man and wife. One paragraph, which has never been quoted, is this:

> Interference from others is greatly to be feared—members of either family too often are the causes of estrangement—a woman does not object to be ruled by her husband, so much as she does by a relative at his back—a man seldom cares to control such matters, when in his power, & lets things glide, or throws his balance on the wrong side which is simply a terrible state of affairs, & may affect unfavourably himself in the end.

With her husband, the "relative at his back" can only have been his mother Jemima, who grew to dominate her family more and more with age. Of course, a more tactful and resourceful woman than Emma might have found ways to overcome this formidable handicap to their marriage. Up to this time, she seems to have had a very good relationship with Hardy's two sisters, Mary and Kate. In failing with Jemima, she cannot avoid some of the blame.

Hardy's return to the family seems to have been only to the immediate circle under his mother's wing, his father, brother, and two sisters. It hardly included the very numerous Hand, Sparks, and Antell cousins, whom Hardy virtually never mentions in his writing, except for one single reference by initials to one cousin, John Antell. Even when members die, he gives no word. Late in 1884, his cousin, Emma Sparks (Mrs. Cary), died within weeks of emigrating to Australia. She had recently been in his thoughts, for just before leaving

Wimborne he had written a story for boys, *Our Exploits at West Poley*, which he called "A Tale of the Mendips", and which described a caving adventure. She had lived in a little Somerset hamlet, full of Mendip miners, and her boys were the ages of those in the story. They were now looked after by Martha Mary Sparks (Mrs. Duffield), who had emigrated earlier to Queensland, and who had been one of Hardy's early loves. In 1885, Rebecca Sparks (Mrs. Pain) also died, at the Topsham home of the fourth sister Tryphena (Mrs. Gale). Rebecca had first attracted Hardy's adolescent attentions, and Tryphena had had some sort of engagement with him. Not a sign of this appears: but his diary is full of his immediate family. There are long descriptions of the plantation behind the Bockhampton cottage, "The Birds' Bedroom" as they called it in childhood, of strange local anecdotes by his mother and father. Even his unobtrusive but much-loved sister Mary provides remarks which he notes, while in August 1884 he goes off on a bachelor holiday with brother Henry to the Channel Isles.

The prophet had come home to his admiring family; but he had little honour in his county town. "Some people say he was a bit queer in the head," remembered one citizen, "But I think he was just strange like the stories he wrote."[12] He wandered about, half-unnoticed, among the scenes of his past loves, only to renounce them. In 1883, he wrote a poem with the chilling title, *He Abjures Love*. Even in its first stanza, he has the Biblical accent of the returned prophet.

> At last I put off love,
> For twice ten years
> The daysman of my thought,
> And hope, and doing;
> Being ashamed thereof,
> And faint of fears
> And desolations wrought
> In his pursuing.

The language is that of Hardy's heavily-marked Bible—the word "daysman" is actually underlined by him in the Book of Job—and the echoes of putting off the old man, putting away childish things, are pervasive. In the clinching final stanza, the prophet speaks, and yet admits a human doubt.

> —I speak as one who plumbs
> Life's dim profound,
> One who at length can sound
> Clear views and certain.
> But—after love what comes?
> A scene that lours,
> A few sad vacant hours,
> And then, the Curtain.

Next year, 1884, one of these loves forced herself into his mind's eye in
A Countenance, which began

> Her laugh was not in the middle of her face quite,
>   As a gay laugh springs,

and ended

> Alas, I knew not much of her,
> And lost all sight and touch of her!
>
> If otherwise, should I have minded
> The shy laugh not in the middle of her mouth quite,
> And would my kisses have died of drouth quite
>   As love became unblinded?

Not only did Hardy turn away from the memories of his own former
loves. In his new serious purpose as a novelist, he turned away from all
former heroines. *The Mayor of Casterbridge*, which he started writing in
1884, has no woman who is like these "Undines of the earth", in Havelock Ellis's phrase, or who is "of the coming-on disposition", as Gosse
wrote a few years later. Such women had been the core of every previous novel; even the colourless heroine of his first published book,
Desperate Remedies, has her moments of caprice and coquetry. Now his
story demanded heroic and masculine stature. Its chief character,
Michael Henchard, is a tragic hero on Shakespearian scale. Some critics
have seen a likeness to King Lear; but Henchard's weakness, violence,
generous impulse, jealousies, mistakes, simplicities, superstitions, large
though often futile gestures, physical strength, and ultimate wish to
"extenuate nothing", are more like a Dorchester Othello.[13] The likeness to Cassio of Farfrae, his successful rival both professionally and in
love, is unmistakable. Hardy saw a performance of *Othello* by strolling
players during the first few months of writing the novel; and though
he records how the chief actor had to stop and rebuke a rustic audience,
he was perhaps more influenced than he realized.[14]

The leap forward in power, purpose, and construction is astonishing.
Even the Greek tragedy pattern of *The Return of the Native* is surpassed,
and there are several reasons for this. Hardy was not writing against
time; the novel was not due to be serialized in the *Graphic* until 1886.
Not only could he finish it well before serialization; he could, and did,
revise it substantially for publication in volume form. He was guiltily
conscious that he had not revised his last book, *Two on a Tower*; he had
gone instead on his Parisian holiday with Emma. Hardy thought he had
still failed to iron out the episodic serial shape of *The Mayor of Casterbridge*; but it remains the best plotted and the most dramatic of all his
novels.

Yet time to write, time to revise, cannot alone account for this advance. Hardy's artistic instinct had been right. He needed Dorchester. Rejecting a first notion of a novel about Roman Dorchester, prompted by the discovery that his building site was a Roman burial-ground, he set it in the town he knew as a child, round about 1850. Even then, it is not merely a historic picture. It evokes the spirit of a nineteenth-century county town at all times; Hardy combines both an older and a newer Dorchester. To start with, on 4 April, he was elected Justice of the Peace for the Borough of Dorchester.[15] Although "according to his own account he plays the part of Justice Silence with great assiduity", this not only brought him in touch with Dorchester affairs but may have contributed to the scene of the magistrates in the novel.[16] He also sought, for many incidents, the files of the *Dorset County Chronicle* for 1826-30. Wife-selling, living with a second "husband", the dinner at the King's Arms, Henchard's honourable conduct at his bankruptcy, his oath to abstain from drink, even his shaming of Abel Whittle, can all be found in these files.[17] Why did Hardy seek these events of the late 1820s? It was because they were the years of his mother's girlhood, and her own stories all come from this period. What he heard by the cottage fireside was supplemented by what he read in Dorchester, though not all the incidents he used had occurred in the town itself. Yet this picture of the generation past was itself supplemented by material from the immediate present. Dorchester was no longer the town of Hardy's childhood. From 1870, expansion and industry had appeared. When Hardy began to write *The Mayor of Casterbridge*, Eddison's Steam-Plough Works was well established in Dorchester. Francis Eddison was a Leeds man and the works were run by North-countrymen and Midlanders, whose ability, jobs, and pay were objects of local envy. Hardy simply shifted his fictional newcomer's origins a little north of the Border. Farfrae's northern skill and enterprise, even his new machinery, were intensely topical in the Dorchester of 1884-85. So was that accompaniment of industrial life, the cycle of boom and slump. Failures and bankruptcies abound in Dorchester of the 1880s; even Francis Eddison only saved his credit by ingeniously adapting his works from steam-ploughs to road-making machinery.[18] The ways of "foreigners" were resented. Hardy himself protested without sucess against the noise of Eddison's 5.45 a.m. factory hooter, while, later, Hardy's little pageboy, Fred Randall, was induced, probably by higher wages, to work for Eddison's as a water-cart boy.[19]

In the novel, this composite Dorchester is frequently seen through the eyes of one of Hardy's most remarkable characters, Elizabeth Jane, Henchard's supposed daughter. Her literary origins clearly derive from an unlikely source. In his last year at Wimborne, Hardy copied this passage[20] from J. H. Shorthouse's novel, *John Inglesant*:

> From those high windows beyond the flower-pots young girls have
> looked out upon life, which their instincts told them was made for
> pleasure but which year after year convinced them was, somehow or
> other, given over to pain.

It is an almost exact picture of the girl who sees so many passing events
of Hardy's "Casterbridge" from "high windows"—indeed, sometimes
from windows in a house Hardy has called High Hall Place. Hardy
ends the novel with her, in words that closely recall those of Shorthouse.

> And in being forced to class herself among the fortunate she did not
> cease to wonder at the persistence of the unforeseen when the one to
> whom such unbroken tranquillity had been accorded in the adult stage
> was she whose youth had seemed to teach that happiness was but the
> occasional episode in a general drama of pain.

The self-effacing Elizabeth Jane is all the more moving for her personal
origins. Hardy had returned to the one person who could move his
sympathy almost as deeply as his mother. This was his sister Mary.
She was now beside him in the streets of Dorchester itself; for just at
this time, she moved from teaching in the village of Piddlehinton, and
became head teacher at the "National" school in Bell Street, Dorchester,
helped by her sister Kate, who took charge of children in the first
class.[21] Mary's silent witness pervades the novel. Summing up Elizabeth Jane, Hardy wrote, "that she was not demonstratively thankful
was no fault of hers". Years later, hearing the parson read over his
sister's grave the verse, "I held my tongue and spake nothing: I kept
silent, yea, even from good words," Hardy exclaimed, "That was my
poor Mary, exactly."[22] Hardy's work at this stage displays a paradox.
There is an enhanced tenderness, connected with close family relationships, yet an almost ruthless manipulation of the fortunes of men and
women, as if he had cut his sympathies off from all but those nearest to
him. Emma was not far out when she perceived that exclusive attention
to his family could be a harmful influence.

Hardy's gloomy isolation was not decreased by the move on 29 June
1885 to Max Gate, the newly-built home called after Mack the toll-
house keeper. The house was undistinguished and ill-designed, resembling any one of the turreted, nondescript suburban villas he and
the local architect Crickmay had put up in the Greenhill area of Weymouth in the 1870s. It was cramped and inhospitable. The spare bedroom was at first only large enough for a bachelor visitor. Nor had
brother Henry done his job too well as a builder. Within three years, a
portion of the drawing-room ceiling fell down. Moreover, Hardy felt
depressed in this way of life, which he called "cottage-like and lonely".
In mid-November he recorded that for three days he suffered "a fit of
depression, as if enveloped in a leaden cloud". This was followed by a

two days' sick headache, and just over a month later he wrote, "the end of the old year 1885 finds me sadder than many previous New Year's Eves have done". He doubted the wisdom of building; but he had other doubts he could not put into words.[23] To add to his depression, he had a return of his bladder trouble. Though the family doctor, Fisher, claimed to cure him, it returned, at intervals, for the rest of his life.

It has been pointed out that the Hardys did not by any means spend all their time at Max Gate. Hardy spoke of "four or five months a year spent in London or elsewhere" and later claimed to be "half a Londoner". Yet according to the Hardys' fashionable friend, Mrs. Jeune, they were "very little in London".[24] It seems that their real centre was Dorchester. They usually came to London for "the season", that is, the three-and-a-half months from just after Easter until late July; but a sympathetic observer noted that, even after twenty years of this, Hardy and Emma were never at home in London society, appearing still as two dowdy and rather pathetic bourgeois provincials.[25] With the self-conscious deprecation of the country-dweller, Hardy wrote in 1886 of "us small people down here", and in London he was always quick to suspect a snub. At the following year's Royal Academy dinner he commented, "I spoke to a good many; was apparently unknown to a good many more I knew."[26] It was more than the two or three thousand Austrian pines he planted at Max Gate that isolated Hardy from his fellows.

One of the few to break through to him was Edmund Gosse. During the early 1880s, a slow friendship had grown between the two. Gosse had overcome in himself a restrictive childhood; now he began to overcome Hardy's reserve. In Hardy's last days at Wimborne, Gosse lured him up to London to stay a week-end at his own Paddington house— "Lord, how we would talk!"—and to join a literary and artistic party at the Savile on Monday 25 June 1883, to meet the American man of letters, William Dean Howells. Hardy's shyness made Howells feel, "I had only shaken hands with Hardy across his threshold", but it was a feat for Gosse to get him there at all.[27] Gosse, in turn, was the Hardys' first and probably for a long time only house-guest at Dorchester. He actually stayed with them during their first weeks in the town in 1883. He and Hardy visited William Barnes, now rector of Winterborne Came, attended one of his services there, and afterwards looked at his pictures in the rectory. Gosse was also the first to stay at Max Gate in 1886, when he was again able to see Barnes, just before the latter's death.

Gosse had other tastes in common with Hardy besides literature. His father and grandfather had lived in Poole and Blandford, and he himself knew East Dorset well as a boy. Another shared interest was a passion for cats. Gosse's London household was ruled at this time by a proud Persian tabby professional beauty called Atossa, the gift of

Walter Pater, whom she resembled in appearance and manner. She sat for her portrait to Laurence Alma-Tadema and was sculpted by Hamo Thornycroft, both mutual friends of Gosse and Hardy.[28] The cat in Hardy's Dorchester household in the 1880s had the very eccentric name of Kiddleywinkempoops-Trot. He (or she) was the forerunner of a long succession of cats, who inspired Hardy to poetry. One, Snow-dove, drew from Hardy one of his finest serious elegaic poems, *Last Words to a Dumb Friend*. All lie, named, under their respective head-stones in the garden at Max Gate. There were other elements of light distraction. Though the Hardys faced their tragedy of childlessness—Emma was now forty-five—they were not without a child in the house. Emma's tiresome brother Walter, though in a safe job as a Post Office official, had the habit of dumping his children on country relatives. Between 1885 and 1887, his daughter Lilian came several times. This little red-cheeked, round-faced creature, like a Dutch doll, charmed Hardy, and he drew a series of comic sketches for her. Over the next fifteen years she and her brother Gordon came to live for long periods, almost as adopted children.

Such diversions were welcome, for Hardy was now more continuously at work than ever before. In October 1884, while he was still in the midst of *The Mayor of Casterbridge*, John Morley asked for a new serial for *Macmillan's Magazine*. In the middle of March 1885, just before finishing *The Mayor of Casterbridge*, Hardy finally agreed.[29] A new full-scale work, begun immediately after such a highly-wrought performance, taxed Hardy's powers severely. He decided to use "the woodland story" he had put aside in 1875, when he wrote *The Hand of Ethelberta* instead. Even so, he was not sure whether its original design would do; but in mid-November 1885, he decided it would, and set himself to work from half-past ten in the morning till midnight. One instalment was actually finished in the taproom of a village inn.[30] It was a for-midable programme, even with Emma's considerable fair-copying and a ready-made plot.

The Woodlanders, in fact, naturally looks backs to his manner of a decade before, when the story was first conceived. It resembles out-wardly the plot of *Far From the Madding Crowd*, in its combination of faithful suitor, flashy rival, and a heroine who makes the fatal choice. With variations and minor excursions, this had been the basic Hardy plot in many other works. Yet here tragic realism is a new factor, already hinted in a much lighter work, *The Trumpet-Major*. There it had been the subject of a sardonic exchange between Hardy and Leslie Stephen. Stephen had said, "The heroine married the wrong man." Hardy replied that they mostly did. "Not in magazines," was Stephen's saturnine rejoinder. Now, although writing for a magazine, Hardy set out to demolish the "doll" of English fiction, which demanded a happy ending. There is no respite for his faithful suitor or his heroine. One dies, the other is left married to "the wrong man"; not even the new divorce laws can help her.

Many people have connected Hardy's increasing pessimism about marriage in his novels with the stresses of his own. One critic hints at finding, in the 1930s, evidence of an attachment between him and an unhappily-married local woman soon after his move back to Dorchester.[31] Stresses were certainly there; yet this theme of misalliance and mismating, always seen from the woman's point of view, sprang from his own deepest family history. The woman, who had made the first fatal mistake, was his mother's mother, Betsy Swetman; she married George Hand, and condemned herself to lifelong poverty and parish charity, at first eked out by taking in parish lodgers, later by the dole after her husband's death.[32] This was the burden of Hardy's own mother's fireside discourses, her unhappy beginnings as a charity child. It explains why he set *The Woodlanders* where he did, roughly in the rectangle of North Dorset bounded by Sherborne, Yeovil, Holywell, and Minterne. In 1912, on re-reading the novel in proof for the Wessex Edition, he remarked, "On taking up *The Woodlanders* and reading it after many years I think I like it, *as a story*, the best of all. Perhaps that is owing to the locality and scenery of the action, a part I am very fond of." Many critics, mistaking what Hardy said, believe that *The Woodlanders* comes closest to the terrain of his own childhood. It does not; *Far From the Madding Crowd* and, even more, *The Return of the Native* represent the places of young Hardy's playground. He was "very fond of" the locality of *The Woodlanders* because it was the place of his mother's childhood; doubtless, he liked it best "as a story" because it was of a piece with the stories she told. The cottage where her own widowed mother had brought up seven children including Jemima in shameful poverty was in the east quarter of the Melbury Osmond parish, in the direction of Hermitage and Minterne. Hardy was at special pains to point out, both by letter and postcard written to Gosse from abroad just after publication, that Great Hintock in *The Woodlanders* was largely based on Melbury Osmond, with Little Hintock as a hamlet two miles off.[33] The novel is lovingly constructed out of his mother's past, and some of its tragedy is that of his own mother and grandmother. Like *The Mayor of Casterbridge*, the inspiration had elements of the remote past, a middle past, and an immediate present. Hardy's sister Mary had spent some time in 1867 on the deeply-afforested Digby estate at Minterne, where Hardy had visited her. One can again see her character of silent witness in Marty South, while Marty's father, old South, resembles, in one respect, their own father in the Bockhampton cottage at the time of writing. The bedridden John South is the last "life" of a lifehold possession. So was Thomas Hardy senior, now failing and crippled by rheumatism. The Bockhampton cottage was held on the usual three-life lease from 1835,[34] for the lives of Hardy's grandfather, Hardy's uncle James, and Hardy's father. The first two were dead, the grandfather long ago, uncle James in 1880. When Hardy's father died, the home would revert to the landlords, though they in fact, unlike the capricious Mrs. Charmond in the novel, allowed the family to stay on after the death of Thomas Hardy senior in 1892.

It is no accident that the novel opens unforgettably with the poverty of a woman; historians have singled out this district to illustrate the hard lot of working-women in nineteenth-century England. In this rectangle of coppice, woodland, and hedge, life was lived just above subsistence level. A single coppice meant security, its loss disaster. Giles Winterborne is a typical coppice-holder, and the subtle gradations of society where so little meant so much is wonderfully caught in his relations with Melbury, the timber-merchant. Similarly, life for men could only be maintained by the subsidiary tasks of the women. Marty South's miserably-paid spar-making, mocked by the barber who tempts her to sell her hair to Mrs. Charmond, embodies the thousand minor employments of all forest women, in which Jemima and her sisters must have shared.[35] *The Woodlanders*, more than even *Far From the Madding Crowd*, shows a community linked together by desperately hard patterns of common work. When *Far From the Madding Crowd* appeared, *The Times* commented that all its characters were, in one sense or another, working-people. *The Woodlanders* shows a people even more unified in their labour, their reality contrasted with exotics like Mrs. Charmond and the doctor, Fitzpiers. For Hardy, perhaps to enhance the oddity of these extraneous characters, but more likely through haste or carelessness, throws realism to the winds with these two. In his first unpublished novel, he had conscientiously taken the advice of a doctor for medical details. Here, Fitzpiers stops his own bleeding from the capillaries of the scalp by making a self-applied tourniquet from a handkerchief and half pennies; this improbable treatment perhaps garbles one of Hardy's boyhood encyclopedias. Hardy's hero dies in comparative peace of some kind of delayed typhoid, which would realistically have been agonizing. The heroine kisses his dying lips, and the doctor gives her a preventative medicine, which she does not take, though when she does get typhoid, it unaccountably cures her. Finally, we are asked to believe that the doctor, a trained medical observer, cohabits with Mrs. Charmond for many months without realizing she wears false hair, until apprised by letter. Similarly, Mrs Charmond, who we are told with somewhat bated breath had been an actress, keeps an attic full of stage-properties and make-up, with which she disguises Fitzpiers so that no one in the area recognizes him.

Artificial treatment of the ruling classes had been a charge against Hardy since his earliest writing days. Yet, now that he aspired to the upper levels of society, Hardy may have believed he was treating them as realistically as the rest of the novel treated his woodlanders. When he went to visit his wife's aristocratic relative by marriage, in the later stages of writing the book, he

> Called on Mrs. Jeune. She was in a rich pinky-red gown, and looked handsome as we sat by the firelight *en tete-a-tete*.

Dr. Fitzpiers pays his calls on Mrs. Charmond, in the second half of the book. She is in "a deep purple dressing-gown", and, at a later stage, she has "a red-shaded lamp and candles burning . . . a large fire was burning in the grate . . . the rosy passionate lamplight".

This is far from saying, though, that in *The Woodlanders* Hardy merely brought his new-found realism to play on one of the poorest communities in Dorset—and therefore in all England—among his own mother's kin, and added to it his new appraisal of London society. For all its hard realism, *The Woodlanders* is also perhaps the most poetical and impressionistic of all his novels. A few years before, he had laid down his principles as the poet-prophet-novelist—"the seer", as he calls it.[36]

> *June* 3 [1882] As, in looking at a carpet, by following one colour a certain pattern is suggested, by following another colour, another; so in life the seer should watch that pattern among general things which his idiosyncracy moves him to observe, and describe that alone. This is, quite accurately, a going to Nature; yet the result is no mere photograph, but purely the product of the writer's own mind.

Now, a few weeks before finishing *The Woodlanders*, he wrote:[37]

> . . . I feel that Nature is played out as a Beauty, but not as a Mystery. I don't want to see landscapes, i.e., scenic paintings of them, because I don't want to see the original realities—as optical effects, that is. I want to see the deeper reality underlying the scenic, the expression of what are sometimes called abstract imaginings.
>
> The "simply natural" is interesting no longer. The much decried, mad, late-Turner rendering is now necessary to create my interest . . .

These principles are enacted in the novel. Its whole portrayal of Nature, especially when mingled with the human scene, is idiosyncratic and impressionistic. On one occasion even, a "late-Turner" painting reveals itself.[38]

> . . . the whole western sky was revealed. Between the broken clouds they could see far into the recesses of heaven, the eye journeying on under a species of golden arcades past fiery obstructions, fancied cairns, logan-stones, stalactites and stalagmites of topaz. Deeper than this

their gaze passed thin flakes of incandescence till it plunged into a
bottomless medium of soft green fire.

Hardy's poetic and impressionistic descriptions of the woodlanders in
relation to their woodland excel in this new technique. The trees have
human attributes; the men and women, often, treelike ones. The young
trees, in a famous passage, sigh humanly when they are planted, though
indeed, Hardy had found this to be literally true while planting at Max
Gate.[39] The death of a tree and the death of old South are interwined.
Winterborne is presented as a spirit of the trees and of their fruits.

The effort of such a conception took its toll. Hardy ended with the
exhausted comment:

> *February* 4 1887, 8.20 p.m. Finished *The Woodlanders*. Thought I should
> feel glad, but I do not particularly—though relieved.

The tremendous feat of writing two such novels with hardly a break in
under three years could not have been achieved without some help
from circumstances, For one thing, he was encouraged in the summer
of 1886 by the flood of good reviews for *The Mayor of Casterbridge*.
Nearly all agreed that Hardy had retrieved his sagging reputation as a
novelist and moved into a new phase as an artist. Only the *Athenaeum*
kept up its usual complaint about the unnatural use of rustic dialogue,
while the *Saturday Review* concentrated, as Hardy complained to
Gosse, on alleged "improbabilities", such as Farfrae's way of improving
bad flour.[40] Otherwise, it was a complete triumph for his fresh, serious
approach to novel-writing, and an incentive to press on with *The Woodlanders* to a climax, with Marty South's ultimate poetic soliloquy.

Some large-scale break in Hardy's life was now needed. At Max Gate
he was intellectually more isolated than ever by the death of his old
mentor, the poet William Barnes, on 7 October 1886. Hardy had sat
and talked regularly with him in his illness and Emma was probably
the last person, outside his family, to converse with him. Hardy busied
himself with subscriptions for a memorial in the shape of a runic cross,
suggested by the Bishop of Salisbury, but abandoned because some of
the subscribers were Evangelical, and objected. The memorial eventually took the form of a lifelike statue by Roscoe Mullins. Hardy
himself provided the best memorial, an article on Barnes in the *Athenaeum*, which caused Gosse to exclaim, "What a biographer was lost
when Nature stamped novelist on your brow!" Barnes's death emphasized the need to leave Dorchester for a time, directly the novel
was finished, and Emma felt it too. The cheerful Gosse might find, on
his visits to Dorchester, that the bustle and life, the brightly-coloured
uniforms from the barracks, the military bands, gave it "quite a foreign
air",[41] but that was not how it appeared to Emma, who protested to

the end of her days that her tastes were *"Continental"*,[42] and French, though, in strange contradiction, she suspected foreigners were all papists, and signed letters to the press "An Old-Fashioned English-woman".[43] Hardy had often longed to visit the scenes of his classical reading, the galleries and the architecture of his youthful study. On 14 March 1887, the day before *The Woodlanders* was published in volume form, he and Emma left for a spring holiday in Italy.

5

The Original Tess

THE southern journey, their first experience of the Mediterranean, is witness that the Hardys still enjoyed some tastes in common. Long travel and uncertain hotels did not seem to damp a sense of freedom and pleasure in each other's company. Their actual relationship at this time drew conflicting accounts from two visitors to the newly-built Max Gate. In late summer 1885, Mrs. Robert Louis Stevenson called there with her husband on their way to Dartmoor. She described the Hardy ménage curiously and critically.

> A pale, gentle, frightened little man, that one felt an instinctive tenderness for, with a wife—ugly is no word for it!—who said "Whatever shall we do?" I had never heard a human being say it before.

One perhaps needs to set this often-quoted and ambiguous remark against an impression, by another American, of Mrs. Stevenson herself, written at about this time. Henry James's sharp-tongued invalid sister, in discussing "our own vulgar ones" from the western States, took Mrs. Stevenson as an example.[1]

> From her appearance Providence or Nature, which ever is responsible for her, designed her as an appendage to a hand organ, but I believe she is possessed of great wifely virtues . . . —but such egotism and so naked! giving one the strangest feeling of being in the presence of an unclothed being.

In the face of such powerful pot-calling-kettle statements, one can only remark that this was not to be the last time a dogmatic American lady weighed in with her verdict on the Hardys. A kinder and perhaps more balanced view comes from the English minor novelist F. Mabel Robinson, who stayed a week with the Hardys at this time. She later wrote:[2]

> Max Gate was then raw-new and I never thought it showed talent in the designer, but it was pleasant. . . . after dinner Emma lit a bright fire and he read aloud from the novel he was engaged on [*The Woodlanders*]. . . . Mrs. Hardy was inconsequent. Her thoughts hopped off like a bird on a bough, but never then or at any other time did the idea cross my mind that her mind (such as it was) was unhinged . . . as I saw her she was a perfectly normal woman without much brain power but who wanted to be a poet or novelist—I forget which. I found it hard that no one took her literary accomplishment seriously.

Certainly the Hardys must have seemed two "perfectly normal" British tourists, breaking their journey for a day or two at Aix-les-Bains. The South of France caught them out, as it does many travellers, and plunged them in snow, but the weather improved as they made their way south via Turin. One sign of happiness was that Hardy began to write poems, though his characteristic lines on seeing Genoa from the train through a tangle of clothes-lines were written "a long time after".[3] Leghorn gave him a poem on *Shelley's Skylark,* and, after a visit to Pisa with its architecture, and Florence, they reached Rome itself by the last day in March when he picked violets on Keats's grave.[4] As he himself teasingly wrote in his old age, "A visit to the graves of Shelley and Keats was also the inspiration of more verses—probably not written till later."[5] As for Rome itself, he felt "its measureless layers of history to lie upon him like a physical weight",[6] and even to be, as he confessed to Gosse,[7] "like a nightmare in my sleep". The physical dangers of Rome were successfully forestalled, on one occasion at least, by the energies of Emma.[8]

> . . . when Hardy was descending the Via di Aracoeli carrying a small old painting he had bought in a slum at the back of the Capitoline Hill, three men prepared to close on him as if to rob him . . . They could see that both his hands were occupied in holding the picture, but what they seemed not to be perceiving was that he was not alone, Mrs. Hardy being on the opposite side of the narrow way. She cried out to her husband to be aware, and with her usual courage rushed across at the back of the men, who disappeared as if by magic.

Though Emma confided to her own diary, "The attack by confederate thieves dreadful fright to me,"[9] three lazzarone were evidently no match for one "old-fashioned Englishwoman", who showed the same fearlessness when she found any of them ill-treating an animal, though one cabman disarmed her by thanks for taking an interest in his horse —"Italian suavity," she commented. It is interesting that the second Mrs Hardy removed from the printed *Life* several of Hardy's tributes to the courage and impulsiveness of her predecessor. Emma's enthusiasms, in fact, led to an attack of malaria, contracted, Hardy thought, by too long a stay in the romantic labyrinths of the mouldering Colosseum; the disease dogged her each spring for the next three or four years, but then subsided.

The Hardys spent Easter in a return visit to Florence, where, as before, their hostess was Lucy Baxter, the married daughter of the poet Barnes, who showed them the sights and took them to Fiesole, where the usual Italian child offering a Roman coin set him off on a poem about the Etruscan theatre. In spite of a gloomy note, also echoing the usual English travellers' surprise at the bitter Easter weather, particularly in Rome—"all our Money gone in Coals and Gas"—and the fact that such weather pursued them to Venice, Hardy found more pleasure there than anywhere else in his Italian stay. He obviously disliked what he thought the "humbug" of Ruskin about the architecture, distrusted the semi-Oriental style, and clearly hated the mosaics, but clasped to himself a typical source of comfort, when he found that the Campanile sounded exactly the same bell-tone as the chimes of Piddlehinton and Puddletown. Evening parties with friends of Browning and memories of Byron completed Hardy's pleasure in the city itself. The whole tour was rounded off by visits to places which fed Hardy's Napoleonic obsession, never far from his mind when in Europe. The Cathedral at Milan reminded him of the crowning of the Emperor, the Bridge of Lodi not only of the battle, but, typically, of the song of that name sung by his father.[10] Like many provincials, Hardy found reassurance in some parochial reminders in foreign parts, a "gentle anchor", in Keats's words, that drew him home.

Emma, on the other hand, for all her innate Englishness, was far more adaptable to travel, and often childishly delighted by foreigners for the simple reason that they were foreign.[11] "Italian gentlemen wear black gloves," she noted. Whereas Hardy was "very vexed, dyspeptic" (her word), after one of those excellent French station buffet meals, she adapted to continental food, and seldom felt as "weary" as he did. The colour and sounds of Italy enchanted her. Genoa presented "a mass of . . . red & blue & green & purple, the rest a soft harmonious mosaic . . . I never saw such a superb city". Florence pleased her with its "exquisite tone of bells", and the road to Rome had "fig trees pollard, low like spread hand". There were irritating human elements, "a dirty Italian man" in Santa Maria Novella, and a shoeblack in Rome so importunate that she broke her umbrella "beating off" his attentions. Her appreciation of Rome's wonders was deeply felt and spontaneous. In the catacombs, "We seemed like magnified ants burrowing under ground as we walked" in another era. Returned to Florence, the Arno was a blue "with a dash of opal in it . . . a great contrast to the yellow Tiber". Her appreciation of early paintings was often as primitive as they themselves: the haloes in the Fra Angelicos struck her as being "like straw hats", and she confided "old frescoes are horrid, entre nous". Venice was a dream. "You are in a planet where things are managed differently, or you are gone to the bottom of the sea & this is a phantom city." The only real disappointments were the cats in the Forum at Rome, in churches at Venice. "*No* lovely cats in Italy as in France"—remembered from her honeymoon there—"all short-haired ones."

By the time Hardy returned to London in the second week of April, two letters were waiting which both, in their way, pointed to his future as a novelist. Macmillan's serialization of *The Woodlanders* had attracted other magazines. On the day after it appeared in volume form, Tillotson and Son of Bolton, a newspaper syndicate, for which Hardy had already provided three short stories, wrote to suggest that Hardy should write another novel of the same length for them, and offered him £1000 for the serial rights. This was a gratifying result of the new technique Hardy felt he had successfully used in *The Woodlanders*. Yet, considering that the novel Tillotson's encouraged him to write turned out to be *Tess of the d'Urbervilles*, another letter inspired by the serialization of *The Woodlanders* was ominous. On 10 April, Macmillans had received a protest about the appearance of that story in their *Magazine*. Written from the Vicarage, Crewkerne, Somerset, it concluded:[12]

> A story which can hinge on conjugal infidelity, can describe coarse flirtations, and can end in pronouncing a married woman's avowed lover to be a "good man who did good things", is certainly not fit to be printed in a high-toned periodical and to be put into the hands of pure-minded English girls.

Warning had been given; Hardy might well have considered also that the proprietor of Tillotson's too had been a Sunday school worker, and that his magazine served the same type of public.[13]

As things turned out, during the coming half-dozen years Hardy needed some disinterested, practical advice in literary matters. Too often he is found in awkward situations, which he himself had manufactured, and with which he dealt by a mixture of blind indignation and grumbling. His chief literary adviser and regular correspondent at this time was Edmund Gosse. One cannot be sure, in spite of their long friendship and loyalty, that this association was wholly good for either. Both were abnormally sensitive to hostile criticism. Gosse, who, like many Victorians, concealed his homosexual inclinations under conventional marriage,[14] was almost embarrassing in his praise of his chosen friends; he was uniformly adulatory of all Hardy's work, of any sort. Easily moved, he often appears to be in tears, so he says, at quite run-of-the-mill poems by Hardy. His preference for the pastoral Hardy of *Under the Greenwood Tree*, from which Hardy had long been trying to escape, led Gosse to some fallible pronouncements on his friend's more mature work. In his reviews of *Jude*, he seems to suggest that the novel was not so attractive because it was set in North "Wessex", and not in the familiar area of true Dorset. Hardy, on his part, grossly overvalued Gosse as a poet, and even printed two quite trivial stanzas by Gosse in the middle of *The Woodlanders*. Each leapt to the other's rescue over any fancied slight. In the previous year, 1886, the American writer James Russell Lowell had been reported as describing Hardy as "small and unassuming in appearance—does not look like the genius of tradition''. The touchy Hardy greeted this harmless remark with a wail of protest to Gosse that he had been "awfully belittled—corporeally".[15] Gosse rushed to write to friends in America his protest at "the sneer at Hardy's personal appearance", which he himself found "singularly cruel", and which had "very much wounded" his friend. Similarly, at this very same time when the axe-men among Victorian critics, Churton Collins—"Shirt and Collars" to the irreverent—attacked Gosse, quite rightly as it proved, for inaccuracy and sloppiness in his literary biographies, Gosse let out a howl of injured pride which Hardy hastened to soothe by long letters arguing that all critics were fools.

The fact was that each encouraged and sympathized with the other's neuroses. In August 1887, when the Hardys had returned to Max Gate after a London season spent at Campden Hill Road, the two men had a long exchange about their morbid fears and depressions. Hardy confessed to many nights when he had gone to bed never wishing to see daylight again. Victorian medicine tried to treat depressive illness as arising from stomach disorder; but Gosse and Hardy, though admitting some truth in this, knew better.[16] However, Hardy hoped, wrongly as it turned out, that the worst of these depressions were now things of the past. He made his usual New Year's Eve summary of the last year, on what was for him an almost excessively cheerful note: "The year has been a fairly friendly one to me." He instanced his successful Mediterranean expedition, from which he had returned "unharmed"—thanks to Emma's promptitude—"and much illuminated"—thanks to his own poetic imagination. He might have added that, while in London, he and Emma had seen the Jubilee procession from the Savile Club, then in Piccadilly, and that at Lady Carnarvon's he apparently cleared up the misunderstanding with Lowell, over in England for the occasion. What he did add was an impressive list of books and poems read or re-read. Its breadth and comprehensiveness shows that he was preparing himself for another step forward in his art.[17]

The main inspiration was, however, as always not in books but in people. In his last novel, *The Woodlanders*, he had looked deeply at his own family history on his mother's side, the mystery and tragedy of her own mother and the marriage at Melbury Osmond, whose overtones of mismating and class difference run throughout the book. Now, on frequent visits to the Bockhampton cottage, he heard Jemima talk of his other grandmother, her own mother-in-law, Mary Head.

From scattered hints and diary jottings over about a year from autumn 1887 to autumn 1888, it seems that two stories presented themselves as possible candidates to his mind for the new novel, whose contract he had signed with Tillotson on 29 June 1887, promising to deliver the manuscript by 30 June 1889. Both were deviously connected in some way with his own family history; they became eventually

Tess of the d'Urbervilles and *Jude the Obscure*. The idea of *Jude* seems to have been fractionally first in the field, to judge by the well-known note he made on 28 April 1888.[18]

> A short story of a young man—"who could not go to Oxford"—His struggles and ultimate failure. Suicide . . . There is something in this the world ought to be shown, and I am the one to show it to them— though I was not altogether hindered going, at least to Cambridge, and could have gone up easily at five-and-twenty.

Leaving aside the last remark, which was not altogether truthful, this was, as Hardy realized and noted in his old age, "the germ of *Jude the Obscure*". On the other hand, another note at the end of September shows him working on the background of *Tess*, and meditating on the fall in status of old Dorset families. His mother's anecdote, a year before, of a girl called Priddle, descended from the Paridelles, who clung to her far-off aristocratic origins by insisting on using her maiden name after marriage,[19] actually persuaded him to make her one of the dairymaids who companioned Tess in the novel. Another maternal anecdote, now remembered, of a parson's son working with "yarn-barton-wenches" gave him the idea of Parson Clare's son Angel working in the barton with the dairymaids.[20]

Hardy's father, as usual, weighed in with anecdotes about convicts, transportations, and hangings, to feed Hardy's mind with the dramas of a past age. They talked of how his grandmother remembered the exact details of what she was doing when she heard of the execution of Marie Antoinette, even down to the pattern of the gown she was ironing at the time: how she remembered William Keats, the tranter, their nearest neighbour in the cottage opposite, beating out time for dancing to the fiddle, so that they could hear it in their own cottage a hundred yards away. This paternal grandmother came back to his mind as the archetypal figure of his first seventeen years. Her home in Berkshire was well known to the whole family. When Mary Hardy had been a schoolmistress only a few miles away at Denchworth, all the Hardys, her father, Kate, Henry, Hardy himself, had visited there. Hardy, in 1864, visiting his sister, would find members of the Head family still farming that area. He knew it well, long before he was to explore it again as the setting for *Jude the Obscure*. He could have known, too, in his usual pottering about country churches, that a branch of the Turbervilles, remotely connected with the Dorset family of Bere Regis, had their arms quartered on monuments in that part of Berkshire.[21] Above all, the Fawley parish register told him that his own great-grandmother had an illegitimate son, who died in infancy.[22] Yet there was one even more vital influence for him.

Hardy's paternal grandmother, Mary Head, had been baptized on

30 October 1782 at Fawley. Her father had died earlier in the same year, and her mother died when Mary was five-and-a-half. She lived in Fawley, and perhaps also in its neighbouring parish of Chaddleworth, where there were Head relatives, until 1785, when her mother's father, William Hopson or Hobson, also died.[23] These first thirteen years were, Hardy said, so "poignant" that she would never return to Fawley. Hardy, however, was almost totally silent about her next fourteen years; for it was not until 19 December 1799 that she appeared in faraway Puddletown in Dorset, and married Hardy's grandfather, being herself already three months pregnant.[24] There is only one very brief reference in all Hardy's writing to these lost fourteen years. When in 1896 he visited Reading, he described it as "a town which had come into the life" of Mary Head, who, he added vaguely, "had lived here awhile".[25] Such phrases of studied vagueness in Hardy's careful autobiography usually conceal some important personal knowledge. Moreover, Reading, under the name of Aldbrickham, is consistently the setting for scenes and memories of disaster in *Jude the Obscure*.

The registers of the three Reading churches in these fourteen years, 1785 to 1799, produce only one entry for a Mary Head. It is sufficiently startling. Sometime in 1796, an illegitimate girl was born to Mary Head and John Reed. The child was baptized at St. Mary's, Reading, at the age of six or seven, in 1803, the entry recording also her year of birth.[26] She was christened Georgiana Reed, which suggests her mother had by then left the district, and that she was being brought up by the father; it may also suggest he was a person of standing.

Though this is the only church entry for a woman of this name in this period, there is a legal entry in the year 1797. On 3 February of that year, Mary Head was committed by a magistrate to the Bridewell or House of Correction at Reading, on the oath of Rosanna, wife of John Farmer of Winterborne, charged with having feloniously stolen a copper tea-kettle, the property of Mr. and Mrs. Farmer. She remained in the House of Correction for nearly three months, for it was not until the Quarter Sessions of 25 April that her case came up. When it did, the Farmers did not appear to give evidence, and the justices discharged her.[27]

She had by then spent nearly three months under the fear of death by hanging. The laws respecting larceny were in a confused state, but they were appallingly severe, and if the statutes had been strictly applied, executions would have occurred for a huge number of small thefts. A legal authority in 1771 had enunciated that "it is and hath been the law of England that in general all persons guilty of larceny above the value of 12 pence shall be hanged". Such severity often made witnesses, after the first accusation, loth to give evidence; this is probably what happened with the Farmers and Mary Head. If they had appeared, and convinced the Justices, Mary Head would almost certainly have been sentenced to death and probably hanged. In a case in that exact year, 1797, concerned with an article of similar value, a woman called Margaret Kennedy was sentenced to death for stealing a silver button, which she had attempted to conceal in her mouth.[28]

Winterborne, where the theft was alleged to have taken place, was part of the parish of Chieveley, the next parish to Chaddleworth and Fawley, where Hardy's grandmother was born. Mary Head in Reading House of Correction was listed as two years younger than Mary Head of Fawley, but an orphan with a chequered history might well not know her exact age. Hardy's poem about her speaks of her hearing shrieks "under the lash"; the judicial whipping of women in private was not abolished until 1820, and there were scenes of brutality in some Bridewells. The company was brutal too; Mary Head was incarcerated with Kitty Curtain, "a rogue and vagabond who refuses to give an account of herself" and Elizabeth Bloxham, "committed for a year as a lewd woman".[29]

These sole appearances of a Mary Head in Reading seem to dovetail in the story of Tess. A cousin of Hardy, John Antell, said positively, "Tess's life and adventures and final death are practically what happened to a relative of ours."[30] Hardy spoke of her as a real person. Mary Head, like Tess, had been seduced and had borne a child. She had not been executed, but had lived under the fear of execution for nearly three months. Hardy's grandmother had, like Tess, made a fresh start, just as Tess movingly does in Part Three of the book, "The Rally". With Tess, it takes place in another part of Dorset, remote from the district of her first disasters. With Hardy's grandmother, Mary Head, it took place because of some move from Berkshire, where her memories were so unbearable, to Dorset itself, and the area round Puddletown, where she married Hardy's grandfather. A very tenuous family legend that she had a "husband" already in Berkshire was all that remained of the past. There was one, and one only likely way that she might make the journey into this new life from a hundred miles away, and that was as a domestic servant in a landed family, with property in both counties. Two such families immediately come to mind. The Pitt family of Kingston Maurward House, Stinsford, for whom Hardy's grandfather actually worked, were closely connected with the Pitts of Stratfieldsaye, on the border of Hampshire and Berkshire, and very near to Reading. As a boy of twelve, Hardy's own father had been given a book of psalms by Lady Pitt.[31] Another possible employer is the Williams family, of Herringston, Dorset, very near Stinsford, which also had a branch in Berkshire. There is a curious and possible link here. Hardy told Edmund Blunden that he could have had a presentation to Christ's Hospital, but that the Governor, who would have sponsored him, died. When Hardy was just the age that such a presentation could have been made, a Governor, William Williams, of this family, did die.[32]

It is practically certain, then, that the story of Tess is a version of the true story of Hardy's much-loved grandmother. He did not use it at once. With the common background for both *Tess* and *Jude* equally in his mind, Hardy used some of the ideas for *Jude* in a powerful short story, *A Tragedy of Two Ambitions*, which he wrote and published in 1888. In this, two brothers "could not go to Oxford", because their drunken father squanders their mother's small inheritance. They manage to enter a theological college and be ordained, while they succeed in educating their attractive sister, who becomes engaged to a local landowner; but these successes are threatened by the reappearance of their father. After meeting and threatening them, while drunk, he falls into a culvert. They do not rescue him, and he drowns; but the brothers are haunted by guilt, and the story ends with forebodings of their own suicide. While this is obviously some rehearsal for *Jude*, it is also a rehearsal for aspects of *Tess*, which he was just beginning to write. The father is a foretaste of John Durbeyfield, whose drunken folly ends in tragedy for his children, Tess in particular. Another curious anticipation is that not only this story, but two others he wrote about this time, *Alicia's Diary* and *The Waiting Supper*, both depend for their dénouement on a man slipping from a plank and drowning in a stream. This is echoed, strangely and poetically, in *Tess*, when Angel Clare, sleep-walking, carries Tess across a narrow footbridge, and she has a momentary fear that he is going to drown her after her revelation, the previous night, of her seduction by Alec d'Urberville.

Hardy seems to have limbered up for the great effort of writing *Tess* by this succession of short stories. They included a macabre little sketch, *The Withered Arm*, which contains many of his own schoolboy obsessions: hanging and hangmen which form the melodramatic climax, a witch's curse, familiar to his fireside childhood, and even his own juvenile love-affair with the lady of the manor, Julia Augusta Martin, who had just written to him. The thrilling *frou-frou* of Mrs. Martin's silk dress, as she entered Stinsford church in those far-off days, is reproduced exactly in the fictional lady of the manor. Such stories brought in some money during the long haul of constructing yet another major novel. On 4 May 1888, Macmillans, having done well out of *The Woodlanders*, produced *The Withered Arm*, together with four previous short stories by Hardy, in a two-volume edition, which sold enough to warrant a single-volume reprint within a year.

Hardy now had the financial security, and comparative leisure, to explore the new depths he had uncovered while writing *The Woodlanders*. For that novel, he had tried to see "the deeper reality" beyond what was merely visual, a technique akin to Turner's later paintings. This search appears in many of his scattered notes at this time. "At a concert at Prince's Hall I saw Souls outside Bodies", he wrote on 25 June 1887.[33] In the British Museum Reading Room on 9 March 1888, he commented, "Souls are gliding about here in a sort of dream—screened somewhat by their bodies, but imaginable behind them."[34] "I have", he wrote three months later, "the habit of regarding the scene as if I were a spectre not solid enough to influence my environment."[35] Early in 1889, he feasted on the exhibition of Turner at the Academy. He singled for special mention, among others, the painter's *Snowstorm*, which has been brilliantly shown[36] to be the basis for the weird impressionistic passage about the Arctic birds in the Dorset uplands which he eventually used in *Tess*. Hardy's lack of interest in prose techniques was a later pose, when poetry had again become all to him; at this stage he was clearly striving to surpass himself in the novel. Tess's vision that "our souls can be made to go outside our bodies when we are alive", which both puzzled Dairyman Crick and attracted Angel Clare, derives directly from Hardy's determination to seek the spiritual nature of the material world about him.

During early 1888 Hardy deliberately gathered material, from past history or from present inspiration, as a way well known to all authors of putting off the plunge into a large and exacting work. Among his tactical expedients was a 6000-word article for the New York *Forum* on "The Profitable Reading of Fiction". This collection of not very well expressed platitudes about a writer and his public probably served its main purpose of postponing the evil hour. It was followed, during most of June 1888, by another long foreign trip with Emma, this time to Paris, where they stayed in the Rue du Commandant Rivière, went to museums, archives, tombs, and famous buildings, but lightened the culture with a day at Longchamps race-course for the Grand Prix de Paris. Hardy noted with surprise that "the starter spoke to the jockeys entirely in English, and most of the cursing and swearing was done in English likewise, and done well". He had not realized that the starter on this occasion was, in fact, an Englishman, Dick Fijus, and that the French jockeys' swearing was meant to intimidate the foreigner in his own terms.[37] July brought the London season, Kensington lodgings at Upper Phillimore Place, opposite Walter Pater, but with constant early-morning disturbance from market-carts on their way to Covent Garden. Hardy, about to create his most attractive heroine, began to make notes, even more obsessively than usual, about the feminine beauties he encountered. On 3 July, he observed that Lady Portsmouth, with whom he had stayed more than once in Devon, looked like "a model countess, . . . her black brocaded silk fitting her well". On 8 July he noted "red plumes and ribbons in two stylish girls' hats" in St. Mary

Abbots Church; next day he was attracted by Ada Rehan's performance in *The Taming of the Shrew*, in which she played at Daly's opposite her fellow-American, John Drew. Five days later, he met an unnamed and intriguingly Swinburnian type—"an Amazon, more, an Atalanta, most a Faustine. Smokes: handsome girl: cruel small mouth."[38]

Some time in the autumn, however, Hardy got down to writing, and seems to have continued, without any obvious breaks apart from the 1889 London season, for a whole year. At all events, on 9 September 1889, he forwarded to Tillotson "a portion of the MS. . . . equal to about one half I think" of the novel, which at that stage was called "Too Late Beloved" or perhaps "Too Late, Beloved". From subsequent negotiations with other publishers, this seems to have taken the heroine through her seduction, her baby and its death, and into the section afterwards called "The Rally", where she goes as a dairymaid to Talbothays Farm, and meets Angel Clare. Though the seduced village maiden was not unknown in Victorian fiction, Tillotson's took fright at this as a fit subject for their magazine readers. Hardy must surely have anticipated this, for he allowed them to cancel their contract and return both set-up proofs and manuscript on 25 September. In old age, though, he suppressed all memory of his contract with Tillotson, and implied that Edward Arnold of *Murray's Magazine*, to whom he sent the MS on 5 October, was the first editor he had approached. Arnold, already cautious at Hardy's demand for £50 a month for the work, more than the magazine was in the habit of paying, consulted with Murray, and on 15 November rejected the story as "not . . . well adapted for publication in this magazine". He added to this vague phrase the remarkable statement, "I believe . . . it is quite possible and very desirable for women to grow up and pass through life without the knowledge of" matters which he termed "immoral situations" and their "tragedies". The warning from Crewkerne Vicarage about *The Woodlanders* had now been spelled out editorially. Nevertheless, Hardy immediately sent his MS, by now apparently nearly reaching the scene of Tess's wedding night, to Mowbray Morris, editor of *Macmillan's Magazine* itself, the very journal which had received the censure of his former novel. Rejection was inevitable, and only took ten days, during which Morris wrote a long letter, setting out his response to the story; he did not like the sensuous descriptions of Tess, nor the implication that she was ripe for seduction from the start.

He incidently provided some idea of the original plot, which was very different from the finished novel. Briefly, it was a simple and ordinary story of a country working-girl's seduction by her employer's son, almost a commonplace of Victorian life. At this stage, the theme of villain and heroine sharing one apparent lineage, the whole ancestral d'Urberville background, simply did not exist. Her original surname was Woodrow, his Hawneferne; and incidentally, though his Christian name was always Alec, hers showed the mutations Love, Cis, Sue and Rose-Mary, before Tess. The whole atmosphere of inevitable and almost Darwinian replacement, so strong in the final *Tess*, the decay of old families and the theft of their titles by parvenus, painted upon some cosmic canvas, was completely absent. Instead, there was merely, as it must have appeared to Morris, and perhaps to any average reader, an account of the deflowering of a "succulent" innocent village maiden by "a handsome horsey dandy", as the original manuscript had read. Though Tess was aware "since her infancy" of the tradition of past noble blood, this had nothing to do with her fall to Hawneferne, since there was not the slightest resemblance even of names. Her original name of Woodrow was suggested by a true story,[39] on which Hardy drew later for Angel Clare's emigration to Brazil. This is the disastrous event of the 350 British who left Liverpool for Rio on 29 November 1872, one being a Dorset man named Woodrow. *Tess* was apparently at this stage unadorned by the spirit of those Greek tragedies with their suggestions of a malign fate, which formed a large part of Hardy's staple reading at this time.[40]

Hardy was therefore left, after a whole year's work, with a story which seemed unsaleable, in spite, or in certain quarters because, of his previous reputation as a novelist. It was a time of extreme professional crisis. It was also a time of personal crises in the lives of Hardy and his wife. Though Emma had had little contact with her own family since her marriage, apart from one visit to Plymouth in the year 1886, she received regular news, which, at this point, became a matter of horror. Her eldest brother, Richard Ireland Gifford, a bachelor, was a civil engineer in Cornwall. In January 1888, he began to show severe delusions and attempted suicide. He was difficult to feed, believed he was filthy, verminous, and unfit to live, and became beyond the control of his mother and of Emma's sister. After a year in the Cornwall County Asylum at Bodmin and in Bethlem Hospital, London, he was transferred on 15 March 1889 to the Warneford Hospital, Oxford.[41] He had always suffered from ill-health, which Emma, whose medical knowledge was sketchy, put down to a heart condition, angina pectoris.[42] In fact, he had a severe chronic kidney ailment, Bright's disease. Since the searching hospital enquiries showed no history of insanity in the Gifford family, and no sign of it in his four siblings, of whom Emma, of course, was one, it is likely that his mental disturbance would now be diagnosed as stemming from this poisoning of his system.[43]

At the time, however, and specially to one of Hardy's country-superstitious mind—he considered it dangerous even to be weighed—the idea of an hereditary taint in the Gifford family must have presented itself. Emma's "inconsequent" chatter, "without much brain power", as Mabel Robinson had noted, were to seem as sinister to Hardy as her father's previous alcoholic outbreaks, during which he is said to have chased Emma's mother out into the streets in her nightgown.[44] It was a seed of evil omen, sown in his own mind, to his later disquiet, though at this time it may have had the helpful effect of bringing the theme of family doom more powerfully to assist the deepening of the story of Tess, as she had now at last become in his unpublishable pages.

6

Tess and Jude

AT THIS time of literary crisis, Hardy introduced a personal complication. Up to now, Emma had ignored the succession of shopgirls, actresses, and society ladies, whom her husband had wistfully admired from afar. She counted on the shared interests of their marriage, in country life and folklore, in campaigns for the protection of animals, and, above all, in the feeling that, in some sense, they had literary work in common. He discussed this with her still, and fairly fully. She knew all the vicissitudes of the naming of Tess, in a way which suggests she read and commented on all the early manuscript versions of the novel. She also helped him to introduce an incident from her own unpublished, and indeed not very publishable tale, *The Maid on the Shore*. When thinking, as she must have done, about his barely-concealed appreciation of other ladies, she could congratulate herself that he regarded her as his helpmeet where literature was concerned, if only as a copyist and captive audience. No other woman held that position.

Yet in 1889 and 1890, her position revealed its basic insecurity; for from that date, and for the next decade, Hardy began to share his literary confidences with a succession of ladies. To add to Emma's chagrin, these were all ladies who not only had printed publications to their credit, but who were recognized in London society. It is not at all certain that Emma ever really made her often-quoted remark about the London ladies who "spoilt" Thomas—"they are the poison, I am the antidote".[1] Yet their advent now surely poisoned the deepest well from which, she had felt, she and Thomas could still draw for their love, the springs of literary creation.

This was all the more galling to her because she could and did produce, at this time, work of a highly literate character. The tradition of her virtual illiteracy, so universally stressed by Hardy's biographers, aided by his second wife, is simply not true. Reading only her breathless and erratic private letters, hearing only accounts of her inconsequent conversational manner, all have ignored her serious pieces of writing. On 5 September 1891, for instance, the *Daily Chronicle*, a most responsible paper, printed her letter[2] of over 1000 words—virtually an article —on a serious topic, the education of the young. The letter is sustained and extremely well expressed. It is advanced in its view of education as the right and the salvation of all classes: "the houseless, bedless, ever-comfortless poor should not exist in a *rightly-taught* nation". She saw education as beginning in the cradle, where "almost always the plastic minds and hearts are in ignorant hands". She drew a picture of poor children, starved of education, and pleaded for reform: "start another way altogether, get instructors of the Arnoldian stamp", who should be looked up to, not despised by society, especially the women. It is a well-reasoned, direct, enlightened, and admirable piece of writing. Yet Emma was despised by her husband, and other writing women preferred.

The first of these intruders can be detected just at this time. The beautiful Rosamund Ball had published an anonymous little book of verse entitled *Tares* in 1884, when she was only twenty-one. Shortly after, she married the artist Arthur Graham Tomson, and took the semi-pseudonym of "Graham R. Tomson". In June 1889, she inscribed a copy of her new collection, *The Bird Bride: A Volume of Ballads and Sonnets* to "Thomas Hardy, with the sincere admiration of G.R.T."[3] In the next few years she gave him two other books, written or edited by her, one an anthology concerned with one of their common interests, cats. There was also an exchange of letters, of which hers, embellished with a self-designed art-nouveau letter-head, still survive.[4] Nor were her attractions solely intellectual. She was "a tall, slight, brown-haired woman, with large grey eyes, that at times seemed to be a deep hazel".[5] In other words, she was of the slender brunette type that held such physical attraction for Hardy, noticeably akin to the actresses Mary Scott-Siddons and Helen Mathews. Her beauty was enhanced by "a striking individuality pervading her carriage, manner, and dress". The susceptible Hardy entered and preserved in his diary that, at a party at Mrs. Jeune's, he "Met Mrs. T[omson] and her great eyes in a corner of the rooms, as if washed up by the surging crowd."[6] He was sufficiently struck to obtain and keep her portrait, and to write an oddly-moving poem about it, *An Old Likeness* (*Recalling R.T.*), about ten years after her death, which occurred in 1911. In it, he recalled

> Our early flows
> Of wit and laughter,
> And framing of rhymes
> At idle times.

The rhymes that Rosamund Tomson actually framed can hardly be said to be worth such recall. Empty little lyrics in artificial forms, the villanelles, rondeaux, ballades, made fashionable by Austin Dobson, were all that her poems display. They contain two undistinguished poems dedicated to Hardy himself; but her one possible direct inspiration to Hardy's own writing occurs in the title poem of the book she inscribed to him, *The Bird Bride*. This ballad, said to be on an Eskimo legend, could, at a stretch, be associated with Tess's strange vision of the weird Arctic birds, flown from the far north, where the ballad and its own birds originate. The lady was divorced by Tomson in 1896, married Henry Brereton Marriott-Watson, a prolific Antipodean popular novelist, produced other books of verse, but died comparatively young, deeply mourned by her second husband. To Hardy, she was a portent of his personal life during the coming decade of the 1890s. Some sort of shy flirtation, during which he wrote her wistful letters about seeing two lovers under one umbrella in the rain, or hesitated between two portraits of her, neither of which, he thought, did her justice, soon faded at the touch of reality. It has been assumed that she was the "enfranchised woman" who disgusted him "by exhibiting him as her admirer";[7] but this may equally have been another woman poet he knew about this time, Agnes Mary Francis Robinson, who wrote verse in much the same style, and appeared in the same anthology as Rosamund Tomson.

The next half-dozen years, from November 1889 to November 1895, were both packed with personal incident and the most prolific of Hardy's writing career. Something in his withdrawn and passive nature seemed to require the stimulus of other personalities to touch it into full creative life and output. The literary tally of these six years is remarkable. First, there was the virtual rewriting and reconstitution of *Tess*, far more extensive than his retrospective memory allowed,[8] and the production of that novel, his finest work, in serial and in volume form, both entailing large adjustment from one to another. Then came the writing and the publication in serial form of two other novels, *The Well-Beloved*, under the title of *The Pursuit of the Well-Beloved*, serialized in October, November, and December 1892, and *Jude the Obscure*, under the title of *Hearts Insurgent*, serialized from December 1894 to November 1895. This was by no means all. In 1891, he collected together and published the short stories called *A Group of Noble Dames*, and at this time wrote most of the stories collected in *Life's Little Ironies* (1893). In addition, two important essays on literature, "Candour in English Fiction" and "The Science of Fiction" were published in January 1890 and April 1891 respectively.[9] Then, on Christmas Day 1890, he woke feeling "the viewless wings of poesy" (in Keats's phrase) spread themselves, in a series of deeply-felt lyrics, which filled the next few years. These were not wholly given over to what he afterwards seemed to regard as the arid wastes of prose.

Hardy's personal life showed an equal complexity and variety. His "framing of rhymes", or at any rate literary correspondence, with Rosamund Tomson went on until at least late 1891. Such feverishly-begun but soon exhausted attractions to literary ladies show a consistent pattern. A new female personality, intense excitement, and hectic letter-writing, some stumbling-block, when reality contradicted the initial fantasy, and, to be just to Hardy, a milder but long-lasting friendship formed the usual sequence. His wilder hopes seldom lasted more than a few years, sometimes even months, before the ideal proved to be not what he had thought. A perpetual adolescent, even into his eighties, Hardy was out of love only shortly after he was in. "Love lives on propinquity but dies of contact", he had just remarked in the summer of 1889.[10] An average of about two or three years seems to be common, before a new idealization takes the place of a partly-disappointing one.

Death, on the other hand, proved a stimulant whose effects did not so easily wear off. The death of a woman remained the most powerful and lasting factor in his creative life. There were certainly three deaths of women in 1890 to rouse "the viewless wings of poesy" he felt beating again by the end of that year. The first fell only on the margin of his consciousness. In January 1890, Helen Mathews, the young actress he had so much admired in the early 1880s, died at Birmingham.[11] She had been acting in Henry Irving's Lyceum company, to which she had returned after a few years' absence, until very shortly before her death. Quite apart from his frequent play-going to the Lyceum—he saw Irving in *The Bells* only a few months later—Hardy met Irving a good deal socially at this time. He must have known of Miss Mathews's death, though he does not mention it in any diary notes which have survived.

A note about another woman's death,[12] at almost the same time and age, has survived, and has become a subject for speculation. This recorded the death on 11 May at Topsham of Mrs. Gale—Hardy's cousin Tryphena Sparks—to whom he had been so strongly attached in his late twenties and early thirties. According to his own account, he wrote the beginning of a poem to her without realizing, after years of complete separation from her life, that she was at the time on her death-bed. "A curious instance of sympathetic telepathy" he called this incident, which resulted in the finished poem, entitled in his manuscript *T—a, At news of her death*. Thirdly, and not usually noticed, came the death that summer of an older woman, his mother's sister, Aunt Mary Antell. She had looked after him in infancy, and virtually brought him up during the rather mysterious period when his own mother, by family hearsay, suffered an attack of "brain-fever".[13] Certainly his aunt's house in Puddletown had been a second home to him from a very early age; he was deeply attached to her, and to her wild, erratic, picturesque husband, the Puddletown cobbler, with his frustrated dreams and ambitions, who had died a dozen years before.

Finally, one cannot discount the death in this year of Hardy's father-in-law, that now-extinct volcano of a man, John Attersoll Gifford. Though he had long moved back from Cornwall to his more accessible native Devon, Hardy does not himself seem to have seen him. His former outbreaks of alcoholic violence were things of the past. Yet his death, and the recent news that his eldest son, Hardy's brother-in-law, was hopelessly insane, served to strengthen the idea of a family curse. The effect on Emma herself cannot be discounted either. Her father's funeral, which she attended, contributed to a latent violence which, as his favourite and spoilt child, she inherited from his temperament. Perhaps Hardy's fresh weakness for literary ladies wore her temper thin, or perhaps she began now to adopt the attitude of her contemptuous father. For she began from this time to keep a diary of bitter denigration of Hardy, of his ways, of his own family, which, according to later witness, she christened with the ominous title, "What I think of my Husband". John Gifford had written off Hardy as a "base churl"; his daughter now began to speak darkly and pejoratively of Hardy's "peasant origin". About now, she cut off relations with the women of his own family. Hardy had just bought a house in Wollaston Road, Dorchester, which his two schoolmistress sisters, Mary and Kate, shared conveniently for their teaching at the Girls' National School in Bell Street.[14] Jemima was companioned at the Bockhampton cottage by Mary Antell's daughter and namesake, whom Mary had implored Jemima to give a home. Emma may well have thought that Hardy was over-occupied with these domestic arrangements for his own family, and may have resented particularly his spending money to house his own sisters, and his special and obvious affection for the elder, Mary, his early inspiration.

All these recent deaths strongly influenced the novels Hardy produced in the next few years, the highly-reconstructed *Tess*, the deeply-conceived though in many ways imperfectly realized *Jude the Obscure*, and, sandwiched between them, the strange half-symbolic and wholly-personal "sketch of a temperament" remarkably like his own, *The Well-Beloved*. All three have their origins in a remote yet intimate past, of people, events, and family traits, which, it has been suggested,[15] he was trying to exorcise by writing them out of his system. Yet the novels transcend therapy. When we come to disregard all the circumstances of its initial rejections, its "dismemberment", its bowdlerized serial-form, and its final book publication in November 1891, *Tess of the d'Urbervilles* is his masterpiece, the fruit of over twenty years of a novelist's career, and of the chrysalis passion of a poet spreading new wings. Its heroine is perhaps the most memorable in all English literature. It has been argued she took a new, intimate reality from the death of Tryphena Sparks. Whatever the truth of the many explanations by Hardy that Tess "had a real existence"[16]—and they range, rather incongruously from a chance-seen girl driving a cart to the mixture of two Dorchester girls and a Weymouth waitress—he has used all his professional resources to convince us of her personal reality. Her basic story, of course, originates in his grandmother's tragedy; its portrayal belongs to his utmost art. On the mechanical note-taking side of an author's craft, he combed the files of the *Dorset County Chronicle* with more than usual care for incidents from the late 1820s to the late 1880s. The fatal horse-accident of an early chapter, the blood-stained ceiling of a later one, were all garnered in his own methodical way from these sources.[17] The puzzlement felt by critics at Hardy's obscure personal remarks about Tess, such as "I have not been able to put on paper all that she is, or was, to me", which certainly suggests a recent death, such as Tryphena's, should not distract attention from the fruition of his hard-won lifework as a prose-writer. To expand one casual true incident which Hardy witnessed, a drunken man boasting of a noble family vault, into the whole conception of ancestral decay, which runs throughout the novel, shows his power to grasp a huge general theme from a trivial particular. If, as has been suggested,[18] he owed much to the atmosphere of Zola's novels, several of which he had recently read, the poetry of his approach everywhere transcended them.

Similarly, the bare facts of his grandmother's story, deeply impressed on Hardy's adolescence, become a study of a woman's development through every stage of innocence to experience. Tess is unique in Hardy's work, since she literally seems to grow under our eyes. This is partly due to the poetic construction of her story. It is an epic in seven books, an Odyssey or an Aeneid, with Tess's journeys to each part of Hardy's Wessex forming a new emotional stage. The outward scenes are linked with Tess's inward development in a way which is more poetry than prose. This is achieved not by "poetic" fine writing, but by an artist's conception of the wholeness of life. Every scene is fitted to its human counterpart. The straggling valley of the early phases corresponds with the desultory though harmless life of Tess with her feckless family; the dark forest of the chase connives at her seduction. The lush, fruitful vale of the next phases is one with the slow full-bearing workings of recovery and love. The wonderful winter scenes in the barren uplands of Flintcombe Ash mirror the bleak horror of her desertion by Angel, and her bewildered, faithful efforts to maintain love in extreme adversity. Though physically they echo the actual experiences of Hardy's grandmother, who told him of walking on snow that reached the height of hedgerows, they are given the emotional force of a universal poem, as moving as the expulsion from Paradise in the last book of *Paradise Lost*. Indeed, with Alec reappearing as tempter here, it is not fanciful to compare Milton's epic with Hardy's. The new-rich, false Bournemouth becomes the scene of her shame's second surrender, which only murder can resolve; the price for this is paid among the stones of sacrifice at primitive Stonehenge. Every part is planned as a poem; within each part are separate poems, such as Angel's sleepwalk in the misty water-meads. Yet nothing is merely decorative. Every natural scene is calculated to underpin Hardy's concern, the growth of Tess's soul. The intensity of each image comes from the intense interest he feels for Tess as a person. However much the trials of his own family Tess, Mary Head, had coloured the imagination of his susceptible youth, his is the rarest of a novelist's creations, a character we accept without question as a revealed part of life, as real as if we knew her.

The effect on Hardy's popular reputation as a novelist was unprecedented, and surely comes from the complete reality of his main creation. From being the novelist of a discerning few, whose sales had barely satisfied various patient publishers, he became a best-seller. His last-minute designation of Tess as "a pure woman" was endlessly debated in circles which often had little notion of the whole novel. His men were held up for examination which often revealed more about the commentators than it did of the novelist's characters. John Addington Symonds, for example, found in Hardy "the right democratic spirit", which he himself had discovered in his "exile in the Alps" among handsome Swiss guides, and which enabled him to provide Edmund Gosse with photographs of Greek fisher boys to enliven Robert Browning's Abbey funeral on the last day of 1890. He became vehement about Angel Clare, "the loathsome male . . . I should have liked to kick . . . the fellow"—presumably for the "middle-class maudlin" sexual intolerance, which Symonds was still wistfully resenting as he neared the end of his own self-tormented life. Unlike some critics, he half-confessed a personal involvement. "My vehemence please take as a sign of the intense interest I took in the novel."[19]

Tess carried Hardy to fame, and, incidentally, fortune, thanks to the lucky coincidence of the U.S.A. Copyright Act, passed just a year earlier in December 1890. He now had prospects of vast, unpirated reward from the popular work which lay ready to hand. *Tess* also took him, finally and decisively, into the fashionable society he affected to despise, but really enjoyed. He might note, "But these women! If put into rough wrappers in a turnip field, where would their beauty be?" Yet such cynical speculation was sheer disguise; he admitted one of these beauties, Mrs. Hamo Thornycroft, as yet another physical model for Tess. He obviously revelled in fashionable dress, manners, aristocratic connections, distinguished company. He marked off each distinct social triumph like a schoolboy's tabulation of goal-scoring feats. He began to go to gatherings where royalty were guests, and met the future Queen Mary. A year before *Tess*, Lord Rowton, of the tramps' lodging-houses, had called him, not without sarcasm, Mrs. Jeune's "dosser". One lady carried away the impression of "a rough-looking man, dressed very unlike his fellows, with . . . a decided accent".[20] Now those who met the shy figure in Mary Jeune's drawing-room vied for his further acquaintance. Specially pleasing, among early landmarks, was an invitation from Sir Henry Thompson, whose patient he had been ten years before. At that time the famous society surgeon had barely noticed the still-struggling novelist. Now, "recalling I admit very slightly a personal acquaintance", he selected Hardy for one of his celebrated "Octaves", dinners of eight top people.[21] Hardy refrained from cynical comment on the delayed accolade. He was also elected a founder-member of the Omar Khayyam Club, started by the rationalist Edward Clodd in 1892, and took chief part in a notable dinner a few years later, when the Club went to Burford Bridge to honour the invalid Meredith.[22]

Fashionable interest and private appreciation for *Tess* was seconded by critical acclaim. Despite the author's occasional growls at critics' obtuseness, they were almost unanimous in praise. To quote one,[23] "the most difficult of all the tasks which a writer of fiction can attempt —the portraiture of a living woman" was generally acknowledged everywhere to have succeeded. A fellow-novelist, George Meredith, felt a falling-off in the later stages of Tess's story, but his opinion was not widely shared. Andrew Lang in *New Review* was the sole important dissentient, and he was at once countered by other critics. His doubts about the men in the novel, however, were echoed elsewhere. Angel was often judged the unrelieved prig that J. A. Symonds had found him; Alec was pilloried in *Punch* as luridly melodramatic. Yet altogether, 1891–92 provided a year of reviews flattering to any author, though Lang's criticism made Hardy momentarily think of resigning from the Savile Club, of which they were fellow-members, and making his West End base the Athenaeum, which had just elected him. Any adverse criticism was reserved for his uninspired collection of short stories, *A Group of Noble Dames*.

Success certainly inspired Hardy to a burst of fresh writing in 1891–92. He was under contract to Tillotson's to make up for the broken agreement over the original *Tess*, and to supply their syndicate with a shorter serial in a lighter vein, and so he embarked on *The Pursuit of the Well-Beloved*. Whether or not the death of Tryphena Sparks affected the characterization of Tess, it clearly called up memories which he took as the ground-plan of his newer and slighter novel. In his youth he had been attracted, to greater and lesser degrees, by his three girl-cousins, Rebecca, Martha, and Tryphena Sparks herself. In the large Sparks family, where the youngest, Tryphena, was actually twenty-one years younger than her eldest sister, Rebecca, these three girls had seemed almost like three generations. This, and their marked physical resemblance, led Hardy to construct a fantastic plot, in which his artist-hero falls in love with three generation of girls, when he himself is twenty, forty and sixty. Not only does this spring from Hardy's own past history, but the hero's temperament, the mainspring of the action is, perhaps, more self-centred than any other self-portrayal by Hardy. It is a study of a search for an ideal in a rapidly and constantly changing series of women. Actual women are hinted at throughout, actresses like Helen Mathews, literati like Rosamund Tomson, even half-remembered adolescent loves. His recent impressions of high society are packed into two more photographic and generally heavy-handed chapters. Here a good deal of exact identification has been worked out,[24] for instance a portrait of Ellen Terry, almost identical verbally with a diary note by Hardy on meeting her in society at this time.

This work, which Hardy never valued greatly, was written mainly in the year 1892. The same year saw the death of his father, whose sensible, reasonable nature Hardy compared with that of Hamlet's Horatio. It left his mother at the cottage, by courtesy of the landlord, since Thomas Hardy senior had been the third and final "life" of the lifeholding. His father's death gave Hardy further thought about the Grandmother at Fawley in Berkshire. The major theme, put aside for *Tess*, that of a young man "who could not go to Oxford", seemed ready to be written, in a setting akin to his own ancestry. *Tess*'s story, after all, had largely arisen from the tragic history of Mary Head. He visited Fawley in October 1892, and brooded on family history. "I can only see the dead here," he wrote, though no one knows quite what he found of those long-dead but to him living ghosts. The most recent dead spirit, that of his mason father, inspired him to sketch his hero, at first called by the name of an actual Berkshire relative, Jack Head, as a journeyman stonemason. This craft of the Dorset Hardy family was introduced into the Berkshire setting of the Head family. Later stages of the writing actually led Hardy to seek more exact detail by restoring a local church himself; he obtained from architectural work on a church near Max Gate, West Knighton, much of the physical background he always wanted for his characters.[25]

The novel, however, hung fire, perhaps because of the painful memories and discoveries it aroused, perhaps through lack of any creative inspiration in his over-clouded private life, with marriage tacitly worsening every day. Like the hero of his last serial, Hardy needed a fresh feminine excitement to set him forward. This came when on 19 May 1893, on a visit to the late Lord Houghton's son, viceroy of Ireland, he met one of Houghton's married daughters, Florence Henniker, "a charming, *intuitive* woman apparently".[26] Florence was acting as hostess for her widowed brother, in the weirdly-isolated colony of Dublin Castle, whose members went to church protected by armed police and detectives, one of whom had been blown to pieces under the walls the previous Christmas Day. From her earliest years she was accustomed to high society, cosmopolitan and literary, as befitted a daughter of Houghton, one of the best-known hosts in Europe. Swinburne had fallen at her feet, though not in a proposal but to observe her hair was getting darker. Her father had been the first biographer of Keats, and she, in spite of a country-house reputation for being "fast", followed a serious literary career, supplementing the income of her impoverished soldier-husband. Inheriting, like her handsome brother, the aristocratic features of their mother—their father's face, according to Disraeli, looked as if it had been cut out of an orange—Florence had looks, dash, style, and a moderate literary ability, with three tolerably successful novels already to her credit.[27] Tall, slim, and graceful, in her late twenties, she also had a slightly gamine sense of humour; her father, after all, had combined a Unitarian upbringing with a famous library of erotica. She wrote with fatal ease, and had dashed off her first society-novel during a summer holiday.[28]

The susceptible Hardy at once decided that this society woman-novelist with "apparently" liberal views was the "enfranchised" spirit of inspiration he needed. She was, he said, "Pre-eminently the child of the Shelleyean tradition"; for was she not daughter of a man who, as early as 1829, had publicly defended Shelley, at the time still an outcast in England?[29] She went to the plays of the advanced and daring Ibsen, in their translations by Hardy's friend Gosse and by Archer. Blinded by this, by her considerable charm and lack of family ties—she was childless—Hardy failed to see, for some weeks at least, that Florence's unconventionality did not preclude sincere religious belief, church attendance, and an entirely faithful marriage to a heavily-moustached and non-poetical military husband. A flurry of letters followed their return to England, interspersed with visits to the theatre (Ibsen, of course), and plans to educate her in the historical niceties of church architecture—"I want you to be able to walk into a church, and pronounce upon its date at a glance."[30] He was pro-prietorial, tender: "If you go to the ball . . . Don't fag yourself out . . . Promise you won't." In their private Ibsen-based language, he, architect son of a mason, was her Master Builder, she, the young in-spirer, Hilda Wangel. Some unsurviving early letters were "trollish", that is, in the language of the same play, containing hints of sexual feeling.

The crash of these hopes, in this whirlwind progress, was bound to come sooner rather than later. On 16 July, only two months after their meeting, he was writing desperately but ominously, "as the mentor" of her hoped-for enfranchisement, "Depend upon it there are other valves for feeling than the ordinances of Mother Church."[31] Disillusion on this score came within another month. On 3 August he wrote her a letter expressing to the full his "enfranchised" views, presumably on love, marriage, and the relationship of men and women. On 8 August, slipping away together, he from Emma at Max Gate, she from her out-of-Town home at Southsea, they met at Eastleigh Junction for an expedition to Winchester. Here, in the typically Victorian setting of a railway carriage, she put paid to all his wilder hopes. He was crushed. Never again would he write such a letter, though "I am always your friend", as he told her in a slightly stunned communication nine days later.[32] What he had hoped will never quite be known; perhaps he did not know himself. An elopement? What his own Emma was to call "Eastern ideas of matrimony", with some platonic extra-marital relationship for both Hardy and Florence Henniker? Speculation must fail in the face of conventional phrasing and the loss of letters such as that of 3 August. Did she encourage him more than she intended? She certainly sent him many portraits of herself, in fashionable décolletage, and her own lush translation of Gautier's poem, *Affinity*. A daughter of the notorious Lord Houghton too may have had a deceptively on-coming manner. She succeeded in arousing passion, cooling it, and establishing a more comfortable relationship. By 6 October he was writing, "if we are not to be the *thorough* friends in future we have hitherto been, life will have lost a very great attraction".[33] Passion had dwindled to the milder temperature of collaboration in their joint short-story, *The Spectre of the Real*, on whose probable reception he ruefully and correctly prophesied, "all the wickedness . . . will be laid on my unfortunate head, while all the tender and proper parts will be attributed to you". This[34] might be a summing-up of his own six-month illusion.

What these six months certainly gave was an impetus to his neglected novel, *Jude*. "What name", he wrote to Florence Henniker on 22 October, "shall I give to the heroine of my coming long story?"[35] In point of fact, he called her Susan Florence Mary Bridehead. The Christian names were constructed by inserting the Florence of Mrs. Henniker's between the two first names (Susan Mary) of their mutual friend Mary Jeune, whose country house, Arlington Manor, was in Jude's part of the county of Berkshire. For whatever Florence Henniker did or did not contribute to Sue Bridehead's nature, one must consider Hardy's prefatory statement about the beginnings of the novel.

The scheme was jotted down in 1890, from notes made in 1887 and onwards, some of the circumstances being suggested by the death of a woman in the former year.

Three women, it has been seen, died in 1890. While the one intended as supplying "some of the circumstances" was undoubtedly Hardy's cousin Tryphena Sparks, since the protagonists, Sue and Jude, are cousins, the other two deaths also play a part. Helen Mathews, the actress, had made her London success in *Two Roses* as Ida, a part which has strange affinities with Sue—cool, independent, yet sudden in instinctive impulses. Mary Antell had been the wife of the man Hardy acknowledged to be partly the model for Jude, John Antell the Puddletown cobbler, with his self-taught Latin, Greek, and Hebrew, his little school, his changeable, violent black despondencies, his untoward surrenders to drink. Hardy had designed this man's tombstone, and composed an inscription which might have been an epitaph for his own fictional Jude.[36]

> In Memory of John Antell. He was a man of considerable local reputation as a self-made scholar, having acquired a varied knowledge of languages, literature and science by unaided study, & in the face of many untoward circumstances.

The death, in 1890, of the widow of this lonely, self-taught scholar must again have suggested "some of the circumstances" of the novel.

The external *circumstances* of the novel were suggested to Hardy by happenings in the early 1890s; the same is not necessarily true of the internal *characters*. This is specially so with Sue Bridehead. It is too neat an equation to say she began as Tryphena Sparks and developed as Florence Henniker, though she was, according to the second Mrs. Hardy, drawn from the latter.[37] It is only in circumstances, not in character, that this process took place. On her Tryphena side, Sue was a cousin, a pupil-teacher, and went to a training college. Among other minor circumstances, Tryphena actually signed a round robin asking the college staff for longer holidays, while Sue's fellow-students petition the staff about her with a similar document. Yet these are only, as Hardy truthfully wrote, the circumstances. There is evidence that the delicate, literary, fastidious, palely-sexed Sue was nothing like Tryphena in real life. Set beside the letters written by Sue in the book, bloodless, humourless, intellectual, the following section of a typical letter actually written by Tryphena Sparks to her brother Nat[38] tells a different story.

> . . . if only girls might propose—but alas! Well, there is a young schoolmaster of 34 or 35 has went and gone and done it in our place—married a young girl of 21—about a fortnight since—and hasn't he burnished himself up for the awful event with a new set of teeth—set bells ringing and people drunk—painted, papered and fitted his landlady's house with gas—sported Brussels carpets, walnut inlaid tables, chimney glasses of monstrous size and other things too much for my small brain to comprehend—(don't your sister wish she had baited her hook properly, that's all?)

Nothing could be less like Sue in character than this rumbustious young woman; Tryphena's letter might rather have been written by the novel's coarser symbol, Arabella Donn.

Similarly, the circumstances of Hardy's passage with Florence Henniker suggested some circumstances in the story of Sue and Jude. Sue, like Florence with Hardy, first appears to Jude as freethinking and enfranchised; she ends, in the hour-glass construction of the novel, as self-destructively wedded to Christian orthodoxy. Yet these are circumstances only. There is absolutely no hint that the character of Sue in the novel was drawn from the character of Florence Henniker as we know it, sophisticated, poised, calm, though at the same time imaginative and keenly humorous.

Once more, it is the *circumstances* of Hardy's passage with Florence Henniker which have been incorporated into the novel, not her character. Hardy was a thorough-going rationalist of a really rather old-fashioned sort, the kind of self-taught critical unbeliever of the mid-nineteenth-century stamp. G. K. Chesterton noted at this time that Hardy defended his views "with the innocence of a boys' debating club".[39]

His childhood religion, which he had abandoned with such pain in his middle twenties, had left him just as dogmatic about agnostic unbelief as he would have been about belief. To him, religious orthodoxy was something as horrifying as its agnostic opposite would have been to a conventional Christian. The one thing he could not stand about Florence, and which he satirized so obsessively and cruelly in Sue, was her belief. He could not keep his horror at this out of his letters to her, nor even, almost incredibly, out of the would-be eulogistic article he wrote about her for the *Illustrated London News* just a year after his disastrous disillusion with her on this score. Quite unnecessarily, he puts down her writing ambitions partly to her having shown in childhood "a quaint devotional fervour not unknown in imaginative children, taking the form of an enthusiasm for the writing of hymns".[40] Whether he consciously knew it or not, he was dismissing Florence's religion, which she herself was to declare, in a magazine interview, to be "very High Church", as something childish, which she had not grown out of. They are the terms in which Jude, in the horrendous last chapters of the book, raves against Sue's new-found orthodoxy, to him a betrayal almost to the point of obscenity.

Hardy wrote to Gosse, concerning Sue, that she was "a type of woman which has always had an attraction for me, but the difficulty of drawing the type has kept me from attempting it till now". He did not find her in Florence Henniker, whom he told bluntly, when his first illusions faded, that he "would have to trust to imagination". His admission that such a type "always had an attraction" may draw attention to his remote past. Hardy himself said that the novel was set in the 1860s, when he was in London.[41] The shadowy girl of his early London career, whom we only know by her initials, H.A., or the "H. Lond." of a note in his Bible may be the basis for this type and for Sue.[42] Again, we have little but circumstances to go on. "H. Lond." and Sue, for example, are both associated in Hardy's mind with the Epistle to the Thessalonians. Yet some huge emotional and spiritual shock, apparently associated with this girl, took place in Hardy in his middle twenties. Jude's continuous though changing sense of shock over the enigmatic character of Sue may be connected with this deep subliminal past. This must include Hardy's attachment to his own sister Mary, to whom he gave a copy of the novel. Sue and Jude, as a character remarks, are like brother and sister, and his sister's training college is chosen as Sue's. All through the 1890s, Mary and Kate shared the small house in Wollaston Avenue, Dorchester, where Hardy visited them frequently, and renewed sympathies he failed to find at Max Gate.

For one strand in the character of Jude, though Hardy at times hotly denied it, is the character and experiences of the young Hardy himself. Perhaps one should confine it to the boyhood and youth of Jude, but here it is almost photographic. The tenderness for wild things, especially birds, the schoolboy ambitions, the earnest self-education, hopes of the Church career, even the named books in his personal library, are all common to the fictional Jude and the real-life Hardy. Another strand, as also confirmed by the second Mrs. Hardy, is the real-life story of Hardy's uncle, John Antell, the self-taught. The third strand is the disastrous failure, defeated by drink and sex, of the man who was always to Hardy "my friend", Horace Moule. Moule's entanglement with a coarse girl like Arabella, the child he owned or was persuaded to own his, that child's shadowy history of going to Australia and being hanged, and Moule's eventual suicide, all add up to a set of circumstances unmistakably pointing to Moule as part-model. They also seem to point, more deeply, to his character as well. In the final, tragic flaw of an outwardly promising and noble character, Moule gave Hardy more than a hint of the heavy loading of life against happy fulfilment, which runs like a scar through the whole tissue of *Jude*.

The serialization of *Jude* under the title of *Hearts Insurgent*, with considerable bowdlerization for the magazine, *Harper's New Monthly*, did not arouse much critical notice except some which pointed out inconsistencies caused by the cuts. What it did arouse was a different kind of reading public. *Tess* had interested the fashionable, the conventionally-literate, the established. *Hearts Insurgent* spoke to the emerging, the new popularly-educated, the young, In the summer of 1895, its instalments were read avidly by the twenty-eight-year-old H. G. Wells. Just beginning his second marriage after a divorce, Wells had set up house at Woking, where he taught himself to bicycle by practising every day on the sandy tracks of open heathland, and suffered severe bruises in this novel sport. Seeing Jude's career as some parallel to his, he conceived a sort of Sue and Jude story of his own, carried out on a bicycle tour, the new symbol of emancipation, in a vein of light comedy, but with occasional serious social overtones. In Wells's *The Wheels of Chance*, Hoopdriver, the draper's assistant, and Jessica, the would-be emancipated girl, are Jude and Sue in another setting. Wells even provides a counterpart to Sue's mysterious Oxford graduate, who disillusioned her by wanting her to be not his companion but his mistress. When Jessica tries to take in hand Hoopdriver's education by encouraging him about self-educated working-class authors, she asks particularly if he has read *Hearts Insurgent*, by name; she desists (without mentioning Hardy's own name) when Hoopdriver confesses to reading only authors who "didn't seem to have much to do with me", the romantic novels of Walter Besant, Mrs. Braddon, Rider Haggard, Marie Corelli, and Ouida. To a representative of a really new literate class, Hardy now seemed "to have much to do with" life as Wells knew it to be.

It is perhaps ironic, then, that when the final instalments of *Hearts Insurgent* were appearing, Hardy plunged yet again into one more of his aristocratic literary infatuations. On 4 September 1895, he danced, as the guest of General Pitt-Rivers, with his married daughter Agnes Grove, at the Larmer Tree festivities, held at an ancient landmark of that name on the General's estate at Rushmore in Wiltshire. Through her mother, Agnes was of the progressive and liberal—though quarrelsome—family of Stanley, into which Mary Jeune had first married. Agnes herself had her share of vivid, imperious, sharp-tongued personality. She broke away early from her parents, whom she called "the Man" and "the minor one", and married the mild-mannered heir to a baronetcy, Walter Grove, who in later life referred to her philosophically as "my little pepper-pot". Dazzlingly beautiful in her extreme décolletage, flamboyant and vigorous, she was more robust, talented, and intellectual than Florence Henniker. She had a genuine journalistic gift, which she deployed with considerable success. Her articles which make up *The Social Fetich* (1907), dedicated to Hardy, anticipate, and indeed were probably copied by Nancy Mitford, in their witty demonstration of what was U and non-U in Edwardian times. Her attacks in these on the genteelisms of the middle-classes must have come uncomfortably near home to Hardy, and particularly to Emma, over whom she seems to have ridden rough-shod.[43] As a genuine unconventional aristocrat, she had a complete fascination for Hardy.

Hardy all too easily fell into a hopeful fantasy about Agnes Grove. He began to write innumerable letters, and tried to coach her still-inexperienced attempts at journalism. It was a familiar pattern with his literary ladies. Rosamund Tomson had felt encouraged by his interest to ask him for a contribution to her new artistic magazine;[44] Florence Henniker had obtained his collaboration in a short story, in addition to his adulatory though back-handed article in the August 1894 number of the *Illustrated London News*. Whatever the cost to his increasingly-strained marriage, Hardy must now have a literary lady— not his wife—whom he could mastermind, and who would appreciate him in return. It was a situation which clearly brought him satisfaction and happiness.

7

Prose to Poetry

ON I NOVEMBER 1895, the day of the volume publication of *Jude the Obscure*, Hardy might well feel happy. *Tess* had weathered the storm raised by a few critics, and was a popular success, generally acknowledged as his finest book. The dramatized version, which he himself had just completed for a rising actor-manager, Johnston Forbes-Robertson, was eagerly awaited by a most distinguished leading-lady, Mrs. Patrick Campbell, who had scored such a success in 1893 as Mrs. Tanqueray. *Tess* had quickened public interest in all his previous novels. Since the beginning of the year, he had been revising these for collected publication in a uniform edition by Osgood, McIlvaine, to which *Jude* was added as the latest title. He had used his reputation over *Tess* to make some of the sexual expressions in these other novels more frank. For the first time, in this edition, the heroine of *The Woodlanders* was allowed to say to her rival, "O, my great God! He's had you." On the personal side, he now had two well-born ladies with literary ambitions under his tutelage. He was helping Florence Henniker with her forthcoming book of short stories, including their own collaboration *The Spectre of the Real*.[1] He was encouraging Agnes Grove to use her fine and decisive mind in topical journalism.[2] To both he at once sent copies of *Jude*. To Florence he wrote a little nervously, "not because I thought you narrow—but because I had rather bored you with him during the writing".[3] To Agnes he confidently wrote with her copy, "You are, I know, sufficiently broad of view to estimate without bias a tragedy of very unconventional lives."[4] Though he must have been uneasy at the effect of these talented ladies on Emma, he could congratulate himself that she seemed now able to compete as hostess with the best of them. That summer, the *Weekly Sun* had noticed her afternoon "at homes" at Ashley Gardens, where she had entertained, among others, Florence Henniker and Mrs. Patrick Campbell. Emma had been praised by the gossip-writer: "Mrs. Hardy is an excellent hostess. She sees that her guests are properly introduced and put completely at ease by a kind word or two. And she seems to know instinctively the people who desire to know each other."[5] Perhaps his literary fame would help to bring her satisfaction in her own social success.

The last two months in 1895 shattered what false calm he may have felt. Friends like Florence Henniker, who wrote at once to ask for a key to the great Oxford figures of the past mentioned in *Jude*, might be appreciative.[6] The critics could not have been more damning. The *Morning Post* could see no good in it, the *Pall Mall Gazette* found it full of "dirt, drivel, and damnation", and coined the sneer "Jude the Obscene". The *Athenaeum* dismissed it as the bad book of a great writer. Puritan America was particularly shocked. Jeannette Gilder, in the New York *World*, made her two notorious attacks, one entitled "Hardy the Degenerate". More deeply wounding, perhaps, than all this, and nearest home, were the doubts expressed by his usually adulatory supporter, Edmund Gosse. A week after publication, Gosse reviewed the book in the *St. James's Gazette*. He wrote of "a grimy story that Mr. Hardy has at last presented to his admirers". There were other cutting phrases. Hardy, though beginning a letter of 10 November by praising Gosse's article as "the most discriminating that has yet appeared", was very clearly hurt.[7] He had an even more unpleasant shock from Gosse in December, when he and Emma paid a flying visit to London, to see both Forbes-Robertson and Mrs. Patrick Campbell in *Romeo and Juliet*. At the common luncheon-table at the Savile Club, Gosse told Hardy publicly to his face that *Jude the Obscure* was the most indecent novel ever written.[8] For the first, and, as he afterwards said, the only time in his life, Hardy became really angry with his friend. Even a more "generous view", expressed by Gosse in a new magazine *Cosmopolis* at the New Year, did not easily make up for the shock. Considering how abnormally thin-skinned Hardy was, and how much this novel of all others meant to him, it is a tribute to both men that their friendship survived. Yet worse than the critics, worse even than temporary estrangement from Gosse, was the effect of the novel on Emma. Though this has almost always been exaggerated and distorted, it formed a serious break. Writing in April 1899, she exclaimed, "the last four or five [years] alas!"[9] Emma's jealousy and anger were connected with Hardy's slights, real or imaginary, to her intellect and beliefs. Her objection to the succession of lady authors was that her husband interested himself actively in their writing while paying little attention to her own far from pathetic attempts. So far this had not prevented her from trying to do what she could to help his own work. Now she was faced with a book in which she could not believe, and whose message, as she understood it, she detested. Her nephew, Gordon Gifford, later wrote, speaking of this exact time, a comment on Lord David Cecil's book on Hardy.[10]

> I was living with them at their house, and . . . I consider therefore that I should be in the best position as judge on this matter. The author [Cecil], in a footnote, adds that "Hardy was at odds with his wife at this time"—namely, the publication of "Jude the Obscure". With this I do not disagree, as my aunt, who was a very ardent Churchwoman

and believer in the virtues and qualities of women in general, strongly objected to this book, and, I think, the outlook of some of the characters depicted therein. I should, however, mention that this was the first of the Hardy novels in which she had not assisted by her counsel, copious notes for reference and mutual discussion.

The later part of this statement is true, and is proved by Emma's familiarity with all the complicated stages of writing and rewriting *Tess*, including her knowledge of the various changing names adopted by Hardy for his heroine. She even took an interest in the *setting* of *Jude*, as she had with all his novels, and as late as April 1895, on a visit to Mary Jeune at Arlington Manor, she sketched the church at Chaddleworth, Berks.[11] It is likely, then, that Gordon Gifford's account of the quarrel over *Jude* is true too; it is certainly more plausible than some of the legends woven about Hardy and Emma at this time.

One of the most persistent of these legends is that Emma made a special journey to Dr. Richard Garnett, keeper of printed books at the British Museum, and asked him to suppress *Jude*, proposing herself to burn the manuscript. The more one enquires into the origins of this improbable story, the less likely is it to be true. It comes from Ford Madox Ford, recognized as one of the great literary liars, with his "tricky memory, his carelessness with details, his occasional outright fantasies".[12] Even he does not claim it to be true. He was told, he says, by "the young Garnetts" that Mrs. Hardy, who was "a Dean's daughter", had come up from "a long white farmhouse with roses at the window" to persuade their father. Ford then admits that what he calls "the pother" about *Jude* "took place in circles remote from my own". When he later visited Emma, he found that the young Garnetts "had projected an image" of a household where Emma burnt Hardy's manuscripts which was entirely false, even in its smallest details. Emma was not "a Dean's daughter" but an Archdeacon's niece. Max Gate was far from the "long white farmhouse" described by the Garnetts. The whole story was, in Ford's words, "merely a Garnettian slant on the Hardy household"; they had painted a picture of events which was "all naturally nothing of the sort".[13] If even that arch-romancer Ford Madox Ford was so sceptical, it is all the more astonishing that biographers have accepted the story.

At the same time, the break with Emma was severe. From now onward, she suspected intellectual, society women not only for their monopoly of her husband's literary interest, but if they could be judged as "Jude-*ite*", a term of reproach coined by her.[14] She herself adopted the popular outcry that the novel was in the manner of Zola, the stock pornographic symbol of the English 1890s, his publisher and translator, Vizetelly, having been fined and imprisoned in 1889. She did not, she wrote, wish "T.H. to be hand-in-glove with Zola". In point of fact,

Hardy wrote disingenuously to Gosse that he was "read in Zola very little", and even tried to persuade Gosse that scenes in *Jude* were rather in the style of Fielding, a fellow Dorset author they mutually admired.[15] Hardy, of course, had read at least two of Vizetelly's Zola translations in the late 1880s. In 1891, he was asked by Vizetelly's son to sign an appeal against his father's imprisonment. To Emma, Hardy himself in *Jude* was both irreligious and immoral, and in both like Zola. Her powerful inherited Protestantism made her feel called to combat this tendency, in both Hardy and his friends. Her husband was an example of talents dangerously misused, in view of "the thickening clouds of evil advancing". A year or so later, she rebuked Hardy's freethinking friend Clodd for his *Pioneers of Evolution*.[16] One can guess, too, how the pleasure of her summer success as a London hostess was marred when she felt herself marked down as the wife of a notorious blasphemer and pornographer.

Hardy's busy outward life in 1896 seemed to ride out these storms. Early in January, Mrs. Pat Campbell arrived impressively at Max Gate, only to declare herself "heartbroken" a fortnight later at the slow negotiations over *Tess*. In London, early in February, Hardy took a walk with another thirty-year-old leading lady, Elizabeth Robins. She seems to have understood from him that the play was for her; once again, she expressed herself mortified when she heard next month that he had promised it to Mrs. Pat. In point of fact, Harpers of New York were after it for the beautiful and popular Mrs. Fiske, who was "wild to play it"; Hardy had wired his London publishers early in February to extract the script from the Jeunes' strong-box, where he was keeping it, and to send it overseas. On 28 February, Charles Frohman, the American impresario, offered terms—hence, probably, Hardy's prevarication with actresses in his own country, quite apart from his weakness for pleasing a pretty young woman. At the same time, he took care to have the terms vetted by his friend, the dramatist, Henry Arthur Jones. He was also involved in helping his two English lady literary protégées, Florence Henniker and Agnes Grove. On 9 March, he rescued from the magazine *Temple Bar* an unpublished story that Florence Henniker wanted for her collection, writing a special letter to the editor on her behalf.[17] Simultaneously, he was busy encouraging Agnes to capitalize on a remark she had made about the child in *Jude* by putting her thoughts into an article entitled "What should children be told?"; he offered to read her draft himself. April was spent polishing his "good little pupil's" article, sending it to the *New Review*, and writing to hurry up the editor.[18]

Such activities seem to have kept him happily occupied: and this was as well, since the attacks on *Jude* had now passed from the serious reviewers into the lunatic fringes of literature. In January 1896, the elderly Mrs. Oliphant, just at the end of a long life of penury and struggling journalism, seized on the novel as the pretext for a sensational article in *Blackwood's*, entitled "The Anti-Marriage League". She professed to regard the book as an attack on women and "an assault on the stronghold of marriage". In May, Arthur John Butler, the translator of Dante, wrote in the *National Review* on "Hardy as a Decadent", condemning Hardy's "night-cart" view of nature, and deploring in particular the pig-killing scene. In July, Thomas Gunn Selby, a former Wesleyan missionary to China, outdid nearly everyone in his Fernley Lecture at Liverpool—"Filth and defilement he faces with the calm, unshrinkable countenance of a Local Board labourer", picking up the idea of Hardy as concerned with "night-soil", and adding, "This gifted man has made his home in the slime-pits of Siddim." Not to be outdone by nonconformity, on 9 June, the Bishop of Wakefield announced he had thrown "such garbage" into his fire. Hardy, not appreciating the climate of Yorkshire, said he doubted if the Bishop had a fire to burn a thick novel in summer, adding wryly that, if so, he had done it in default of being able to burn the author; but he was hurt at the Bishop's alleged instructions to W. H. Smith not to stock the book. He also told young William Rothenstein that he hardly dared enter his new club, the Athenaeum;[19] seven months later, he wrote to the anticlerical Clodd about this "miserable second-class prelate".[20]

On top of these disturbances, Hardy was attacked that spring by the familial disease of rheumatism, which had crippled his father; he was subject to bouts of it for the rest of his life. When he and Emma came up to Pelham Gardens, a rented house, pain drove him south to try the air of Brighton in May, though he found more relief in retreating for a few days to Max Gate, in whose chalky situation he had great faith. Meantime, the attacks on *Jude* redoubled, but so did the ironic fame that the book acquired him. He refused to stand for the Rectorship of Glasgow University. More substantially, the sales of the book were enormous, 20,000 in three months. He was able to enjoy the London season, and plan extensive holidays. He found time to sit for Winifred Hope Thomson to complete the portrait she had begun the previous year. He and Emma attended once again the popular open-air concerts at the Imperial Institute. Meeting Agnes Grove at one of these, Hardy, inspired by memories of the Larmer Tree Gardens, took two or three turns with her to the strains of the Blue Danube Waltz "among the promenaders, who eyed them with a mild surmise as to whether they had been drinking".[21] It was not, perhaps, the most tactful behaviour towards Emma, who had been ill with shingles, a stress condition possibly caused by tension over *Jude*, and was just now suffering from one of her periodic attacks of lameness. However, he determined to take her on a more extended holiday than usual when the season ended. After briefly looking in at Dorchester early in August, where he found his mother well though aged—"her face looked smaller"—he and Emma set off for Worcestershire and Warwickshire. They returned south via Reading, where Hardy, still haunted by the family history that produced *Tess* and *Jude*, remembered his father's mother had lived. They then spent a fortnight at Dover before going abroad. Here he read *King Lear*, which he had begun at Stratford, and wrote against Arnold's *Dover Beach* "Sept. 1896—T.H./E.L.H." Some have seen this entry as a pathetic or remorseful comment on Arnold's lines

> Ah, love, let us be true
> To one another!

though, with Hardy's literalness of mind, it may simply record the parallel of the place where they found themselves.

Similarly, the month's holiday that followed in Flanders may have been both an attempt to relive their honeymoon tours of over twenty years before, and a further exploration of the epic scenery for a work about the Napoleonic Wars. There was one difference from their long-ago visit. Hardy perhaps remembered how exhausted Emma had become previously on the battlefield of Waterloo; she was twenty years older now, and more lame. Fortunately, the Hardys were in the forefront of the dominant craze of the 1890s, bicycling. Hardy himself had found in February "the loveliest 'Byke' for myself . . . 'The Rover Cob' ".[22] Emma had acquired for herself a splendid green-painted steed, named "The Grasshopper". Always more daring than her husband, and encouraged by the numerous lady bicyclists she saw boarding the Channel ferry, she took it abroad, where it became a constant source of adventure, disappearing again and again in train-transit but always emerging with triumphant cries of "V'la le veloze de Madame!" She was run into, hurt her shoulder, but continued defiantly in Ostend, Bruges, Dinant, Spa, and Liège. Only Brussels, which they visited twice en route, was too busy to bike in. Hardy explored the field of Waterloo alone. The memories of twenty years ago, the attempt to stay at the same hotel in Brussels, proved saddening. "I ask myself why I am here again and not underground", he confided in a letter to Florence Henniker, whom he emotionally addressed as "my dear little friend", adding, "if you should write put *Mr*", in case a response in the same vein should fall into Emma's hands.[23]

Emma and the Grasshopper returned to menace the steep streets of Dorchester, and Hardy went back to his study at Max Gate. Here, on 17 October, he made a note which marked what he called "the end of prose". In fact, it crystallized all that had been happening for the past year. The busy, social, literary, external events of his life were nothing

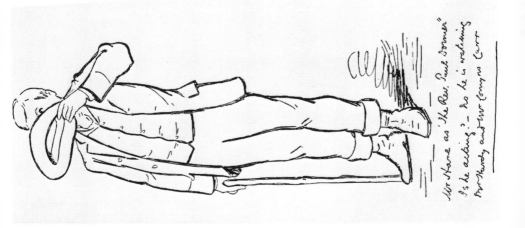

1 Two sketches from *The Illustrated Sporting and Dramatic News*, 7 January 1882

Hardy, J. Comyns Carr and George Lewis (*left*) watching John Hare (*right*) playing in Pinero's *The Squire* at St. James's Theatre; they are concerned about alleged plagiarism of Hardy's own play, based on *Far From the Madding Crowd*

2 Scene from *Two Roses* with Helen Mathews (*right*)
Artist's impression by Harold Ludlow, January 1882

(a) Mary Jeune (hostess)

(b) Rosamund Tomson (poet)

3   Hardy's four ladies of fashion in the 1890s

(c) Florence Henniker (novelist)

(d) Agnes Grove (journalist)

(*a*) Henry Hardy

(*b*) Kate Hardy

4   Hardy's brother, sisters, and best friend

(*c*) Mary Hardy

(*d*) Horace Moule

beside his inner, emotional existence. This was now to be expressed completely in poems. In his note, he saw poetry too as a way of expressing intellectual beliefs freely. "If Galileo had said in verse that the world moved, the Inquisition might have let him alone."[24] This decision, after what he called to Gosse twenty-five-and-a-half years of prose, reckoned from his first novel publication of spring 1871, had already been taken, and had helped to fulfil his secret emotional needs ever since *Jude* had appeared. The new-found techniques of half-a-dozen years, since he renewed "the viewless wings of poesy" in 1890, resulted in three of his finest poems, written in the year from December 1895 to December 1896. These were *In Tenebris, The Dead Man Walking*, and *Wessex Heights*. All three, totally different from each other in form and method, fitted with new mastery the most urgent themes of his inner life.

That three such fine poems were written in the year from December 1895 shows that Hardy's decision of mid-October 1896, to write poems only, was neither arbitrary nor abrupt. The idea that it was taken in pique or resentment at the critical reception of *Jude* is almost certainly false, as Max Beerbohm pointed out.[25] One very simple explanation, seldom given, is that poetry needed far less weight of words. As Hardy grew older, novel-writing was becoming a physical burden. In summer 1895, revising *The Woodlanders*, he wanted to add a verse epigraph. Not finding a quotation, he invented four lines himself to fit the book:

> Not boskiest bow'r,
> When hearts are ill affin'd,
> Hath tree of pow'r
> To shelter from the wind!

It is an extreme case; but if three volumes of prose could be summed up in four lines of verse, Hardy may well now have decided for poetry. Secondly, the highly personal themes of his secret youth were now beginning to force themselves uncomfortably into his novels.[27] When he attached them to a novelist's human characters, they became too self-revealing. Poems could reveal more of the emotion, but less of the biographical circumstances. Lastly, and again very simply, he had alienated his help and amanuensis, Emma. From *Jude* onward, he could no longer count on the faithful copying in her hand, which many of his other novels had enjoyed. A new novel might now literally be beyond his physical powers, especially as rheumatism began to affect his fingers.

The first of this group of poems was written in late 1895 and early 1896, and was at first called *De Profundis*, and published under that title in 1901. Oscar Wilde's posthumous autobiography of the same name in 1905 probably caused Hardy later to alter his title to *In*

Tenebris. It consists of three parts, the first in notably short, and the next two in notably long lines. All bear the stamp of personal disillusion with the world and his own life, and the second has explicit reference to the reception of *Jude*, to whose author he imagines his fellows saying,

> Get him up and be gone as one shaped awry; he disturbs the order here.

This section also characterizes himself, in words which he was often to use later to refute charges of mere pessimism, as one

> Who holds that if way to a better there be, it exacts a full look at the worst.

All carry the message, if not of suicide, that he might as well be dead. The third embodies a series of highly personal and mysterious unrecorded incidents from his very early life as a child at Higher Bockhampton,

> Ere I had learnt that the world was a welter of futile doing:

he describes clearing the winter snow from the garden, with childish springtime hope, an incident in the evening on the Heath with his mother—"She who upheld me"—and a moment from his delicate childhood, "the smallest and feeblest of folk", by the cottage fireside, weak from some "baptism of pain". Now, he wishes he had died at one of those early moments, before adult disillusion had come.

The poem, *The Dead Man Walking*, written later in 1896, and in the clipped, laconic metre of the first section of *In Tenebris*, also recalls past and personal history. Its theme is how, though apparently alive, his soul has died gradually through the years of his life, since the time of optimistic "Troubadour-youth". Incident by incident, he has been "inched" on to living death. He was first "iced" by struggles and failures of ambition, "the goal of men". Then,

> When passed my friend, my kinsfolk,
> Through the Last Door,
> And left me standing bleakly,
> I died yet more.

The term "my friend", always used for Horace Moule, who committed suicide in 1873, leads on to the many "kinsfolk", who had died in the past decade, three of his Sparks girl cousins, his kindly Aunt Mary Antell, and finally his own father in 1892. Then, as a last and most recent blow,

> And when my Love's heart kindled
> In hate of me,
> Wherefore I knew not, died I
> One more degree.

Emma, since *Jude*, had abandoned sympathy with him; though his "Wherefore I knew not" may seem ingenuous, he was genuinely surprised at the violence of her rejection, implied by the word "hate".

The third and last great poem of 1896 was written in the December of that year, *Wessex Heights*. It is at once the most moving and the most enigmatic, and though it is grouped in feeling with the others, and even echoes an occasional phrase, some of its special aspects lie in what he was doing at the time of writing. In December 1896, he was particularly "hard-pressed in sending off a copy of *The Well-Beloved* to the printers". This was his volume-revision of the serial of 1892. He found this revision immensely difficult; he confessed to Gosse that he did not rewrite from beginning to end as he had intended, but only substantially altered the first part and the ending—though, it is true, both these gave very much a different bearing to the story.[29] This is again a reminder that he now lacked Emma's help in fair-copying; it also shows how weary he had become with prose generally. The story, partly conceived in youth as a poetic Shelleyan symbol, had become a burden of words, a dead weight.

Against this background, the long-lined quatrains of *Wessex Heights* were written. Apparently simple, even at times naïve, their tension and dramatic rhythm quiver with such intensity that one feels an intention far deeper than at first appears. The surface idea is one of extreme simplicity. Like his father, who used to take him to high places in Dorset to look through his telescope, Hardy seeks the hilltop view-points of his Wessex countryside—Ingpen Beacon, Wylls-Neck, Bul-barrow, Pilsdon—and feels at home and at peace there. He avoids the valleys, the "lowlands", the towns, where he cannot feel happy or at ease either with the inhabitants or his own past there.

Yet it seems clear that there is a strong current of emotion below this surface, which many critics have tried in various ways to explain. A factual start to some kind of explanation lies in two letters of the second Mrs. Hardy to Alda, Lady Hoare, written on 6 and 9 December 1914.[30] She wrote,

> When I read 'Wessex Heights' it wrung my heart. It made me miserable to think that he had ever suffered so much. It was written in '96, before I knew him, but the four people mentioned are actual women. One was dead & three living when it was written—now only one is living . . . 'Wessex Heights' will *always* wring my heart, for I know when it was written a little while after the publication of 'Jude', when he was so cruelly treated.

Though these letters reveal something, mainly that the distress of the poem is partly connected with the reception of *Jude*, in other ways they deepen the confusion, especially over the "four . . . actual women", and their respective lives and deaths when related to the year of composition, 1896, and the year Florence Hardy wrote, 1914.

For one thing, no critic has been able to agree which parts of the poem are allusions to "actual women", so veiled are Hardy's references. One of the oddest mistakes has been to take a reference in stanza two to Hardy's favourite text from 1 Corinthians, chapter 13, "Her who suffereth long and is kind"—that is, Charity—which he uses in several other poems, as one of the women. It is, however, common sense to assume that the "four women" would be self-evident, in reading the poem, to Mrs. Hardy's correspondent, Lady Hoare. Otherwise, Florence Hardy's explanation of the poem would be meaningless to her. This, and Hardy's usual simplicity of construction, makes it certain that the four women are not teasingly embedded in different parts of the poem, like plums in a cake, but quite straightforwardly catalogued in these two consecutive stanzas.

> There's a ghost at Yell'ham Bottom chiding loud at the fall of the night,
> There's a ghost in Froom-side Vale, thin-lipped and vague in a shroud
> of white,
> There is one in the railway train whenever I do not want her there,[31]
> I see its profile against the pane, saying what I would not hear.
>
> As for one rare fair woman, I am now but a thought of hers,
> I enter her mind and another thought succeeds me that she prefers;
> Yet my love for her in its fulness she herself even did not know;
> Well, time cures hearts of tenderness, and now I can let her go.

Expanding what she had written about the four, Mrs. Hardy identified, to most people's satisfaction, the fourth "rare fair woman". Later in her letter of 9 December 1914, she added

She has always been a sincere & affectionate friend to him, staunch & unaltering—& I am glad to say she is my friend too.

This has been taken, almost certainly rightly, to mean Florence Henniker. At Mrs. Henniker's death in 1923, Mrs. Hardy wrote to another woman friend that Mrs. Henniker had been "my dear friend for 13 [years]".[32] That is, they had been friends since 1910,[33] and therefore were so in 1914. It is difficult to find another common friend of Hardy and his second wife who fits these facts. Complete uncertainty, however, still exists over the three "ghosts" from Hardy's past in the previous stanza. Since Hardy, while writing the poem, was revising *The Well-Beloved*, and since that novel was, at least in part, based on Hardy's own youthful attraction towards his three girl-cousins, Rebecca, Martha, and Tryphena Sparks, it would seem an easy solution if these were the three. Yet Florence Hardy's formula of the dead and the living will not allow this; for, by the time of *Wessex Heights*, not one but two of the cousins, Rebecca and Tryphena, were dead. Possibly Florence, as she confessed, did not always know the details of the times before she met Hardy; for instance, she thought that Winifred Hope Thomson's

portrait of Hardy, painted at this period, 1895-96, had been painted in
1892.[34] Still, over a poem which moved her as much as *Wessex Heights*,
she would surely have every reason to be accurate. It is only possible
to say, then, that these three women, all associated with local places,
are loves of Hardy's youth, just as the fourth, Mrs. Henniker, was that
of his middle-age. A guess—but only a guess—is that the "ghost at
Yell'ham Bottom" is Elizabeth Bishop, the beautiful red-haired
daughter of the gamekeeper, who lived in the cottage at the bottom of
Yellowham Hill, and who was celebrated by Hardy in the poem *To
Lizbie Browne*. The "thin-lipped" ghost "in Froom-side Vale" might be
Louisa Harding, another youthful love, who used to pass him without
speaking. The "one in the railway train" could be Tryphena Sparks,
who in 1870 chose to go and study in London, putting her career before
their attachment, and thus "saying what I would not hear". Yet these,
though fitting Florence's conditions, are pure conjecture.

In any case, the identification puzzle should not distract from the
main meaning of the poem. Though these two stanzas have their own
heartbeat, there is a pulse of urgency throughout the whole work which
suggests great spiritual importance. The "lowlands", where Hardy
seems "false to myself, my simple self that was,/And is not now",
peopled with "phantoms" are a chilling symbol of real horror. One
reasonable conjecture for this feeling is that these "lowlands" are
associated with his works in prose, a lower level of writing, he now felt,
than the "heights" of poetry, which he had assayed when very young—
"my simple self that was"—and was attempting again now. This echoes
his "Troubadour youth" of *The Dead Man Walking*. Probably this
should not be pressed too exactly; but it gives meaning to the dark
stanza which immediately precedes these other two:

> I cannot go to the Great grey Plain; there's a figure against the moon,
> Nobody sees it but I, and it makes my breast beat out of tune;
> I cannot go to the tall-spired town, being barred by the forms now passed
> For everybody but me, in whose long vision they stand there fast.

Here Florence Hardy's hint that the whole poem is concerned in
some way with *Jude the Obscure* may help. In his note-gathering for that
book, Hardy recorded, as we saw, a ghastly experience at Fawley, the
scene of Jude's childhood, in what he calls a valley of melancholy—
"though I am alive with the living, I can only see the dead here".[35]
These "dead", who are the relatives of Hardy's mysterious grandmother, Mary Head, are connected, in the book, with a gibbet and a
hanging. Was this the ancestral "figure against the moon" of "the
Great grey Plain", seen only by Hardy himself? "The tall-spired town"
is, of course, Salisbury, one of the other main scenes in *Jude*, where
Hardy had had some traumatic experience—what, one does not quite

know—in youth, when visiting his sister Mary there in 1860 at her training-college, so largely drawn on for the background to this part of the novel. The horror of these places seems to be associated in the poem with the horror felt in revulsion at the reception of his last prose work, and all that it had cost him spiritually.

The writing of *Wessex Heights*, at all events, seemed a release, and Hardy appeared to breathe more freely in the early months of 1897. News came from New York of the success of Mrs. Fiske in *Tess*, though the simultaneous reading of the script, to protect Hardy's copyright, at the St. James's Theatre on 2 March, cost Hardy twenty pounds and nervous dyspepsia.[36] Hardy's version had, in fact, been totally rewritten for New York by Lorimer Stoddard, who found it, as an English producer did later,[37] unplayably undramatic. In the middle of March 1897, the volume-form *The Well-Beloved* was published, and was at once highly praised by Gosse. Most other reviewers were puzzled, but generally respectful, and often relieved that it was not another *Jude*. Only the *World*, cashing in on the clamour about that novel, found this one immoral. "Of all forms of sex-mania in fiction we have no hesitation in pronouncing the most unpleasant to be the Wessex-mania of Mr. Thomas Hardy." Unluckily, Hardy showed over this one irresponsible and trivial comment the obsession, which had haunted him ever since his first printed book, that of letting one bad review outweigh all others. He wrote bitter protests to Gosse, to Mrs. Henniker, to everyone who would listen. Months later, he still refered to "that horrid *World*".[38] In fact, he protested too much for complete truth. It might have occurred to him that a hero who tried to marry three generations of girls might seem questionable, and invite personal comparison—he had just admitted privately to Gosse, after more rheumatism, that he himself was "getting old, like Pierston". Instead, he chose to regard the review as inspired by "personal malignity". Happily, his decision to let his secret and real life be expressed no more in novels, but in poetry, was gaining ground. On 4 February, he entered in his diary, "Title: 'Wessex Poems: with Sketches of their Scenes by the Author'." Two other entries, bracketing this one, show his poet's way of looking at things dominant. On 27 January he entered, "Today has length, breadth, thickness, colour, smell, voice. As soon as it becomes *yesterday* it is a thin layer among many layers, without substance, colour, or articulate sound." On 10 February, he wrote, "I cannot help noticing countenances and tempers in objects of scenery, e.g. trees, hills, houses."[39] The next two years were mostly spent in assembling and decorating his first printed volume of verse.

1897 was, of course, also Queen Victoria's Diamond Jubilee year. Emma and Hardy decided to spend it in an individual way, simply by not being present. Though compelled by habit to come to London for the start of "the season", they did not compete for a house or flat there, but stayed at Basingstoke, travelling up on day-trips by fast train. As usual, they went to the Imperial Institute, where Edward Strauss's Viennese band was playing that summer; in Hampshire, they visited the Roman city of Silchester, which Hardy found as sufficiently mournful as he had found Rome itself just ten years before. Then, in the middle of June, they left England for an empty Europe, everyone travelling the other way for the great occasion. On the actual day, 20 June, they were at Berne. At Interlaken, the rosy glow of the Jungfrau could be seen from Hardy's bedroom at three in the morning. With solemn humour, he read *The Times*'s account of the Jubilee "in the snowy presence of the maiden-monarch that dominated the whole place".[40] Looking at the peak, he conceived his impressive poem to the mountaineering literary man, Leslie Stephen, which was to be so much admired by the latter's daughter, Virginia Woolf. At Lausanne on 27 June, with an older literary association, he spent from eleven to midnight in Gibbon's old garden, where *The Decline and Fall* had been finished precisely 110 years before, a coincidence which also provided Hardy with a poem. A poetic note from Zermatt—"Could see where the Matterhorn was by the absence of stars within its outline"—gave him another sonnet, not unluckily as good as the original note. Over-fatigue made him ill at Geneva; Emma, "in excellent health and vigour", actually thought of hiring a bicycle. At all events, she found "the tomb of an ancestor" in the town.[41]

Returning to a post-Jubilee England, the Hardys toured cathedrals and great houses in the West country. At Salisbury, always an evocative place with memories of his sister Mary's sojourn there, Hardy was moved both by the reading by an old canon of a chapter from Jeremiah and by the beauty of the Close at night. The autumn was spent in a flurry of bicycling, accompanied for some days by Kipling, who was playing with the idea of making his home in Dorset. Winter, as usual now with Hardy, brought complaints of ill-health. In December he visited London but "retired ignominiously" with a three days' sick headache. In the first two months of 1898, he was involved by Gosse in an address to be presented by fellow-authors to George Meredith, on the occasion of his seventieth birthday on 28 February. Hardy approved strongly of Leslie Stephen's composition of this address. The summer season of 1898 found the Hardys, though less active, back in their London rhythm. They took a flat in Wynnstay Gardens, Kensington; but the bicycling craze brought them home to Dorset earlier than usual. Hardy was often joined on these tours by his brother Henry, whom he had introduced to the pleasures of the bicycle, and they visited their Sparks cousin in Bristol. In August, Hardy entertained Florence Henniker's military husband, who was on Southern Command manœuvres, and wrote to her, somewhat archly, of a "mysterious occupation" on which he himself was engaged. This was the sketching of his projected illustrations for the volume of *Wessex Poems*. He made the final decision to publish this, his first collected volume, in mid-September.[42] By mid-October, he was groaning over the numerous printing errors, and complaining that the news of his illustrative sketches had somehow got into the papers.[43] In mid-December, *Wessex Poems* was published. It was the first fully visible and public sign of his poetic resolve; it had consequences which he himself cannot have anticipated.

8

War at Home and Abroad

"WELL", wrote Hardy to Edmund Gosse, "the poems were lying about, and I did not quite know what to do with them."[1] Since he had been planning for nearly two years to bring out a volume, the remark seems a little disingenuous. There was, in fact, a certain element of unease in his mind at the step he was taking, and for more than one reason. Would the public accept the well-known novelist as a poet? He fortified himself, as so often, by anticipatory abuse of his supposed critics. "Considering", he wrote, "that the Britisher resents a change of utterance, instrument, even of note, I do not expect a particularly gracious reception of them." Hardy's doubts, expressed in this way, do not themselves sound gracious; but there are signs that he was thinking not only of the critics, but of one Britisher in person. This was his own wife, whose reaction he tried to avert by a brief Preface. "The pieces", he claimed, "are in a large degree dramatic or personative in conception; and this even when they are not obviously so." What he meant by the second part of this cryptic sentence was that poems in which the poet, "I", speaks to or about women, should not be taken as his own personal feelings. This false claim was a naïve attempt to throw Emma off the scent for it was repeated in the two successive books of verse before her death, but never again after. Nor was Emma fooled. Plain for all to read was her husband's extreme susceptibility to women all through his life. Many of the twenty-odd love-poems, two-fifths of the total contents, were dated from the 1860s to the 1890s. Only one, *Ditty*, written during their courtship in 1870, was addressed to her. Hurt and indignant, she wrote at once to a friend and admirer. Alfred Pretor, a Cambridge don, Fellow of St. Catherine's, had earlier in the year actually dedicated his book of mild and animal-loving short stories "to Mrs. Thomas Hardy, who suggested and encouraged the publication of these tales", a gesture that, for all her encouragement of his novels, her own famous husband had signally failed to make. Pretor therefore seemed a fit confidant for her grievance about Thomas's implied insult to their love and marriage. The bachelor don, whose own schoolboy past included a sensational scandal at Harrow, did his best with the angry wife.[2] Hardy, he wrote, "has said again and again to me little casual things that are absolute proofs that all his reminiscences are little fancies evoked from the days of his youth and absolutely without bearing on the real happiness of his life." All the same, even the gentle Pretor could not help feeling disturbed. "I *do* wish T.H. wd. dedicate a book to you." Hardy showed no sign of doing so in the 1900s, and the faithful Pretor was forced to repeat his own gesture in 1905, when he again dedicated a book about his pet dog, Judy; "to my friend Mrs. Thomas Hardy, a true lover of animals, to whom I dedicated Judy's first memoirs, I dedicate the last".

It is clear that Emma's indignation with her husband had been coming to the boil all through the 1890s. According to the second Mrs. Hardy, Emma round about 1891 began to confide to her diary "bitter denunciations" of Hardy, "full of venom, hatred and abuse".[3] According to another though less reliable witness, she actually gave these the heading "What I think of my Husband".[4] The literal truth will never be known, since Hardy, horrified by reading the manuscript in the months after Emma's death, eventually burned it. Yet a summary of her feelings during this decade has survived in a letter written by Emma in August 1899.[5] This was addressed to the sister of Winifred Hope Thomson, who had recently painted Hardy's portrait. In 1899, Elspeth Thomson married the writer Kenneth Grahame. It was a late marriage, and Grahame, set in the bachelor ways he presented with such loving sympathy in the all-male establishment of furry animals in *The Wind in the Willows*, was something of a domestic disaster. His wife, in some perplexity, and perhaps acting on hints, wrote for advice to Emma Hardy. Emma's reply was barbed by the knowledge that Hardy had been indulging in one of his minor literary flirtations with Mrs. Grahame just before her marriage. On 20 May 1897, he had been shown her verses by Justin McCarthy, and liked them so much for their "tender humour—slyness, if I may say so"[6] that he had kept them by him. In February 1898, he praised a valentine she had sent him.[7] Emma therefore had the double satisfaction of showing the younger wife she was not to be trifled with, and of trumpeting the wrongs she felt she had suffered from her own husband during the past decade. Her opening, in all the circumstances, was itself sufficiently remarkable.

> It is really too "early days" with you to be benefitted by one who has just come to the twenty-fifth year of matrimony: (I knew T.H. in 1870 (April) married Sep[r]. 1874). You are *both* at present in a Benedict state (Women can be anything in these days.)

Having established her long-standing authority as a wife, Emma then launched on the experience of nearly twenty-five years.

> Do I know your choice, perhaps I have met him, perhaps not. However it is impossible to give "directions for use"—besides characters change so greatly with time, and circumstances. I can scarcely think that love proper and enduring is in the nature of men—as a rule—perhaps there

is no woman "whom custom will not stale". There is ever a desire to give but little in return for our devotion, & affection—theirs being akin to children's—a sort of easy affection*eness*—& at fifty, a man's feelings too often take a new course altogether. Eastern ideas of matrimony secretly pervade his thoughts, & he wearies of the most perfect & suitable wife chosen in his earlier life. Of course he gets over it usually somehow, or hides it, or is lucky!

Since Hardy had notably failed to hide or get over his "Eastern ideas" about other women, one wonders if Emma reckoned he had been "lucky", and what form the luck had taken. She then proceeded to the attack on the influence of her husband's relatives, which was noticed earlier,[8] and in which her deep-laid resentment at all she had suffered from the possessive Jemima Hardy found full expression. She continued with her own rules of conduct.

Keeping separate a good deal is a wise plan in crises—and being both free—and expecting little neither gratitude, nor attention, love, nor *justice*, nor anything you may set your heart on—Love interest— adoration, & all that kind of thing is usually a failure complete—some one comes by & upsets your pail of milk in the end—If he belongs to the public in any way, years of devotion count for nothing—Influence can seldom be retained as years go by, & *hundreds* of wives go through a phase of disillusion—it is really a pity to have any ideals in the first place.

"This is gruesome, horrid, you will say", Emma continued, with the alarming fancy that Kenneth Grahame might be actually "looking over the bride's shoulder as bridegrooms often do". However, after somewhat obscurely advocating stoicism—"The Spartan style was wise doubtless" —she concluded with a grudging concession to exceptional happy marriages, by adding, "Yet I must qualify all this by saying that occasionally marriage undoubtedly is the happy state, (With Christians always if *both* are) which it was intended to be." The forceful underlining of *both* shows the nub of the main difference between Emma and Hardy after *Jude the Obscure*. She then gathered up her forces for a final onslaught on him.

There must of necessity be great purity in the mind of the *man*, joined with magnanimity, & *justice*, and where, or *rather* how often are these qualities to be found combined? Similarity of taste is not to be depended upon, though it goes some way, but rivalry, fear, jealousy, steps in. Often a love-match has failed completely over & over again—Christian philosophy is the only oil certain to work the complication. I see that continually.

Emma ended her bizarre and pathetic diatribe with characteristic congratulations—"though I rather congratulate a man in these cases" —and an invitation to "drop into our roadside cottage". Her eccentric grammar and phrasing cannot obscure the real bitterness and hurt she had suffered in the 1890s at the sequence of talented women, Rosamund Tomson, Florence Henniker, Agnes Grove, who had "come by and upset her pail of milk" with the "similarity of taste" she had once believed unique to herself and her husband. Any hope of a shared belief in orthodox Christianity had been killed by the writing and publication of *Jude*. The final betrayal, as Emma must have seen it, was the publication of *Wessex Poems*, ranging from her husband's "little fancies" of the 1860s before he had known her, through dated poems from the early 1890s, such as *Thoughts of Phena*, on the death in 1890 of one of these earlier loves, Tryphena Sparks, and still more hurtfully through poems written a few years later and clearly addressed in the most deeply-felt terms to Florence Henniker. Illogical and ill-educated as the letter shows Emma to be, it is sincere in its portrayal of "What I think of my Husband", and a succinct summary of "that awful diary" which her death thirteen years later left as her legacy to Hardy. A similar letter of about the same date to Clement Shorter[9] sums up her openly-expressed disillusion with Hardy—"he is like no other man—nor himself as he *was*". A final, terrible blow was his poem, *The Ivy Wife*, in which Emma saw, all too clearly, Hardy's own bitter reaction to herself.[10]

Both husband and wife were adult enough to make, each in characteristic fashion, gestures of reconciliation, at this time. Just a month before *Wessex Poems* appeared, Hardy, seemingly conscious that Emma was so poorly represented in its pages, started to write a poem recalling their earlier, happier love. Its title alone would remind Emma of those days, since the lines were an attempt to fit words to Mozart's well-known Symphony in E Flat, the minuet and trio movement. The refrain of each stanza, as it emerged, is an invocation of their past happiness and his magical wooing in Cornwall.

> Show me again the time
> When in the Junetide's prime
> We flew by meads and mountains northerly!—
> Yea, to such freshness, fairness, fulness, fineness, freeness,
> Love lures life on.
>
> Show me again the day
> When from the sandy bay
> We looked together upon the pestered sea!—
> Yea, to such surging, swaying, sighing, swelling, shrinking,
> Love lures life on.

Possibly technical difficulties put him off, to leave the poem for completion many years later. According to a distinguished musicologist, the stanza form suggests but does not finally fit either minuet or trio of

Mozart's composition.[11] Yet the association with Emma and the past is evident and poignant. Hardy was remembering the themes in the popular piano duet version played by Emma and her sister long ago. Now Emma was estranged, and the sister, the widowed Catherine Holder, dying in a nursing-home at Lee-on-Solent in Hampshire, far from Cornwall.

Emma too made her attempt to revive in her husband a happier past. On his birthday, 2 June 1899, while staying for the London season at a flat in Wynnstay Gardens, near the one they had rented in the previous year, she gave and inscribed to him a Bible. She may have thought that there was even now some chance *"both"* could share the Evangelical Christian worship that meant so much to her, or at any rate the church attendance which was Hardy's lasting legacy from his "churchy" upbringing. Hardy actually spent his birthday listening to the beautiful Duchess of Manchester reciting Gray's *Elegy* by the poet's grave. Yet he appreciated Emma's gift enough to copy into it the date of the last time they had gone to church together, at Salisbury Cathedral in the summer of 1897. He had been so moved then by the old canon's reading of Jeremiah that he now put the initials of himself and Emma against the text.

Yet none of this lasted. The poem, revised and completed, was not published until after Emma's death, and the Bible contains to this day hardly any other markings.[12] The flicker of middle-aged reconciliation went out almost before it began. Its brief life was recorded by Hardy in another poem, which movingly summarizes this abortive effort by both to revive their first, inspired meeting, "thirty years after". He gave it the title *A Second Attempt*. It ends "Twice-over cannot be!"

Yet the picture could not all be gloom, nor gloom all the time, a fact of nearly everyone's married life which Hardy's biographers have too often forgotten. Looking back, at Hardy's death, Sir George Douglas, who knew both well, thought that Emma and Thomas were as well assorted as most of the happily married couples that one comes across in life, and that each had sacrificed something to the other.[13] They had, moreover, even at this time of crisis, interests in common to paper the cracks of a strained partnership. One was their mutual passion for the defence of animals. Emma shared hers with Alfred Pretor, Hardy his with Florence Henniker, which may partly have reconciled Emma to other aspects of the lady. Emma and Hardy themselves were allies in the cause, and also members of the London Anti-Vivisection Society, whose secretary, Sidney Trist, visited Max Gate in September 1898. Emma doubtless approved of Hardy's letter to the journalist, W. T. Stead, who asked him for an opinion on movements for peace, to be printed in a new periodical in the first half of 1899. Hardy wrote that "As a preliminary, all civilized nations might at least show their humanity by covenanting that no horses be employed in battle except for transport", a message to be horribly ignored in the South African War later that year.[14] Hardy equally must have approved of Emma's forthright letter to the *Daily Chronicle* of 8 September in the same year, lambasting the English excursionists who on 3 September had gone to a bull-fight in Boulogne, and "thus trailed our national reputation in the dirt".[15] When the American professor W. L. Phelps came to tea at Max Gate in summer 1900, primed with enquiries about Hardy's novels, and desiring to exchange opinions about the relations of poetry and prose in Hardy's work, he found himself to his evident amazement surrounded by an army of cats. "Are all these your own cats?" he exclaimed. "Oh, dear, no," replied Hardy. "Some of them are, and some are cats who come regularly to have tea, and some are still other cats, not invited by us, but who seem to find out about this time of day that tea will be going."[16] After this pronouncement by the great literary man, it must have been even more inexplicable to Phelps that Hardy was "evidently pained" by the idea that his poetry was less good than his prose, and wished to be regarded as an English poet who had written some stories in prose. The eccentricity of the English is a constant theme in the writings of many of Hardy's American admirers, and his preference for poetry and cats, and even his poems *about* cats, seemed to these transatlantic ladies and gentlemen "too funny".[17] In fact, man's injustice to his fellow-creatures, with the conviction that he could now powerfully express his deepest sympathies about this, and other topics, in verse of increasing effect, were from now onward among the ruling forces in Hardy's life. The first was a passion he could still share with Emma; the second, the passion for poetry, and his vision of himself as primarily a poet, was one she totally failed to grasp, though it was in the end to immortalize her.

At the same time, Emma, as we have already seen, was most certainly not the ninny that many biographers of Hardy have assumed. She studied and deeply appreciated the latest Ibsen, *John Gabriel Borkman*, in Archer's translation, finding it "pathetically powerful and true".[18] She read Tolstoi's *Resurrection* (though she could not spell its title) in a French translation.[19] She tried to cope with a certain amount of "modern" poetry, though perplexed by Yeats, and preferring the easier O'Shaughnessy.[20] Her blind eye in the way of literary appreciation was now reserved for her husband's work, and for what she took to be its message. A not unkindly visitor, Bertha Newcombe, described her in the year 1900 to Mrs. Gosse.[21]

> I felt a great sympathy & pity for "Emma" this time. It is pathetic to see her struggling against her woes. She asserts herself as much as possible and is a great bore, but at the same time is so kind and good-hearted, and one cannot help realising what she must have been to her

husband . . . [She told me] that she had a fresh complexion and was nick-named "the peony". Now imagine, to this full-blown young girl, coming an ill-grown, under-sized young architect . . . I don't wonder she resents being slighted by everyone, now that her ugly duckling has grown into such a charming swan. It is so silly of her though isn't it not to rejoice in the privilege of being wife to so great a man?

Emma, anticipating later attitudes, did not see this "privilege". She commented, "I often wonder if women's rule of the world would not have produced a better world than it is".[22] Yet she felt no urge to do anything publicly about this, "getting shyer as I get older".[23]

All through January 1899, Hardy read the reviews of his first so-long-delayed book of verse, and brooded on the function and nature of a poet. "No man's poetry can be truly judged till its last line is written. What is the last line? The death of the poet."[24] Some of Hardy's "last lines", if he had known, would have amazed even him. For the present, he went into his characteristic growling cavern of determination to be misunderstood. On 25 January he wrote, "A principle of conduct: acquiescence but recognition"; a few days later, stung by a casual review, "Pessimism. Was there ever any great poetry which was not 'pessimistic'?";[25] on 30 January, to Florence Henniker, "The reviews have . . . had their say about the poems—a poor say."[26] She evidently rallied him briskly on his unreasonableness, and in another letter a fortnight later he retracted his strictures on the book's reception. In this fortnight, the first half of February, he wrote a new cluster of poems, proof that the venture into public had encouraged his verse, and not damped it.

In this little group, *I have Lived With Shades* (2 February), *The To-Be-Forgotten* (probably 9 February), and *On a Fine Morning*, the first-named and first-written was the most considerable. In form and tone, it resembles the first of Hardy's *In Tenebris* group; all were destined, together with the *In Tenebris* poems, for his next book of verse. *I Have Lived With Shades*, because of its direct simplicity, has tempted some rather metaphysical speculation.[27] The "Shades", however, are surely and straightforwardly his memories of actual dead people—ancestors, friends, relatives from family history. After showing him visions of the past and what is to be, they show him a picture "Of man, So commonplace. He moves me not at all." The man is, of course, his unrecognized self, whom to contemplate realistically would cause Hardy "Deep pain". The message of morbidity, repeated in *The To-Be-Forgotten*, and only half-allayed in *On a Fine Morning*, might have set his future verse into a mould of monotonous introspection, but for a historical accident, lucky for the poet though shattering for the nation, which occurred later in the same year.

This was the outbreak, early in October, of the South African War

against the Boers of the Transvaal. Ironically, this sordid struggle gave
Hardy the poet an objective interest and a theme which resulted in a
dozen poems, many of considerable stature. It also gave him another
much-needed link of sympathy with Emma, to match their shared
concern for the animals in war. Both were what came to be known as
"Pro-Boer". Many English "liberals" were, though in point of fact the
Boers were almost totally illiberal. The common "liberal" view was
put by Emma in her usual vivid if breathless way. Well before the war
started, she wrote, "The battles will be on a huge scale that's certain—
& a terrible ending it will all have. But the Boers fight for homes &
liberties—we fight for the Transvaal Funds, diamonds & gold!"[28] She
did not see, any more than Agnes Grove, the Stanley ladies, and other
typical English "liberals", that the Boers were also fighting for Hotten-
tot slave labour and their own command of the huge Rand profits,
hitherto pillaged by foreign outlanders. Emma's "terrible ending",
whether she foresaw it or not, included the introduction by Kitchener
of the shame of our century, the concentration camp. As a minor compensation, the poor physical condition of young British recruits resulted
in the first School Meals Service; but "this is a man's world", as Emma
wrote. "It is in fact a terrible failure as to peace & joy."[29]

Hardy's practical concern was not with such issues, but with the
personal, human, and purely local domestic effects of the war. In spite
of his own "dreadful langour" after a bad summer—he was convinced
a bout of influenza had permanently affected his eyes—and feeling
"weak as a cat", he bicycled fifty miles and back to see the embarka-
tions from Southampton, with Dorset lads in the troopships. He missed
the departure on 9 November of the troopship carrying Florence
Henniker's husband, though some of the Major's character may have
gone into the laconic Horatian form of a poem Hardy had already
written, *The Colonel's Soliloquy*. His feeling for Florence's anxiety may
be traced in several poems about the suffering wives of soldiers. *The
Going of the Battery* was, Hardy told her, "almost an exact report of the
scene & expressions I overheard".[30] *A Wife in London* was first written,
as the manuscript shows, in the first person, with the woman speaking.

The most remarkable, though so far unremarked, feature of these
War Poems, is that many are partly in the style of other poets. It is as
if Hardy were flexing his muscles at this chance of exercise in his chosen
art. Notably, they are in the styles of poets who had engaged his
attention, in reflection or by actual contact, earlier in this year of 1899.
On 6 March, he had written his celebrated meditations to Gosse about
the mystery of Robert Browning.[31] On 18 June, he met A. E. Housman.
On 20 June, he visited Swinburne at Putney.[32] It can hardly be for-
tuitous that three (and three of the best) of the War Poems Hardy
wrote late in the same year are strongly in the respective manners of

5 Hardy with Emma at Max Gate, circa 1900

6   Hardy without Emma in London, circa 1900
From the painting "First Night at a Theatre" by Alfred Stevens. Joseph Conrad
(smoking) is also portrayed, giving an approximate date

7   Hardy by Jacques-Emile Blanche, May 1906

Best Times. ~~Not Again~~.

We went a day's excursion to the stream,
And climbed the bank, & looked at the rippled gleam,
     And I did not know
     That life would show,
However it might bloom, no finer glow.

———

I walked in the Sunday sunshine by the road
That wound towards the gate of your abode,
     And I did not think
     That life would shrink
To nothing ere it shed a rosier pink

———

Unlooked for I arrived on a rainy night,
And you hailed me at the door by the swaying light;
     And I quite forgot
     That life might not
Again be touching that ecstatic height.

———

And that calm evening when you climbed the stair,
After a ~~bright~~ gaiety prolonged and rare;
     No thought soever
     That you might never
Walk down again, struck me as I stood there.

Rewritten from an old draft.

8 Manuscript of Hardy's poem "Best Times", showing alterations to fit his version of events

these three poets. The Browningesque effort, *The Going of the Battery*, has almost a touch of pastiche or unconscious parody, particularly in its last stanza.

> —Yet, voices haunting us, daunting us, taunting us,
> Hint in the night-time when life beats are low
> Other and graver things . . . Hold we to braver things,
> Wait we, in trust, what Time's fulness shall show.

Yet even more astonishing, since it uses, masters, and revivifies its model, is *Drummer Hodge*, first printed under a title that underlines still further its A. E. Housman pattern, *The Dead Drummer*. Housman's *A Shropshire Lad* had appeared three years earlier, and its classical monodies for adorable, scarlet-clad soldier lads and strong youthful rustic heroes were therefore well known to Hardy. His own *Dead Drummer* could have appeared in Housman's sequence. Yet Hardy somehow outdoes the acidulous but passionate bachelor don in human sympathy, even when he is most like him in thought and technique.

> Yet portion of that unknown plain
> Will Hodge for ever be;
> His homely Northern breast and brain
> Grow to some Southern tree,
> And strange-eyed constellations reign
> His stars eternally.

Hardy's poem remained the finest war-time expression of how "the poetry is in the pity" until Wilfred Owen's own First World War poem *Futility*, which resembles it in personal feeling, with the added accent of a personal experience.

As for Swinburne, Hardy, though reduced almost to a delirium of admiration as a young man in the 1860s, had never before written in his manner. Now he used it openly in the most considerable poem of the whole sequence, *The Souls of the Slain*. In its deliberate use of universal alliteration, its six-line stanza form with a long fifth line followed by an ultra-short sixth, it has the exact accent of Swinburnian works such as *Hertha*, *The Deserted Garden*, or those choruses from *Atalanta in Calydon*, on which Hardy had feasted in his twenties. It is, too, in its own right, a very fine and accomplished poem, individual to Hardy. Its vast, imaginative panorama was emphasized, in its first printing in the *Cornhill* of April 1900, by a note:

The spot indicated in the following poem is the Bill of Portland, which stands, roughly, on a line drawn from South Africa to the middle of the United Kingdom; in other words, the flight of a bird along a 'great circle' of the earth, cutting through South Africa and the British Isles, might land him at Portland Bill . . .

The flocking spirits of slain soldiers "homing", like migrant birds, on the Bill, the ironies of their return, the world-span against which their lives are measured, anticipate the final form in which Hardy was soon to cast his epic *The Dynasts*. Though the ending is technically most Swinburnian, it is typical of Hardy, in that the poet himself remains, when all is over, the solitary figure in the huge, natural Dorset land-scape—

> And the spirits of those who were homing
> Passed on, rushingly,
> Like the Pentecost wind;
> And the whirr of their wayfaring thinned
> And surceased on the sky, and but left in the gloaming
> Sea-mutterings and me.

The Biblical reference leads to Hardy's own lifelong vision of himself as the seer or prophet of his generation: "like some terrible old prophet crying in the wilderness", as one admirer wrote to him half-a-dozen years later.[33]

Not everyone appreciated Hardy's cries in the wilderness of a nation deeply at odds about its own warring role. A seemingly innocent poem, *A Christmas Ghost Story*, was attacked in the *Daily Chronicle* on Christmas Day, of all times, for its pacifism. Hardy gave as good as he got in reply;[34] it must be remembered that, at the New Year, British garrisons in Ladysmith, Mafeking, and Kimberley, were all besieged, there were many casualties, and feeling was high. Even after Lord Roberts's successful spring campaign, Hardy reported to Emma, while on a visit to Town, "Hardly any London season. No balls, no money: people in mourning."[35] Jubilation only returned in summer 1900, with the flight of Kruger, the annexation of the Transvaal, and British possession of the real issue at stake, the Rand mines.

In spite of his conviction that "This Imperial idea is, I fear, leading us into strange waters",[36] Hardy probably shared the public impression that the war was over that warm summer of 1900 when he wrote "to make it warmer there is news of the entry into Pretoria",[37] and he greeted the returning troopships gleefully with his *Song of the Soldiers' Wives*. He and the British public were wrong, since the most deadly campaign, punitive on the British side, guerilla on the part of the Boers, was just about to start. He, on the other hand, had to turn his attention back from public to private stresses. One of Emma's answers to his immersion in poetry, and his published poems about other women, was to write and publish poetry herself. On 14 April 1900, twelve days after Hardy's magnificent *The Souls of the Slain* was printed in the *Cornhill*, Emma's lyric *Spring Song* appeared in *The Sphere* with a comment by the embarrassed editor, Clement Shorter.

We all know that Mr. Thomas Hardy began his literary career writing poetry. It is interesting to know that his wife has also written poems. Mrs. Hardy sends me the following verses, which I am happy, as one of the most enthusiastic admirers of her husband's books, to print . . .

Anyone less armoured by indignation than Emma would have felt the implication of the last sentence. Instead, she made Shorter, all through the 1900s, a repository for her injured feelings about Hardy, who, she once wrote with sarcasm, was determined to keep her out of his affairs "lest the dimmest ray should alight upon me of his supreme glory".[38]

Another stress for Hardy came from Emma's nephew and niece, Gordon and Lilian Gifford. Now in their early twenties, and virtually adopted children to the childless Hardys, they were an added burden, for which he felt responsible. Lilian, though of uncertain temperament, was a useful, cheerful companion for her aunt; but her love of parties, company, and gossip was time-consuming to the routine of Max Gate.[39] Gordon was a professional responsibility. Largely and perhaps irregularly educated in Dorchester, followed by a stay in Paris to learn French, he was now apparently unemployed; it seemed to Hardy that he might find a niche for him in his own first profession of architect. In May 1899, Hardy had called on Gordon's egregious father, Walter Gifford, in Maida Vale to discuss this,[40] and in January 1900 he established the young man in the office of his own old London employers, Blomfields. Hardy showed an active interest, taking Gordon to the Kensington Art Library to get out books, and behaving generally as if the youth were himself in the 1860s. Yet, in spite of good reports, punctiliously relayed to Emma, there are hints that the arrangement did not altogether work. There cannot have been anything seriously wrong, since Gordon achieved a reasonably successful career as an L.C.C. architect, but he was a cause for concern at this time. Another, which had already come up, was the possibility that Gordon's unmanageable younger brother, Randolph, might also come to Max Gate, but even his own father vetoed this.[41]

Gifford family troubles, however, persisted. Emma's widowed sister, Helen Catherine, was dying in Lee-on-Solent, near Portsmouth. Emma, who in September had enjoyed several cycle tours with Hardy, spent most of October away from home nursing the dying woman, while Lilian kept house for Hardy, and shared his bike-riding. Emma returned on 9 November, "rather broken down", but was away again a fortnight later. During this second absence, Max Gate was invaded by Hardy's most egocentric and thick-skinned admirer, Miss Rebekah Owen, who had arrived with her own sister from the house they had acquired in the Lake District. She monopolized Hardy, gossiped with Lilian about her aunt's shortcomings, retailed spiteful Dorchester

criticism of Emma, and altogether behaved in an insufferably pro-
prietorial way. When Emma returned unexpectedly, probably because
she wished to arrange for power of attorney to deal with her sister's
affairs, Rebekah Owen found it "so rude in Mrs. T.H." that she herself
was not invited to Max Gate as much as she had expected, in spite of
the fact that Emma had actually found time, in her troubles, to write
a friendly note. Emma had been nursing for two months a woman in
an advanced stage of premature senility, yet this was ignored by the
American lady, who lamented that she herself was being kept from her
literary idol; she regarded Emma's comings and goings between Dorset
and Hampshire as the whims of an unreasonable and jealous wife. Miss
Owen's monstrous complacency was to have still more sinister manifestations later; firm dealing by the second Mrs. Hardy eventually put
a stop to it. Emma and the power of attorney arrived back at Lee-on-
Solent only just in time for her sister's death on 6 December, and she
stayed for the funeral on 10 December. Hardy wrote to her kindly,
telling her how they had pulled the blinds down at Max Gate, how
Lilian had ordered mourning, and advising her to "'take it stiddy', as
they say here"—and indeed still do say in Dorset.[42] If Hardy cannot
quite be absolved from the sin of not keeping his lady admirers in order,
it must be remembered that his habitual lack of confidence gave him
some real need for flattery, even of the most brash kind.

1900 had been a punishing year for Hardy; he wrote its epitaph in
one of his finest poems, *By the Century's Death-Bed*, now universally
known and anthologized as *The Darkling Thrush*. 1901 was a happier,
and, incidentally, healthier time. By June he was organizing a second
book of verse, which at that stage he intended to call *Poems of Feeling,
Dream and Deed*. The War sequence had given him the idea of a book
in several defined sections. He resuscitated as *Poems of Pilgrimage* the
dozen-odd poems he had written on his two last holidays abroad with
Emma, in 1887 and again in 1897. Most characteristically, he included
a poem about refusing an invitation to the United States. In fact, he
never in his life visited America and so, perhaps instinctively, avoided
those women's literary organizations, peopled by their Miss Owens.
About sixty poems came under the general heading of "Miscellaneous".
There was a powerful section of grey philosophy, both recently and
earlier written. There were, by contrast, and also from past and present,
a number of love poems, more fuel for Emma, since they were all to
"miscellaneous" loves, the gamekeeper's daughter, Elizabeth Bishop
of young days, and other girls, jostling poems to be associated with
Florence Henniker, all, as Emma said, "Written *to please* . . . others! or
himself—but not ME, far otherwise".[43] Earlier and funnier poems were
included, slightly bowdlerized to fit volume form, *The Ruined Maid* and
The Levelled Churchyard. There were poems connected with novels,

Tess and *The Well-Beloved*, a little bunch of translations, designated "Imitations Etc.", and finer, recent poems of the dying century—the *In Tenebris* group, *I Have Lived With Shades* and *The Darkling Thrush*. The whole collection, now appropriately called *Poems of the Past and of the Present*, came out in mid-November. In spite of Hardy's usual gloomy prognostications to Gosse—"Alas for that volume"—it was an instant success. The first edition of 500 was quickly sold, and by 3 December he was preparing a second edition. He was established, as he had wished, as a recognized poet, and not merely a novelist turned poet. No longer would a new poem in a magazine be announced as "by Mr. Thomas Hardy, the distinguished novelist".[44] Now was the time for putting into practice the huge poetic idea, whose various schemes had engaged his last thirty years: the Napoleonic, philosophic epic, *The Dynasts*.

9

Dynasts and Destinies

THE SPIRITS IRONIC, who provide some of the catchier moments in *The Dynasts*, with sprightly lyric stanzas such as W. S. Gilbert might have written in *The Sorcerer* or *The Pirates of Penzance*, complete with musical comedy rhymes like "baby" and "maybe", can be held to have presided over Hardy's initial penning of that long-contemplated work. He began writing it in 1902. Only a year or so earlier, by a coincidence of ultra-Hardy irony, his insane brother-in-law, Richard Ireland Gifford, long-term inmate in the Warneford Asylum, entered into a huge poetic epic on practically the same subject, "a poem describing the battle of Waterloo for which he is industriously collecting geographical, climatological and other interesting local facts". Further, according to the hospital case-book,[1] he "has great faith in the success which will attend the publication . . . and is arranging for his discharge in order to attend to the details . . ." The delusion of poetic ability, which this brother shared with Emma, and the subject in which he chose to display it, which he shared with Hardy, provide the weirdest possible backdrop to Hardy's own extraordinary production, on which he lavished his next five years.

Why did he choose this moment to embark upon it? One reason was the feeling, common to all men in their sixties, that time may be running out. Again and again, and particularly in his intimate letters to Edmund Gosse, Hardy stresses how he has pushed on with his great task in case he should not be allowed time to finish it; "flying years compelled me to send out the whole, red-hot".[2] To Henry Newbolt, on 16 January 1909, he admitted "periodic frights lest I should never live to finish". Nor was this the nervous hypochondria of a man in his mid-sixties. Influenza, rheumatism, eye-trouble, sick headache, and intermittent returns of his bladder complaint all seem real enough, though perhaps over-obsessively chronicled. Many eye-witnesses observed that Hardy, in these years, literally looked like death. In 1903, H. W. Nevinson recorded his appearance:[3]

> Face a peculiar grey-white like an invalid's or one soon to die; with many scattered red marks under the skin, and much wrinkled—sad wrinkles, thoughtful and pathetic, but none of power or rage or active courage. Eyes bluish grey and growing a little white with age, eyebrows

and moustache half light brown, half grey. Head nearly bald on top but fringed with thin and soft light hair . . . Figure spare and straight; hands very white and soft and loose-skinned.

In 1906, the painter Jacques-Emile Blanche similarly observed[4]

. . . the hand he extended to me, a gouty hand: white, puffy and limp, with its fingers rigid and awkward like those of Prince Hamlet in the picture by Delacroix . . . The harsh light of mid-day in a sky bleached with heat tinted the scalp, the hollow cheeks, the drooping moustaches . . . with a corpse-like green.

Arthritis, then as now, could be a killer, and Hardy's arthritic hands are common to both accounts. H. G. Wells, who had hailed the closing passages of *Jude* as "the voice of the educated proletarian, speaking more distinctly than it has ever spoken before in English literature", exclaimed, on first seeing Hardy, "What? Not that grey little man!"[5] Ethel Smyth's friend, Henry Brewster, records a similar shock on meeting Hardy.[6] When in 1904 A. C. Benson tried to entertain Henry James and Hardy, he noted how deafness prevented either from hearing what the other was saying.[7]

There were other, more positive, reasons for Hardy to hurry forward with his great work. One was, of course, his commitment to poetry, and his resolve never to be entrapped into the writing of novels again. Then, the excitement of the South African War threw him back to that other and greater war, which had been the background to his grandparents' early lives at his own birthplace, and in which his own grandfather had played a local part. His poems at this time touched on the lives of that generation next but one to his. His other grandmother, his mother's mother, is almost certainly the subject of two poems he wrote in 1901. *Autumn in King's Hintock Park* and *Her Late Husband* (*King's Hintock, 182– *) tell the story of her poverty and of her husband's death in the 1820s at her village of Melbury Osmond (Hardy's "King's Hintock"). *Bereft*, also 1901, may too record her experience, with its sad, haunting folk-song refrain.

Essentially, however, his mind dwelt most on his Bockhampton grandmother, his father's mother, and the subject of his first known poem. Now, on 20 May 1902, he made her the subject of one more tender and moving poem, recalling her at the family fireside during the first seventeen years of his own life. The poem, published in America under the simple title, *Remembrance*, and headed in England by the inscription of pure personal meaning, *One We Knew* (*M.H. 1772–1857*), harked back to her memories of the early days of the nineteenth century, and even the last decade of the eighteenth.

> She told of that far-back day when they learnt astounded
> Of the death of the King of France:

Of the Terror; and than of Bonaparte's unbounded
    Ambition and arrogance.

Of how his threats woke warlike preparations
    Along the Southern strand,
And how each night brought tremors and trepidations
    Lest morning should see him land.

This was where Hardy's mind now was. It is no accident that here, and
at this time in history, he started to write his epic. Indeed, he may even
have written this poem on the same day as the first words of *The
Dynasts*, whose very first scene, once its supernatural machinery is
disposed of, is set on "A Ridge in Wessex" only a few miles from
Hardy's birthplace, and in the year of Napoleon's threatened invasion.
At all events, by the second half of 1902, the huge poem, in all its coils,
was slowly unfolding itself.

Hardy had just proved to his own satisfaction his complete mastery
of the form in which he had first planned to write his epic poem. This
was the ballad form; in one of his earliest relevant jottings, as long ago
as May 1875, Hardy had conceived of his Napoleonic panorama in the
following terms.

Mem: A Ballad of the Hundred Days. Then another of Moscow. Others
of earlier campaigns—forming altogether an Iliad of Europe from 1789
to 1815.

Something of this still remains in the occasional ballad links from
scene to scene in the finished *The Dynasts*. It is no accident that in
April 1902, just before starting, Hardy wrote his finest ballad, or even,
as he himself thought it, his most successful poem. It was written after
a long, thirsty bicycle trip across the Polden hills in Somerset and on to
Glastonbury. The scenery, which offers a splendid view of the county
to north and south, reminded Hardy of a tragic story from his youth,
probably told him by his mother, and dating, like so many of her
reminiscences, from her own youth in the 1820s. This was the recital
of jealousy, murder, and hanging: *A Trampwoman's Tradegy*. It
concerned an actual trampwoman, Mary Ann Taylor, and her lurid and
true story, "though", as he wrote to Gosse, "she has been dust for half
a century". Hardy's confidence that he could write a totally successful
dramatic poem in ballad form brimmed over into the "Iliad" he was
now attempting, though the most obvious feature of *The Dynasts* is the
multiplicity of verse-forms it employs, no less than thirty in all.[8]

The complicated nature of this master-plan was to occupy five exact
years of Hardy's writing life, if we assume he began to draft Part I in
June 1902, and finished the draft, though not the completed version of
Part III, at the end of May 1907. It is, as he himself announced, "an
epic drama . . . in three parts, nineteen acts, and one hundred & thirty

scenes". Later statisticians have found 1470 lines of prose, 7931 of blank verse, and 1152 of rhymed verse, making 10,553 lines in all; but this is to exclude the stage-directions and "dumb-shows"—descriptions of gigantic mimes—which must add several thousand more lines of prose. With such complexity, one can only try to look at the work's different elements; and this, in fact, is suggested by Hardy's own notes through the thirty years when the design was forming. We have seen his first plan in 1875 for an amalgam of long and narrative ballads. In June 1877 he planned "a grand drama, based on the wars with Napoleon, or some one campaign (but not as Shakespeare's historical dramas)"[9]. When *The Trumpet-Major* was published on 23 October 1880, Hardy felt it only "touched the fringe of a vast international tragedy",[10] though by 27 March 1881, he was back to the idea of "A Homeric Ballad, in which Napoleon is a sort of Achilles".[11] On 16 February 1882, a philosophic scheme begins to appear in a note, "Write a history of human automatism, or impulsion",[12] which, Hardy says, he later adopted as a framework for *The Dynasts*. This was developed on 4 March 1886 into a scheme which ruled all his work from *The Woodlanders* onward, and which forms an essential part of the eventual *The Dynasts*:[13]

> The human race to be shown as one great network or tissue which quivers in every part when one point is shaken, like a spider's web if touched. Abstract realisms to be in the form of Spirits, Spectral figures etc.
>
> The Realities to be the true realities of life, hitherto called abstractions. The old material realities to be placed behind the former, as shadowy accessories.

In November 1887, he shaped and abandoned another outline scheme, "in which Napoleon was represented as haunted by an Evil Genius or Familiar, whose existence he has to confess to his wives".[14] This seemed, rightly, too petty, and on 21 September 1889, he confessed,[15] "For carrying out that idea of Napoleon, the Empress, Pitt, Fox, etc., I feel continually that I require a larger canvas . . . A spectral tone must be adopted . . . Royal ghosts. . . . Title: 'A Drama of Kings'." On 26 April 1890, this larger canvas had developed into the idea to "View the Prime Cause of Invariable Antecedent as 'It' and recount its doings."[16] On 26 June 1892,[17] he "considered methods for the Napoleon drama. Forces; emotions, tendencies. The characters do not act under the influence of reason." In autumn 1896, on his attempted second honeymoon with Emma in Flanders, he wrote in his notebook:[18]

Europe in Throes.
Three Parts. Five Acts each.
Characters. Burke, Pitt, Napoleon, George III, Wellington . . .
and many others.

These various elements in its gradual assembly can be assessed separately in the finished work. The first is the element of dramatic writing and particularly of dramatic dialogue. This is almost entirely absent in any normal sense. Hardy never had any ear for effective stage dialogue. His first attempt, the dramatization of *Far From the Madding Crowd*, had had to be very heavily play-doctored by Comyns Carr before it could be put on the stage.[19] Though his one-acter, *The Three Wayfarers*, performed in 1893, was adjudged better than its companions in a quintuple bill, it was soon withdrawn, and Hardy himself revised the dialogue heavily for later amateur performance. His own version of *Tess* had to be almost entirely rewritten by Lorimer Stoddard for its 1897 New York production, and similarly treated by A. E. Filmer for the London production of 1925. Filmer indeed described the script he received from Hardy as "a theatrical impossibility". "That is not *speech*," was his reaction to Hardy's dialogue.[20]

Such criticism applies to nearly all the dialogue in *The Dynasts*. It is "not *speech*". Hardy never got over the dramatist's first pitfall, that of making people tell other people things of which they are perfectly well aware. Many key events are reported to characters who must have known about them already. There are scenes of patent absurdity. Spies discuss out loud, at great length, and frequently in public, minute details of secret information they have just gathered. It is often said that Hardy's prose scenes between Wessex locals are Shakespearian, like similar scenes in his novels; yet unlike Shakespeare, they contain no Dogberry or First Gravedigger, not even a Joseph Poorgrass. The jokes are as laboured as the dialogue, and can be seen coming many speeches ahead. To do Hardy justice he eventually tacitly withdrew his claim, in defence of Part I, that "the methods of a book and the methods of a play . . . are fundamentally similar", and admitted that what he had written was "a spectacular poem . . . more or less resembling a stage-play, though not one".[21]

How then, does *The Dynasts* stand the test as "a spectacular poem"? Since, as the statistics have shown, three-quarters of it is in blank verse, it stands or falls, as poetry, by his handling of this medium. Once more, it must be regretted, Hardy shows little of the skill he had already achieved in lyric utterance. One of the first and best critics of Part I, John Buchan, noted, "his verse throughout is full of the gravest technical faults. He has a habit of falling into that unpleasing form of blank verse where every line is a complete sentence."[22] This end-stopping does, indeed, give a terrible monotony, and must have something to do with Hardy's method of constructing speeches throughout the complete work. As his manuscript often shows, a speech would first be written in prose. It was then literally chopped into blank verse, with dashes to make up the metre and spin out the line, which were then filled in and the whole line finally revised into a regular iambic pentameter.[23] For example, Napoleon's speech in the first scene of Part III began as prose:

Soldiers! war has begun again. The last ended at Friedland at Tilsit
.... At Tilsit Russia swore an eternal allegiance with France war
against England. Today she violates her oaths:

This became four lines of imperfect blank verse, as follows:

Soldiers! wild war is to the fore again.
The — — — alliance Russia swore
At Tilsit for the English realm's undoing
Is violate beyond refurbishing

Hardy's final revision and printed version reads:

Soldiers, wild war is on the board again;
The lifetime-long alliance Russia swore
At Tilsit, for the English realm's undoing,
Is violate beyond refurbishment,

It is noticeable that the flat-footed "lifetime-long" is revealed, by this process, as simply a space-filler, to make up the requisite number of feet in the whole line. This is hardly the way great blank verse is written.

In this, however, Hardy may be viewed as the victim of his age, one of the most uninspired in English dramatic verse. Henry Irving's Lyceum seasons, to which Hardy was a constant play-goer, interspersed Shakespeare with fustian drama of the most stale and undistinguished blank verse. As Shaw wrote in anguish to Ellen Terry, Irving seemed unable to see any difference between the best and the worst writing. Nor was he alone among contemporary actor-managers. In 1901, a verse play called *Herod*, with Frank Benson, was produced by Beerbohm Tree, and in 1902 *Paolo and Francesca*, with the young Henry Ainley, was produced by Sir George Alexander. Both were by Stephen Phillips, whose turgid blank verse and pretentious drama became the target for Max Beerbohm in his *Savonarola Brown*. Yet the critics hailed him as a superlative dramatic poet, finer than anyone since the Elizabethan age. Professor Churton Collins, the *bête noire* of Edmund Gosse and Hardy, actually put Phillips in the same class as Sophocles. The taste of the age, which seems to have been his own taste as a play-goer, must bear some responsibility for the blankness of Hardy's blank verse in *The Dynasts*, though this is surprising in view of the rhythmic originality he always showed as a lyric poet.

One wonders if, as far as poetry was concerned, his own original instinct about telling the story as a succession of long narrative ballads was not a more happy one. It is the lyric links and choruses that one

remembers from *The Dynasts*. The Trafalgar chorus, the song of the
cavalry men at Weymouth, the woman's song, "My love's gone a-
fighting", and, most of all, the lyric of the Spirits before Waterloo, are
in a class of their own. They are among Hardy's finest writing. He himself thought the last-named was an example of his own most original
work, with its entirely characteristic evocation of the small creatures in
the field where the battle is to be fought.

> . . . Yea, the coneys are scared by the thud of hoofs,
> And their white scuts flash at their vanishing heels,
> And swallows abandon the hamlet-roofs.
>
> The mole's tunnelled chambers are crushed by wheels,
> The lark's eggs scattered, their owners fled,
> And the hedgehog's household the sapper unseals.
>
> The snail draws in at the terrible tread,
> But in vain; he is crushed by the felloe-rim;
> The worm asks what can be overhead,
>
> And wriggles deep from a scene so grim,
> And guesses him safe; for he does not know
> What a foul red rain will be soaking him.
>
> Beaten about by the heel and toe
> Are butterflies, sick of the day's long rheum,
> To die of a worse than the weather-foe.
>
> Trodden and bruised to a miry tomb
> Are ears that have greened but will never be gold,
> And flowers in the bud that will never bloom.
>
> So the season's intent, ere its fruit unfold,
> Is frustrate, and mangled, and made succumb,
> Like a youth of promise struck stark and cold.

Yet though the prosody may not impress, the scope and scale of the
work, which we have seen becoming more and more ambitious in
Hardy's mind, certainly does. Just as he was, in some sense, the victim
of the taste of his age in actual verse, so he may have benefited from the
public taste in Edwardian times for the spectacular and the grandiose. It
was a public which loved display, from the opulence of the chorus line
at Daly's and the Gaiety Theatre to the elaborate oratorios and the
richly-orchestrated works of Edward Elgar, rewarded by his knighthood
in 1904. In the theatre, the productions of Tree were lavish and crowded;
Max Beerbohm's sly parody of Stephen Phillips has the stage-direction
"Enter Guelphs and Ghibellines fighting". Hardy's work, however
impossible to stage, had the advantage of being able to impress by sheer
size. This accounts for the favourable reception of the completed work,
after the first doubts and carpings at Part I were overcome by the even

more broadly conceived Parts II and III. By taking all Europe for a setting, he forced admiration at the hugeness of his canvas alone. This accounts for the unreserved praise of such essential Edwardians as Arthur Quiller-Couch, who called *The Dynasts* "the grandest poetic structure planned and raised in England in our time", and the signed tribute of younger writers in 1921 "for all that you have written . . . but most of all, perhaps for *The Dynasts*". The Great War seemed to set a seal on his epic; it even made feasible Granville-Barker's stage abridgement in 1914.

Hardy achieved this sense of space and size, and of relevance to great issues, by employing, as is well known, an Overworld, Here the Spirits, who themselves are automata in the mind of the sleeping "It" or Immanent Will, discuss the affairs of men, who are themselves, without knowing, mere puppets in the universal view of the Spirits. These Spirits, whether of Irony or Pity, Rumour and many others, fulfil what Hardy had found awkward in his later novels, the function of a commentator on events. The Spirit of the Years, for example, in a well-known passage, can speak of

> A local cult called Christianity . . .
> Beyond whose span, uninfluenced, unconcerned,
> The systems of the sun go sweeping on . . .

This is Hardy speaking through a convenient spirit, or rather paraphrasing, for his own purpose, a passage from Mrs. Humphrey Ward's novel, *Robert Elsmere*, to which he has given his own satiric and agnostic twist.[24] These Spirits, helpless as they are to affect the Will's unknowing predestined paths, in which they resemble Hardy's just-published poem, *The Subalterns*, have themselves some minor and impish free-will. They sometimes come to earth in plausible disguise, and try their effect on mankind. They whisper doubts to Napoleon, false information to English politicians. The Spirit of Rumour even has, in Part I, a long discussion about Austerlitz and Trafalgar with a Parisian street-walker, who decides not to sleep with such a "creepy man". This kind of impersonative intervention is the reminder of Hardy's original plan to write "an Iliad"; for in the *Iliad*—and, indeed, though less often, in the *Odyssey*—gods and goddesses appear in the guise of known heroes and warriors, and even take part in the fighting for their own favoured champions.

The epic scope, then, is on the scale of Homer's two great examples, and of other epics, down to Camoens's *Lusiads*, where Vasco de Gama's voyage to India is aided or hindered by favouring or unfavourable deities. *The Dynasts* does, in fact, resemble *The Lusiads*, in that it tells a more or less accurate historical story, but incorporates divine machinery. Though critics admired this sheer size and scope, the philosophy implied

received a cautious reception at first, while later academic critics have
generally concentrated on the philosophic ideas, to the virtual exclusion
of other elements in the work. An impressive roll-call of philosophers,
English, French, and German, has been assembled as influences on
Hardy's final philosophic pattern. Writing to a critic who in 1911
treated the work as an illustration of the philosophy of Schopenhauer,
Hardy claimed, "My pages show harmony of view with Darwin, Huxley,
Spencer, Comte, Hume, Mill, and others, all of whom I used to read more
than Schopenhauer." Yet this disclaimer is similar to his statement,
over the later novels, that he had read very little Zola, and in both the
motive is the same. He did not wish to acknowledge an easy tag-label,
under which lazy critics or reviewers could summarize or dismiss his
original work. Yet the list, to which he could well have added Fourier,
illustrations of whose philosophy he copied into his earliest notebooks,
does far from justice to the breadth of his philosophic reading, and its
effect on *The Dynasts*. There is, it has been shown, a great deal of
Schopenhauer, whom he read and noted industriously in the late 1880s
and 1890s, and still more of Von Hartmann, in particular, and of
Haeckel, though the latter's philosophy has been seen not so much as
an influence but as a reinforcement of what were already Hardy's own
views.[25] Hardy's preoccupation in *The Dynasts* with the idea of an
immanent unconscious Will was, however, highly eclectic; he may have
taken much from both his early reading of English deterministic
philosophers and his later reading of the Germans. Yet the result is his
own, and is repeated in miniature throughout the poems of this period,
such as *The Subalterns*, first printed in November 1901, where, as we
have seen, Climate, Sickness, and Death, personified as forces which
have a considerable effect on mankind's doings, are made to say that
they themselves are helpless servants of a huge Unconsciousness, a
thought which gives the poet an ironic comfort.

> We smiled upon each other then,
> And life to me had less
> Of that fell look it wore ere when
> They owned their passiveness.

The advantages of this Overworld or universal viewpoint are best
seen in Hardy's numerous and lengthy "stage"-directions or "dumb-
shows". Here is the real heart of the epic, and it often appears in phrases
far more poetic than the poetry, far more dramatic than the drama.
Without spoken words, and by sheer descriptive power, these parts of
The Dynasts conjure up an unforgettable scene or plant an undying
impression. They are often like a stage design painted on a gigantic,
world-wide canvas. On the eve of Waterloo, for instance,

From all parts of Europe long and sinister black files are crawling

hitherward in serpentine lines, like slowworms through grass. They
are the advancing armies of the allies.

Grotesque and haunting incidents enhance the action. When the Madrid
mob sacks the rooms of the Minister, Godoy,

> In the rout a musical box is swept off a table, and starts playing a
> serenade as it falls to the floor . . . The mob desists dubiously and goes
> out; the musical box upon the floor plays on, the taper burns to its
> socket, and the room becomes wrapt in the shades of night.

Macabre touches of realism, such as this, also pinpoint the burning
of Moscow.

> The blaze gains the Kremlin, and licks its walls, but does not kindle
> it. Explosions and hissings are constantly audible, amid which can be
> fancied cries and yells of people caught in the combustion. Large
> pieces of canvas aflare sail away on the gale like balloons. Cocks crow,
> thinking it sunrise, ere they are burnt to death.

It is an Overworld view of Europe which opens and closes the whole
spectacle. From the Fore Scene at the beginning of Part I, we see

> The nether sky opens, and Europe is disclosed as a prone and emaciated
> figure, the Alps shaping like a backbone, and the branching mountain-
> chains like ribs, the peninsular plateau of Spain forming a head. Broad
> and lengthy lowlands stretch from the north of France across Russia
> like a grey-green garment hemmed by the Ural mountains and the
> glistening Arctic Ocean.
>   The point of view then sinks downward through space, and draws
> near to the surface of the perturbed countries, where the peoples, dis-
> tressed by events which they did not cause, are seen writhing, crawling,
> heaving, and vibrating in their various cities and nationalities.

After Napoleon's final defeat, we return to where we started:

> Europe has now sunk netherward to its far-off position as in the Fore
> Scene, and it is beheld again as a prone and emaciated figure of which
> the Alps form the vertebrae, and the branching mountain-chains the
> ribs, the Spanish Peninsula shaping the head of the écorché. The low-
> lands look like a grey-green garment half-thrown off, and the sea
> around like a disturbed bed on which the figure lies.

Such images, poetic, natural, yet deeply disturbing, do not have any
counterpart in our literature, except perhaps for Shelley's *Prometheus
Unbound* and a minor work of little value, Robert Buchanan's *The Drama
of Kings*, both of which may have influenced Hardy to some slight
degree. They seem occasionally echoed in Wilfred Owen's First World
War poems, such as *The Show*, though Owen read little Hardy except
Under the Greenwood Tree, and dismissed Hardy's poetry, in the arrogant
and arbitrary way he treated most contemporary verse ("who on earth

are . . . de la Mare etc?"), with the words "Quite potatoey".[26] If he had only known it, his own poignant vision of war had been anticipated a decade earlier by the older poet. In our time, World War Two audiences appreciated the B.B.C.'s radio version of *The Dynasts*, which largely relied on these prose directions by Hardy, arranged as narration.

In the five years of vast concentration, from summer 1902 to summer 1907, it is a wonder that Hardy had time for any personal life. Indeed, he does not seem to have had much. At any rate, his diaries were largely empty of incident, though the outward mechanics of his life, bicycle rides and the yearly London trips for "the season" still went on. Mostly he seems to have been occupied with the effort to keep at bay the spectre that he might die before *The Dynasts* could be completed, as if he saw himself like one of his own soldiers leaving the ballroom at Brussels for the battlefields of Waterloo to the summons of the drums, and in the spectral conduct of "That figure—of a pale drum-major kind" pirouetting before each one, the figure of Death itself. He confessed as much, more than once, to his closest friend, Gosse. Those who observed him noticed not only the extreme marks of apparent ill-health, which we have seen, but the impression of almost total exhaustion which he conveyed. Jacques-Emile Blanche, who painted Hardy's portrait in 1906, wrote not only of Hardy's deathly appearance but of his evident distress of body in the exceptionally hot summer; his straw hat "trickled with sweat; he looked so frail, so pale", that Blanche got his family to revive the poet, in the studio, with fresh iced lemon drinks. Blanche, however, also noted the activity of Hardy's mind, and his concentration, not understood by Blanche at the time, on the theme whose third part he was just beginning, Part II of *The Dynasts* having just been published.

> Without my realising it, his questions on the survival of the Napoleonic legend in France related to some work he was pursuing, which was no less than his tragic poem, *The Dynasts*. This frail old man was brooding over a work which would come to light in a renewed and creative youth . . .

Blanche, incidentally, noticed, with more sympathy than many later observers,[27] the pathetic attempts of Emma Hardy to renew her youth, though

> . . . little remained of that full high-coloured vigorous bloom, described by those who saw her when she was still young . . . Yet although shrunken and shrivelled by age, she posed as a beauty, keeping the fixed smile of bygone days, as if trapped for ever in a photograph.

Though Blanche did not know it, Emma too had had her premonitions of death during these years. In that very summer, only a few weeks earlier, while at Max Gate, she had a sudden fainting fit, and it is probable that she was already suffering acute pain, at times, from the impacted gall-stones, which were the primary cause of her death. She also had her moments of mental anguish from the continued dominance of Agnes Grove over her husband, also noticed by Blanche whose portrait of Hardy had to be submitted to Lady Grove as well as to his wife.[28] It was apparently to assert her own right of judgement that Emma exclaimed to Blanche the often-quoted remark, "Don't make him look miserable!" The further remark, frequently though wrongly attributed to her, "a real gentleman never does", is in fact a garbled version[29] of Blanche's own personal sly and Gallic comment "ce qui eût été si peu d'un gentleman", which expresses the Frenchman's whimsical shrug at fashionable English manners. Emma's own comment was certainly reasonable; Hardy in the portrait, still more in Blanche's revealing preliminary sketch, looks not so much miserable as utterly crushed. It is possible, even with his loyalty to her, that he now found the attentions of Agnes Grove somewhat overpowering. Her Stanley dominance was beginning to be too much even for her own long-suffering husband Sir Walter Grove. Her comment[30] on the expressions of would-be genteel people—"They will always commence, when they ought to begin"—is itself almost a criticism of Hardy's own style. Blanche's description includes an impression of Agnes ruling and directing the guests at the Hardys' own tea-party in their furnished London lodgings in the flat rented to them by Lady Thompson at Hyde Park Gardens, while Emma sat fuming among the literary company, to which she felt she had more right than Agnes. Nor can it have helped that Hardy was still overseeing Agnes Grove's journalistic and other literary work, to the covert amusement of editors. Emma, with no assistance from her husband, had to be content with the columns of the *Dorset County Chronicle* for her innocuous verses.

Husband and wife indeed seem to have kept up a modicum of unity, partly owing to Emma's principle, enunciated in her letter to Mrs. Kenneth Grahame, of "Keeping separate a good deal". In November 1903, Emma took a month's holiday in Calais with her niece Lilian Gifford, leaving Hardy at Max Gate to cope with the cats, Markie, Snowdove, Pixie, and Comfy.[31] Hardy, in his turn, was very frequently at the British Museum, doing the immense historical research for *The Dynasts*; he went on his own in 1905 to receive an honorary doctorate from the University of Aberdeen, the first of the academic honours which so much delighted him. Yet he cannot have been happy that the previous New Year's Eve had found him "quite alone on a bridge".[32]

For both Emma and Hardy, these years brought intimations of mortality. For them, 1904 was a year of deaths. The first was the death of Hardy's old friend, mentor, and best, creative editor, Leslie Stephen. Hardy had not seen much of him recently, but in the days when *Far*

From the Madding Crowd and *The Hand of Ethelberta* were appearing in
Stephen's *Cornhill*, they had been very close in personal and intellectual
sympathy. Stephen had always seemed to Hardy like one of his own
doomed heroes. "I have always felt that a tragic atmosphere encircled
L.S.'s history— & was suggested in some indescribable way by his presence."[33] To him, the great mountaineer as well as editor, Hardy had
written his poem about the Schreckhorn, "gaunt and difficult, like
himself". He included the poem in his considerable contribution, about
half a chapter, to F. W. Maitland's *Life and Letters of Leslie Stephen*,
which came out in 1906. Stephen died in the last week of February
1904. In the next few weeks, Hardy lost another close friend, of forty-
seven years' standing. This was a surviving brother of Hardy's deepest
friend, Horace Moule. Henry Moule had himself become an intimate
friend; in the previous summer he had occupied Max Gate while the
Hardys were in London. Hardy wrote an affectionate little memoir of
him,[34] also printed in 1906.

Hardy's major loss in this year came early in April. For some years
his mother at the Bockhampton cottage had been gently failing, though
keeping almost to the last a bright-eyed independence, typical of her
early days. In May 1901, when a literary and journalist club called the
Whitefriars had visited Hardy at Max Gate, Jemima Hardy had found
that the ladies and gentlemen, with their fine London clothes, were to
pass in open carriages along the Puddletown–Dorchester road, only a
quarter of a mile from her cottage. She got Hardy's sisters, Mary and
Kate, to put her wheel-chair by the roadside, from which she waved her
handkerchief at the well-dressed concourse. Now, on 1 April 1904, aged
ninety, she failed for the first time to recognize her famous son. Two days
later she died. His usual reticence concealed under formal tributes
what she, the real guiding star of his early life, had meant to him. Only
one cry of anguish, in a letter to near relatives, gives a hint.[35]

His more direct and formal expression of grief, in a poem probably
written at her death-bed, ends with a philosophy that echoes much of
the message of *The Dynasts*.

> And yet we feel that something savours well;
> We note a numb relief withheld before;
> Our well-beloved is prisoner in the cell
>   Of Time no more.
>
> We see by littles now the deft achievement
> Whereby she has escaped the Wrongers all,
> In view of which our momentary bereavement
>   Outshapes but small.

"The Wrongers" are not so much, perhaps, those of the Overworld of
spirits, as the physical pains and disabilities Jemima had suffered in

recent years, deafness and the rheumatism which confined her to a wheel-chair. Remembering how, in 1890, at the age of seventy-seven, his mother had walked in slippery winter weather from Bockhampton to Max Gate, and made nothing of it, Hardy felt a sad relief at her final escape. It meant, too, a rearrangement in family affairs that brought him even more back into contact with his boyhood home at the cottage. So that Mary ("Polly") Antell, Jemima's niece, should not be alone there, Mary and Kate let furnished the house Hardy had bought them in Wollaston Road, Dorchester, and moved back to the homestead. With Kate's bustling good humour, still more his beloved Mary's quiet, unobtrusive cheerfulness, the fireside, though bereaved, took on the character of their childhood, especially when brother Henry, the builder, called in with his bluff and hearty presence. Hardy gained in family feeling, much though he lost by his mother's mourned-for death.

Emma too had her griefs and deaths in this year. In October, her brother Walter, whose two elder children she had virtually adopted, died in London. Next month he was followed by her eldest brother Richard, who died in the Warneford Asylum. The supercilious Willy Gifford had died two years before. Emma was the surviving sibling. Though she had seen little enough of her brothers, she felt a sense of isolation. There was a new and slightly ominous symptom of this. The Gifford family had been brought up by their mother and grandmother in a narrow religious fundamentalism. The insane Richard, for some years before he rivalled Hardy in his own Waterloo epic, had spent his time in hospital writing and rewriting a great religious epic in verse, which he sometimes read to other patients in the recreation room.[36] Soon after his death, Emma's own occasional verses show a change. From inept but perfectly coherent poems about garden flowers, trees, and landscapes, she turned to a new strain of somewhat brooding religiosity and dark apocalyptic vision. One such poem, *Ten Moons*, was published in 1907 in the *Dorset County Chronicle*.

> In misery swirled
> Is this one-moon whirled,
> But there's no sorrow or darkness there
> In that mighty Planet where
> There is no night.
> Ten moons ever revolving
> All matter its long years resolving
> To sweetness and light.

This new note, in her otherwise not unusual Protestant theme, sounded increasingly in following years, and was observed by her husband. Not that this yet affected Emma's outward social life or withdrew her from topical affairs. She still took part in the London season, kept up her animal-loving societies and subscriptions, in spite of the death of her friend Pretor in 1907. One topic where she and Hardy agreed was women's suffrage, which he had favoured "for a long time"; and on 6 February of that year, she had shown her interest by marching with other "advanced" women in a suffrage procession from Hyde Park to the Strand, known as "The Mud March" because of the heavy rain.[37] On her home ground at Max Gate she continued her regular garden-parties, and on 1 September 1905 had organized a tea-party on the lawn for no less than 200 members of the Institute of Journalists.[38]

Hardy too had a perennial method for resisting the encroachment of physical weakness, old age, and death. He was, exactly like his hero in *The Well-Beloved*, on perpetual look-out for beauty, particularly the young beauty of women of about twenty-five, successors to his earliest loves, to actresses such as Mary Scott-Siddons and Helen Mathews, and to his more recent and more aristocratic loves, Rosamund Tomson, the Honorable Mrs. Florence Henniker, and Lady Grove.

In his late fifties, he had mapped the emotional course of the rest of his life in the poem with which he appropriately concluded his collection, *Wessex Poems*.

> I look into my glass,
> And view my wasting skin,
> And say, 'Would God it came to pass
> My heart had shrunk as thin!'
>
> For then, I, undistrest
> By hearts grown cold to me,
> Could lonely wait my endless rest
> With equanimity.
>
> But Time, to make me grieve,
> Part steals, lets part abide;
> And shakes this fragile frame at eve
> With throbbings of noontide.

Such "throbbings" occurred, as we know, at fairly frequent intervals. Summer 1907, with *The Dynasts* finished in draft, and Hardy revising Part III at the British Museum, saw the most important, though not the final, manifestation. He met a young woman of twenty-eight, Florence Emily Dugdale. She was always said to have been a "young friend" of Florence Henniker, and introduced by the latter to Hardy in 1904; yet Florence's own letters give the lie to this legend. They prove she did not know Mrs. Henniker till 1910, nor did Mrs. Henniker ask if she could call her "Florence" until 1914.[39] The myth may have arisen because Mrs. Henniker had as a friend the aristocratic Sir William Dugdale of Merevale Hall, Warwickshire,[40] descendant and namesake of the famous seventeenth-century Garter King-of-Arms. Florence Emily Dugdale, however, had far different attractions for

Hardy. She was brown-haired, slim, intelligent, of Dorset origin; above all she shared almost exactly his own social background and working-class family history. At last, at sixty-seven, he had found a natural companion and mate.

10

Florence and the Dugdales

FLORENCE EMILY DUGDALE was the grand-daughter of a Dorset blacksmith, William Dugdale.[1] Her grandmother, Emily Hibbs, was the daughter of a labourer and carter at Langton Matravers, Dorset.[2] Seeking anxiously some more distinguished ancestry for the young woman who became his second wife, Hardy annexed as her great-grandfather another William Dugdale, whose memorial he copied (inexactly) from Hutchins's *History of Dorset*, and who was Mayor of Wareham in 1838 and 1844. Unluckily Florence's real great-grand-father was Elias Dugdale, a carpenter, undistinguished in the borough annals, though both were probably descended from Daniel Dugdale, who had been a Wareham alderman in 1728.

Florence's father, Edward Dugdale, one of four brothers, was born in the crowded working-class back-streets of St. Paul's parish, Portsea, Hampshire. There seems to have been considerable sea traffic between Wareham and the greater port of Portsmouth; the parish showed a little colony of Dorset families at the time of Edward's birth.[3] Portsmouth provided Edward Dugdale with vivid and unusual childhood experiences. He saw the shipping come and go in the busy port, became a fine swimmer, and is known to have saved people from drowning on three occasions before he left the town in his late teens. He entered St. John's College, Battersea, in 1871, and qualified as a certificated elementary teacher. In 1873, he settled in the north London suburb of Enfield, and at once became head of the "National" or church school, St. Andrew's, a post he was to hold for the rest of his working life.[4]

On her mother's side, Florence was of an Enfield family settled in Brighton. Her mother, Emma Taylor, who married Edward Dugdale there on 1 August 1876, was the daughter of a butcher, James Tuckney Taylor.[5] The business of pork butcher was carried on by at least three generations of Taylors in Brighton. The women of the family let respectable furnished apartments near the sea-front at 47 Marine Parade, the address from which Florence's mother was married. When Florence met Hardy, and for many years after, the furnished apartments were kept by her great-aunt, Ann Maria Taylor, and her aunt, Alicia Taylor. One of the men in the butchery business, Charles Taylor, also let apartments at another address.[6]

Florence was born on 12 January 1879, the second of Edward Dugdale's family of five daughters. Their father, according to a former pupil at the school,[7] was strict but just; he was a pillar of the local Conservative, Temperance, and Philanthropic Societies, a well-set-up man, who looked younger than his age.[8] By the 1900s, the Dugdales lived at 5 River Front, Enfield, having seen that town grow from "a green and pleasant little place", in Edward's words, to a suburban sprawl, whose considerable working-class population swelled the numbers of the school. The small hamlets, townships, and clusters of cottages round old Enfield were over-run and fused together by red brick, the market-town atmosphere almost lost in the industrial suburb surrounding the Royal Small Arms factory.

According to a former maid-of-all-work, the Dugdale family was an extremely happy and united one.[9] The mother had a weak heart, and the five girls were brought up to be self-reliant. Three, including Florence, became school-teachers, one a nurse, and the youngest trained at a domestic science college. All five went to the St. Andrew's, Enfield, elementary school for girls, where the education was free. For their secondary education, they all proceeded to the St. Andrew's Upper Grade School, where their father paid ninepence a week for them[10]—a history not unlike Hardy's experiences in Dorchester, first with free education, then at a school for which his father paid a small fee. Florence probably then had four years, from the age of fifteen, as a pupil-teacher, but she never went to college. She began work as an uncertificated teacher in her father's school at the age of exactly nineteen. She taught from January 1898 to April 1908, and did not take her certificate until September 1906, when she received special credit in English Literature, Composition, and the Principles of Education.[11]

Theirs was the standard minimal secondary education for the time, but the girls seem to have entered into it with responsibility and earnestness, fitting for a school-teacher father and a home where there can have been very little money to spare. All, including Florence, were expected to earn a living as soon as possible. There was not much question of choice. Though she taught notably well, Florence was not happy. The classes in the boys' school were between forty and fifty; eight teachers, most of them unqualified, coped with an average attendance of 350 boys.[12] The noise, the frequent need to shout, were exhausting. Moreover, Florence was what her father called "a Radical"; she hated the subservience expected from a church school-teacher. When the vicar called, she must not sit down; she must attend church services where the vicar's wife might object to her hat. Any complaint could not be communicated direct to the school managers; she had to wait for the visiting Inspector in order to state her case. Even after the Education Act of 1902, a teacher could still be dismissed by the

managers "on grounds connected with the giving of religious instruc-
tion", without consent from the local authority. It is no wonder that she
grew up acutely, often morbidly, conscious of social distinctions after a
teaching experience that began in the last years of the reign of Queen
Victoria.

This social background, handicapping and often frustrating, applied,
of course, equally to her sisters; but in addition, Florence had a hard
time physically. The school logbooks record her frequent absences
through illness, feverish colds, chills, and influenza. These began to
take a more serious form over the years. The reason for three months'
leave of absence in April 1908, from which she never returned to teaching, is given as chronic pharyngitis.[13] Bad experience with adenoids
and tonsils probably led to a lifelong horror of operations and to the
depressions from which she suffered. A former pupil remembers her
very quiet voice,[14] also probably due to these illnesses. In spite of the
to-and-fro of a family of sisters, there is a solitary strain in Florence,
which contrasts with the others, and one may guess it developed in
lonely times of illness. She seems to have been not so much a Radical
as a Romantic, slightly the odd one out, Her family affections, however,
were extremely strong, and she kept in very close touch with all her
sisters. Of these, the eldest, Ethel, married in the early 1900s, and the
youngest, Margaret, during the First World War. The two unmarried
sisters, Constance the teacher and Eva the nurse, were deeply loved.
In spite of occasional tiffs between these two,[15] and Constance's later
jealousies of her married sisters,[16] all were prompt and generous to
help one another.

Florence was the only one of the sisters, however, to show an in-
clination towards self-expression, prompted by her somewhat lonely
and introspective temperament. The secret path she chose was literature, though at first in the most humble way, which can be traced in
the files of the local paper.[17] In 1901, at the age of twenty-two, she is
recorded as giving a talk on "The Idylls of the King" to the Enfield
Literary Union at the Bycullah Athenaeum. Later in life, when she
persuaded London acquaintances to speak at an Enfield literary
society, they left unflattering pictures of its provincial dreariness; but
she obviously found inspiration, as many girls struggling with an
unpromising and limited background have done. One can find this
sympathetically treated in the great topical novel of such struggles in
the 1900s, H. G. Wells's *Ann Veronica*, where Ann comes from just
such a suburban setting as Florence. She spread her literary wings from
this beginning in the only way open to her, the children's pages of the
local paper. Her first initial-signed contribution, a little story called
"A Summer Lane", appeared in its columns on 31 July 1903. Other
contributions followed, and encouraged her to apply to publishers of

children's books in the next few years, where, though her efforts were not very distinguished, she at last began to get a hearing.

Pathetic as some of these efforts were, Florence never lost this vision of herself as a creative writer. One of the happiest moments of her later life was when she heard of a boy still reading one of the small children's books she had written as a young woman, and felt her work was wanted. This enthusiasm brought some of the most rewarding experiences of her narrow and dull life. When she began this minor journalistic work, she found that the expenses of having her manuscripts professionally typed swallowed up her meagre earnings. Her belief in herself, however, impressed a well-to-do friend, and he generously gave her a typewriter.[18] She taught herself to type, for, as Hardy wrote in the summer of 1909, "she learns anything",[19] and it was with her own typescripts that she first contributed to the *Tales for the Children* series of readers, a set of little 100-odd-page books, in which she was responsible for No. 10, *Old Time Tales* in 1907, followed by No. 20, *Country Life*. In 1907, she also managed a book of about 150 pages, *Tim's Sister*, for the Christian Knowledge Society, evidently putting aside her radical rejection of organized religion for the sake of getting the small volume published. All through her later life, she spoke of her pleasure in writing, her ambition to write in other forms. Belief in her creative gift, however undistinguished her actual work, buoyed her up in times of sadness.

Such was the young woman whom Hardy met, somewhere and somehow in London in the summer of the year 1907, when he himself was completing what he had felt to be a race against death, and had emerged thinking that there was no more left in life for him. For Hardy, Florence Dugdale held every possible attraction. She was of his own social class, but like him had risen in the world through careful self-education. She was, as he had once been, an apprentice writer, contributing to the local press, and, very recently, composing elementary school books for Chambers and Collins, including some adaptation of stories as supplementary readers.[20] She was the exact physical type to which he always eagerly returned, a slight, willowy, intense brunette, the counterpart of the actresses, Mary Scott-Siddons and Helen Mathews, and of the poetess, Rosamund Tomson. To crown all, like Pierston's last love in *The Well-Beloved*, she was forty years younger than he. There were of course, other attractions, not solely physical. She was, as he had been in his youth, radical in her outlook, shocking her conservative father, who was born of cautious peasant stock. Here again, she brought youth back to Hardy. Perhaps her highest single attraction was that she had, as she confessed, absolutely no religious belief, doubted if there were a God, or, if there were, whether there could be a beneficent one.[21] This view, moreover, was not merely a gesture of youthful rebellion against orthodoxy. It was learnt from a genuinely tragic experience of life, as full of the malignancy of Providence as anything which had caused Hardy's own dark philosophy. Already her past had prepared her for their coming-together.

What did Florence feel about the very distinguished elderly literary gentleman, who wandered eagerly and wistfully eyeing girls in London, where he was at this time, he confessed, "distracted" on the tops of omnibuses "by young women in fluffy blouses"?[22] What did she think when he took her to Liverpool Street Station, kissed her at the barrier, and watched her own "spot of muslin fluff"[23] recede down the platform to catch the crowded Enfield train? If he was moved enough to describe this in a poem, *On the Departure Platform*, what were her own feelings? One fact in her history has never emerged before, and needs now to be considered. Hardy was not the first elderly and distinguished gentleman to play an intimate part in her life. Florence was already the friend of another married man, nearly thirty-five years older than herself, handsome, dark-haired, the possessor of unlimited charm and a knighthood, but also of a secret and central personal tragedy.

Sir William Thornley Stoker[24] was one of the five sons of Abraham Stoker, for fifty years Chief Secretary at Dublin Castle. He was a brilliant member of a highly versatile and distinguished family. One of his brothers, "Bram" Stoker, for many years Irving's manager and right-hand man at the Lyceum and elsewhere, was the author of *Dracula*. Thornley Stoker was a famous surgeon, and one of the leading lights in Dublin society. He was respected by colleagues, loved by medical students at the Richmond Hospital, Dublin, and venerated by the poor law patients for whom he did so much. A man of wide culture and a Governor of the Dublin National Gallery, he built up a fine private art collection in his beautiful residence, Ely House, Dublin. Childless, he was known for his generosity in the causes of young people; he established a school of Nursing in the Richmond Hospital, which was a model of its kind for the training of young nurses.[25] His tragedy— Florence's too—was that Ely House contained a mad wife, who occasionally had been known to escape her attendants.

Such was Florence Dugdale's "dear kind friend in Dublin", about whom she always wrote in terms of the deepest affection.[26] It was Sir Thornley who gave her the typewriter, an expensive present in those days, and continued to show her kindly favours. One does not know how they met, nor when she came to stay at Ely House. To her romantic mind, nourished on books, he may well have been Lancelot to her Elaine, in the idyll she considered the finest poem in the language. Hardy, too, fulfilled a bookish ideal. He inscribed gifts of books to her, in June 1907 his own *Wessex Poems*, in July a copy of *The Rubaiyat of Omar Khayyam*, which came to have a special meaning for them, though Emma had found the sentiments in that poem "pernicious".[27]

Above all, he made instant and strenuous efforts to forward her literary ambitions. The pains he had taken for Mrs. Henniker or for Agnes Grove were nothing to his new endeavours on Florence's behalf. Regardless or innocent of the chance that his letters might be compared or exchanged in the smoking-rooms of London literary clubs, Hardy wrote to nearly every editor or publisher with whom he had any previous connection. On 8 July he wrote a long personal letter to the head of his own publishers, Frederick Macmillan, setting out Florence Dugdale's previous history and her abilities.[28] She had teaching experience, and could do anything they might offer on their educational side, both editorial and contributory. Stretching the point that she had offered to help him check and revise the draft of *The Dynasts* Part III, he wrote that she had helped him with work at the British Museum. She could do shorthand and typing (not altogether skilfully, as later typescripts show) and could make herself useful in any way. Soliciting a personal interview for her, he added that she came from an old Dorset family, well known to himself. The remark, meant to convey a background of gentility or even of landed property, was a smokescreen, in which the blacksmith grandfather, the farm-labourers and carters of her Dorset forebears were conveniently obscured. Whether Florence herself consciously aided and abetted this and similar deceptions, or whether she genuinely had been brought up to know little of this side of her family, is uncertain. She knew she had a Dorset grandfather, but never mentioned his occupation; while, shortly after her marriage, she remarked, "There are Dugdales at Wareham, but, as far as I know, not the least relation to me."[29]

At all events, on the very next day, with well-judged alterations, Hardy wrote practically the same letter to Archibald Marshall, literary editor of the *Daily Mail*.[30] Marshall was a Cambridge graduate of some taste and ability, which included acting, playwriting, song-writing, and, ultimately, novel-writing. He maintained a high standard for the literary page of the *Mail*, where he had recently published Hardy's King's Hintock Park poem about the old woman sweeping up leaves. Attracted by the lyric, Marshall himself had composed a setting for it, and his daughter remembers singing it about the house as a small girl.[31] In May 1907 he had asked Hardy for another contribution. Hardy, away from his papers in Max Gate, and embroiled in revising Part III of *The Dynasts* in London, had asked for time. Now he himself wrote to Marshall, still with no contribution, but using the bait of a future poem to ask an immediate favour. This was, of course, on behalf of Miss Florence Dugdale. Would Marshall consider her work for his columns, or, indeed, use his influence for her in any other suitable department of the *Mail*? Her qualities were listed in the same way as in the previous day's Macmillan letter, with the emphasis on literature rather than on education, the shorthand and typing being added, apparently as an afterthought, in a postscript. Marshall seems to have seen her, and impressed her as "quite a well-bred sort of man",[32] but there is no evidence he found her employment.

There were probably other letters to other editors and publishers in August. In September, Hardy wrote to the editor of the *Cornhill*, Reginald Smith, with whose family and publications he was closely connected. This time it was a most glowing recommendation and eulogy of a short story signed "F. E. Dugdale". Smith was quick and worldly-wise in his response.[33] Yes, he would publish the story, though he wished he might print with it Hardy's letter of praise; that, surely, would attract the interest of readers. Could he know more about Miss Dugdale—he supposed he was right in believing "F. E. Dugdale" to be a lady? He also added a sly postscript to congratulate Hardy on the way he was helping the work of Agnes Grove, whose book, *The Social Fetich*, published this year, was dedicated to him. The insinuation behind Smith's last remark was clear. Agnes Grove's work showed internal evidence of Hardy's hand in its forms of expression and creative editing. Surely, Smith implied, he could detect Hardy's style in parts of Miss Dugdale's story too.

The story, which Smith eventually printed in the *Cornhill* of June 1908, was indeed a remarkable production, not the least for its title, *The Apotheosis of the Minx*, which so confused a later editor of a check-list of Hardy's correspondence[34] in the Dorset County Museum that he catalogued it as "The Apotheosis of the Min*d*". The basic construction and philosophy of the story is typical of Hardy himself. Robert Engle, an innocent, idealistic young schoolmaster, a devotee of Shelley, falls in love with a tawdry, common girl he meets at his landlady's. They arrange a date, and go for a walk together in the country, so reminiscent of Jude and Arabella that this incident, the best in the story, might have come straight out of the earlier pages of *Jude the Obscure*. He is shy; she is disgusted at his lack of "go". Besides, she has her eye on a flashy young grocer. She rounds on Robert for his lack of sexual enterprise; yet, unlike Arabella, she does not tempt him out of it, but chooses to marry the grocer. Robert is stunned and dismisses her as unworthy of his own Shelleyan ideals. Later, he hears she has died in childbed, and meets her widower, who tells him, too late, that the girl had really loved the schoolmaster. The latter begins to idealize her once more, though he cannot rid himself of a repugnance because she had belonged to another. Later still, he meets the grocer again. He is about to be married for a second time. The schoolmaster feels this has released him to idealize the first wife fully. In his memory, he deifies her ideal attributes, associating her with his love of Keats and Shelley. The commonplace, unworthy girl has become a perpetual object of worship for the remainder of the schoolmaster's life. In irony, parodox, mistiming of circumstances, places, and persons, in its Shelleyan idealism, and the author's implied cynical conclusion, the pattern of the story is everywhere typical of Hardy.

How much can one trace Hardy's hand, which Reginald Smith of the *Cornhill* evidently thought he could detect, in the actual writing? The opening paragraphs are obviously taken by Florence from life and from her father's and her own experience, a restless, bored classroom of inattentive boys, to whom the magic incantation of Shelley's *Skylark* means nothing. Robert Engle and his dreary North London school, from which he and the girl go on the traditional country walk of Green Lanes, seems an accurate and individual enough description of Florence's father and his suburban setting, described by a writer,[35] who visited the Dugdales about this time, as depressing and uninspiring. Florence herself hated the North London suburbs, and had some gift for catching an atmosphere. It is rather in small phrases and expressions, which seem to be additional afterthoughts, that one hears an echo of Hardy in his mode of slightly pedantic clumsiness, on which all critics of his prose had commented. A good guide to this type of emendation by Hardy exists in his alterations, some years later, to a manuscript by his first wife. Emma, at her death in 1912, left a charming, spontaneous account of her youthful days up to her marriage, entitled "Some Recollections". Hardy quoted and edited this, not always for the best, in his own autobiography. Emma's vivid description of Hardy's round-about journey to Cornwall, "a sort of cross jump-journey, like a chess-Knight's move", was brought flatly to earth by Hardy's additional explanatory words, pencilled in his hand, "by the route necessitated". Similarly, one suspects, such phrases in Florence's story as "the grocer's assistant aforesaid" must be Hardy's; for the disconcertingly lawyer-like "aforesaid" in this is found everywhere in Hardy's prose, even in his later and more skilled work. On a less prosaic note, Florence's "heavenly singer" in the story is not unreminiscent of Hardy's own descriptions of Shelley—"high singer" and "matchless singer"— though all are equally clichés.[36]

Florence regarded herself as a serious writer, though her small children's books for Chambers and Collins were more or less hackwork, miserably paid. On the basis of *The Apotheosis of the Minx*, though, there is little evidence of much talent, and it seems unlikely that without Hardy's eulogistic covering letter it would have been printed in a leading magazine, which, at this precise time, was publishing the early work of Virginia Stephen (Virginia Woolf). There is no evidence that Florence had any other story accepted, except for one printed early in 1911, under the most curious circumstances.[37] This one successful excursion into serious literature was launched on Hardy's recommendation.

Some small volumes of what are really fictionalized nature studies for children, and some natural history "descriptions", with embarrassing little verses for children, comprised much of her future output. She learnt, however, to write a good, lively, and expressive letter, not without a certain sardonic humour. Her style is strongly in contrast with that of Emma's ungrammatical, illogical, and sometimes ill-spelled screeds, with their occasional touches of maverick imaginative quality. Many perhaps, though, will agree with Beatrix Potter (Mrs. Healis), who preferred Emma's artless style to Florence's "more 'show-off' epistles".[38] Certainly, Emma's printed articles, such as "In Praise of Calais" and "The Egyptian Pet", show more talent than Florence's.

The problem of this new awakening relationship for Hardy was, of course, how to introduce it acceptably into his life with Emma. For the time being, he simply did not dare to try the hazardous experiment. In spite of her alarming forewarning the previous summer of increasing pain and exhaustion from gall-stones, allied with feelings of depression, and distinct weakness of eyesight, Emma was in this year of 1907 at the top of her form as the scourge of husbands. June 1907, two or three weeks before Hardy had written his July letters of appeal on Florence's behalf, brought an incident concerning Emma which has often been retold, though not always with complete accuracy. This was the occasion of Edward VII's garden-party on the 22nd of the month at Windsor Castle. When the trains from Paddington arrived at Windsor station, a number of royal landaus were waiting to pick up the guests for the castle. The carriages proved to be too few for the visitors from the train in which the Hardys had travelled down with Blanche, the painter. Mrs. Hardy was wearing a long green floating "Victorian" veil, a reminder that, as Blanche noticed, she habitually dressed, in her late sixties, in girlish fashions of a bygone age. She and some other ladies settled themselves in the landau, but a lady from Blanche's household at first refused the one spare seat next to Emma, suggesting that the elderly and frail-looking Hardy should sit next to his wife. It is not certain, from Blanche's eye-witness account, that Emma actually made her opprobrious and often-quoted retort to this suggestion—"the walk will do him good"—but the upshot, at all events, was that the poet and the painter followed on foot, while Emma's green veil floated from the royal carriage ahead like a banner: and, as Blanche slyly commented, "such must have been the usual form, the customary rhythm of home life in this illustrious household".[39]

As it happens, there is another eye-witness account of the Hardy's home life, in the following summer of 1908, a little more sympathetic to Emma, and perhaps a little nearer the impression made by Hardy at this time on an observant stranger. In June 1908, Hardy sat again for his portrait, this time to Sir Hubert von Herkomer, who had illustrated some of the serial of *Tess*. Herkomer, was elderly, academic, ponderous, pedestrian, Germanic (he was born in Bavaria), a typical Victorian "subject" painter, well known for his "The Last Muster". This painting, showing a group of Army veterans in Chelsea Hospital, naturally recommended him to Hardy's taste. The portrait was duly despatched to Max Gate, and became the show-piece of Emma's at-homes and garden-parties later that summer. Winifred Fortescue, an intelligent young débutante, described one of these occasions. "Bitterly disappointed", as most people were, by the mean architecture and prosaic setting of Max Gate, the first thing she noticed was a tragi-comic reminder of Emma's attempts to create the setting of a great writer. The hall-porch held a small plaster reproduction of the Capitoline Venus, probably a relic of their visit to Rome twenty years before. From the little wooden bracket on which it stood was suspended a placard addressed in Emma's hand to the housemaid; in rickety capitals it warned, "When dusting, please *blow* but do not touch." Once inside, every guest had to be led by Emma to see what she described with "panting pride" as "the Herkomer of Mr. Hardy". Winifred Fortescue found her pathetic but likeable; she did not form such a favourable view of "her formidable husband".

> To me he made the rather sinister impression of an ancient moulting eagle, with his piercing, restless dark eyes and lean naked neck rising in folds above a low collar, and his bald peering head moving ceaselessly from side to side . . .

She echoes the unfavourable physical shock most admirers had experienced for the last twenty or thirty years on first meeting Hardy. She adds one extra point, perhaps significant at this time: his evident and suspiciously restless sense of unease.[40] The new attachment, outside his marriage, was one more reason for embarrassment in the presence of his wife, quite apart from those she was all too capable of creating on her own account.

Once again, however, it is rather Hardy's biographers than anything really observed about the marriage that has created the legend of an open, public warfare between Emma and Thomas. Among many examples, the biographers have invented an entirely fictitious scene, in which Dame Rebecca West—no less—was present, and heard Emma say to Hardy, "Thomas Hardy, try to remember you married a lady." Since, as Dame Rebecca has pointed out,[41] she herself never at any time met Emma, this story, elaborated to the legend that Emma "often reminded Hardy that he had 'married a lady' ",[42] is not only apocryphal but impossible. It has its origin in something that happened in the 1920s, about ten years after Emma died. An elderly member of a Dorset family, who had known Emma and Thomas, said, in Dame Rebecca's hearing, that the remark was made very naturally

... in a matrimonial flurry ... Hardy and his wife had been going to
some local function and he had appeared before her dressed inappro-
priately at the hour when they should have been leaving the house.

One can even conjecture what this "inappropriate" dress, which
caused such an understandable reaction, may have been. In 1900,
Hardy bought a pair of trousers, which became "his study trousers",
and to which he was inordinately attached. Twenty years later, he was
found mending them with string and a packing needle,[43] though even
the servants at Max Gate commented unfavourably on them, and
defying his second wife to burn them. These trousers are the likely
cause of this particular legend of public discord between Hardy and
Emma, and the incident a commonplace in most married lives.

Whatever his personal manœuvres, Hardy the writer was fully at
work. The main matter on hand was an edition of William Barnes,
about which he had been approached by the Clarendon Press early in
1907. His response[44] was enthusiastic and prompt to accept. Of Barnes,
he wrote:

> Hitherto he has been badly handled by most of those who have given
> specimens of his work—from the point of view of the few of us still
> left who know the dialect as Barnes knew it, which the rising generation
> of rustics do not, on account of the schools whose tendency is to kill
> it off rapidly.

In spite of his prejudice against popular education, the self-taught
Hardy himself got down to work in a way that proved him a better and
more practical scholar than the distinguished men who hired him for
the task, including Sir Walter Raleigh; they, indeed, made elementary
errors of taste and judgement, and the monumental blunder, unforgiv-
able in an academic publishing firm, of not finding out which works of
Barnes were still in copyright. Hardy wrote nearly two dozen letters to
the Press in 1907 and 1908 after he had finally laid aside *The Dynasts*.[45]
He comes very well out of the correspondence, hard-working, meticulous as an editor, patient about copyright difficulties, but above all
intensely loyal to Barnes's poetry and the selection itself.

He offered to make the selection, edit the texts, and provide a necessary glossary, either free of charge, or for a nominal fee at the publisher's
discretion. He worked, on this agreement, for a year, before the Clarendon Press discovered that Kegan Paul's copyright on Barnes's later
improved editions had still two years to run. Rather than reprint
earlier, inferior drafts and printings, Hardy offered all his own textual
work free of charge to Kegan Paul in return for the copyright, though
the offer seems to have been rejected. Hardy was therefore forced to
compromise, using out-of-copyright versions and poems.

It is striking that in all the long, tedious negotiations Hardy does not complain of the quite unnecessary trouble, to which he himself has been put, but only of the injustice to Barnes as a poet, and consequent loss to the book itself. He was even generous about the money involved, and courteous under provocation and incompetence by the high-handed Press. He valued this work more than most, and he inscribed an advance copy to Florence Dugdale with evident affection for both the book and for her.

Hardy's literary career was therefore as full as his emotional life, and the two were intertwined. He was collecting a fresh book of verse, now that Barnes and the monumental *Dynasts* were both safely off his hands, and his new love-attachment made him exhume love-poems to other women, even those of his remotest past, under the comprehensive sub-title of "More Love Lyrics". Among these special two-dozen poems, were many youthful love-lyrics from the 1860s. These included two sonnets to his early theatre infatuation, the dark, slender actress, Mrs. Mary Scott-Siddons. Others can be associated with Weymouth and the brunette Tryphena Sparks. Discreetly sandwiched between them, undated, was *On the Departure Platform*, describing an encounter with his new dark-haired, deep-eyed young lady, Florence Dugdale. In deference to Emma, the whole volume was preceded by what was now his stock disclaimer. He wrote,

> the sense of disconnection, particularly in respect of those lyrics penned in the first person, will be immaterial when it is borne in mind that they are to be regarded, in the main, as dramatic monologues by different characters.

One wonders if he really supposed this would placate Emma. The "different characters" are so patently Hardy himself; the love section ends deliberately with his very personal 1883 lyric *He Abjures Love*. From the manuscript, it appears he had several last-minute thoughts about where to insert the poem silently reserved for Miss Dugdale, *On the Departure Platform*. Far from abjuring love, Hardy was now, in his late sixties, as firmly as ever in love's toils. Florence Dugdale and her distinctive feature, her "large, luminous eyes",[46] begin to dominate his life and work. On her part, she promoted the book by lecturing on him to her local literary society, comparing his lyrics to those of Heine.

The general tone of *Time's Laughingstocks*, published on 3 December 1909, contrasts with his previous collection, *Poems of the Past and of the Present*, almost exactly eight years earlier. That had, on the whole, been weighted heavily on the side of philosophic, sceptical, and quasi-religious poems. The poems in *Time's Laughingstocks*, with the exception of one short sequence, a rural *Set of Country Songs*, are connected with people close to Hardy and the intimate relationships of his life. There are poems concerned with both his grandmothers, Betsy Hand and

Mary Head, the latter immortalized in the superb evocation of her home
in the Bockhampton cottage, laconically entitled *One We Knew* (*M.H
1772–1857*) and ending, with beautiful reminiscence,

> With cap-framed face and long gaze into the embers—
> We seated around her knees—
> She would dwell on such dead themes, not as one who remembers,
> But rather as one who sees.

> She seemed one left behind of a band gone distant
> So far that no tongue could hail:
> Past things retold were to her as things existent,
> Things present but as a tale.

Several poems seem to have more than a shadowy connection with his
other grandmother. She is the old woman "Raking up leaves" in the
verses *Autumn in King's Hinton Park* at Melbury Osmond, where she
made the improvident marriage which earned her an old age of penury.
She is the widow of *Bereft* and *She Hears the Storm*. Hardy's own mother
and father are idealized in *A Church Romance*. Its line about their
meeting, "Thus their hearts' bond began, in due time signed", begs the
questionable fact that their bond of marriage was certainly not signed
until it was considerably overdue, when the baby Hardy was already
four months on the way. Interspersed with poems to his galaxy of
brunette beauties, Hardy included two poems about his previous
Florence of the 1890s, Florence Henniker, one, *The Division*, dated
1893, and the other, a little less surely about her, called *The End of the
Episode*. All in all, this volume is far more concerned with touchingly
portrayed human relationships than his last, though the gritting
grimace at the sour taste of life can be felt in 1909 as it had been in 1901.

This is not to neglect one or two charming comic Dorset dialect
verse-sketches, like *The Curate's Kindness* and *Rose-Ann*, little master-
pieces of sly rural humour, probably derived from his recent editing of
William Barnes. The more ambitious narratives, however, are of
unrelieved and tragic irony. They include two ballad-form tales in
verse, to both of which Hardy applied the term "tragedy": *A Trampwoman's Tragedy* and *A Sunday Morning Tragedy*. The long rolling
ballad-like lines of *The Rash Bride* and the more conventional short
ballad-stanzas, *The Vampirine Fair*, fall into the same group. Finally,
and in a late position, designed to attract attention, Hardy tried an
exercise in narrative blank verse, *Panthera*, using a legend designed—
successfully—to shock the orthodox Christian reader, based on the
second-century story that Christ himself was the illegitimate son of a
Roman soldier.

A Trampwoman's Tragedy was, Hardy thought, his most successful
poem: to the end, he had a prejudice in favour of the ballad-form, with

refrain and repetition. The refrain of another, shorter poem, *Bereft*, has a distinct folk-song echo.

> Leave the door unbarred,
> The clock unwound.
> Make my lone bed hard—
> Would 't were underground!

This is the accent, form, and rhythm of the ballad *Lord Randal*. In *A Sunday Morning Tragedy*, written in January 1904, Hardy reprinted a ballad-form poem, which marked the extreme of his attempts, in prose and poetry, to write "adult" literature. It was a poem about unsuccessful, rural abortion. Hardy had even planned to make a short play of it, called *Birthwort*, since it hinged on a herbal abortifacient, provided by "a subtle man". The poem had first been printed in the *English Review* of December 1907, its first number. The story that the *Review* was actually founded in order to publish this poem of Hardy's, which several other magazines had refused, seems to be one more of the exuberant fancies of its editor, the notorious Ford Madox Ford. Ford, also the inventor of the story about Emma, Richard Garnett, and her attempted suppression of *Jude the Obscure*, persuaded the future that he had made this dramatic literary gesture on behalf of Hardy's controversial poem. In fact, as his own biographer hints,[47] he had already solicited Hardy and several leading writers for contributions to give his new magazine a rousing send-off. Hardy submitted the poem himself, and Ford was glad to accept it, only later casting himself in the flamboyant role of Hardy's broadminded benefactor. The poem, Wordsworthian and direct, had no need of help; it is a picture of real rural life such as, Hardy had earlier told William Rothenstein, the public "would not stand". To that extent, the magazine provided a forum, and Hardy was to use its pages again for verses of an explicit sexual character.

The reviews of this volume, and of the fully-completed *Dynasts*, were more than respectful. Hardy was now acclaimed as a poet as he had been a novelist, his stature assured as the senior figure in contemporary English literature. He began to be sought for, and to make, oracular judgements, some of which sound dubious to modern ears. He was consistently modest about his own work, and when Gosse in March 1908 voted the whole *Dynasts* "one of the most original and beautiful productions of the modern age",[48] Hardy expressed regret that he had not improved it far more by rewriting. On other writers, though, however eminent, he could be obstinately pontifical. On Shakespeare, he wrote to a correspondent,[49] "I do not think that Shakespeare appertains particularly to the theatrical world nowadays, if ever he did . . . I would hazard the guess that he will someday cease altogether to be acted." On a lighter and more domestic note, when asked by the Dorset regiment for a marching tune, he sent them an old one of his grandfather's, called "The Dorchester Hornpipe", which he himself had fiddled at dances as a boy.[50] Official occasions, to which he was deferentially invited, included the John Milton tercentenary celebrations at Cambridge, which he attended in July 1908. Approaching his seventieth year, he was bidding fair to steer a latter-day settled course as a Grand Old Man of English Letters, beginning to relish his stature, and to dismiss as "cheeky" an invitation to the Whitefriars journalistic club,[51] whose members he had entertained at Max Gate a few years earlier. Only his jealously secretive emotional life indicated another side of him, those "throbbings of noon-tide" which were shaking him still, and were to shake him yet further, into the most startling old age of any English poet.

11

Florence and Emma and Thomas

WHAT Florence now drew from Hardy was a tenderness he did not always display to people. Tenderness of the quality he had shown towards his fictional women—Tess, Fanny Robin, Marty South—now appeared rarely in his life. In poetry, it belonged not to human beings, but the small wild creatures—worm, lark, mole, rabbit—in the wonderful Waterloo chorus of Part III of *The Dynasts*. Towards his fellow-men, as we have seen, he was now frequently curt and arbitrary. In letters to his wife, such as those written to her late in autumn 1908, he wrote of being concerned about her welfare, but with no very apparent conviction or feeling. With Florence it was different. Her youth, her difficulties, her ill-health specially, touched springs of sympathy, anxiety, understanding. Real thought for her health seems even to have cured his crushing hypochondria about his own at least for a time. In 1909, he made Edward Clodd his first close acquaintance to know of Florence's existence, and actually to meet her. The free-thinking advanced Clodd perhaps seemed most naturally suitable; Hardy did not reveal Florence's existence to the more conventional Gosse for another five years. He wrote to Clodd about "my young friend" or "my young friend and assistant", in a vein of entire tenderness. She was so delicate, so susceptible to illness; she must be made to wrap up well against the damp night air. "Please make her wrap up", he wrote to Clodd, "as she is so very delicate." Sea air was good for her; she must have holidays at the seaside, and Hardy would take her on them. So it was that they went together to Aldeburgh in August 1909, and again probably later that year, Ventnor in March 1910, Aldeburgh again in October 1911 and in May 1912.[1]

When Hardy wrote his autobiography, a few years later, he either did not mention these visits, or, more often, when he did, invariably concealed the fact that Florence had been with him. Sometimes the concealment took a highly devious form. On this first visit to Aldeburgh, in summer 1909, he wrote in his autobiography that he had had to put off his trip to Clodd owing to an attack of influenza, but recovered sufficiently later in the summer to go. His letters to Edward Clodd at Aldeburgh, however, reveal that this was far from the case. Hardy did not have influenza at all. It was Florence who had recurring trouble with her throat, which the visit was intended to cure—"it will be an excellent restorative", Hardy wrote about her to Clodd. The stay with Clodd was postponed twice because of her renewed illness, and only took place in August, when she was well again.[2] Hardy, not mentioning her name at all, has accounted for the postponed visit by pretending that he, not she, was too ill to travel to Suffolk,[3] and, of course, equally, pretending that he went alone to Clodd.

Hardy was caught in a web of concealment in more ways than one. One of its more complicated enmeshings, in this same summer of 1909, surrounded the performance at Covent Garden, on 14 July, of the opera of *Tess of the d'Urbervilles* by Baron D'Erlanger. Hardy wanted to take Florence to the first night; but the question was whether Emma would want to come up for it from Dorchester, where she was spending a semi-invalid existence for the second summer in succession. On 9 July, Hardy wrote to Emma, stressing the fatigues and difficulties of London, and mentioning that she could come to a later performance. Emma, decided, however, to come to this one. At short notice, Clodd enrolled himself as the understanding friend. He would be Florence's partner to Covent Garden, having first—something Hardy himself had forgotten —taken her out for a light dinner—"this bright idea of yours she highly appreciates",[4] Hardy wrote. Hardy would visit them, if he could, in the intervals, and at curtain-fall Clodd would put her into a cab for her London aunt's, while Hardy took Emma back to the hotel. So it was that both Florence and Emma heard "a Dorset dairymaid singing her woes in choice Italian", as Hardy described to Gosse the performance of Destinn.[5]

All this sounds like the exercise in real life of a novelist's craft, yet it is too much to accuse Hardy of completely deliberate plotting. Half the time, he may scarcely have known what he was doing, or what its remoter consequences might be. Many of his statements, even to the trusted Clodd, have an ambiguity which could either be studied, or the result of sheer bewilderment. Writing from Max Gate on 1 May, he spoke to Clodd of "my domestic circumstances which, between ourselves, make it embarrassing for me to return hospitalities received".[6] This may hint at some domestic human tangle, or it may simply recall the lambasting that Clodd had received from Emma a dozen years before over his open irreligion;[7] for, in fact, many other people continued to be invited to Max Gate about this time. The general impression is that Hardy, during these years, was like his own Napoleon in *The Dynasts*, swept along helpless by forces beyond control, however much he might appear to be master in outward life.

Yet some step must be taken to avoid the to-and-fro, the manœuvres, the reliance on the secrecy and goodwill of friends, which had taken place in summer 1909 over the opera seats. Somehow Emma and Florence must get to know each other; ideally, Florence should be introduced so that she could come and go freely at Max Gate. This was the problem Hardy now set himself to achieve. It cannot have been easy; but, according to a passage in Hardy's autobiography, by at least summer 1910, Florence had become an accepted visitor at Max Gate, and a partner in its strange atmosphere.[8]

The Max Gate household in 1909 consisted of Emma, Thomas, a visiting gardener called Trevis,[9] and three living-in maids, Jane, Daisy, and Florence Griffin.[10] The last-named was slightly better-educated than the others, and was entrusted with small tasks, such as paying the gardener, forwarding letters, and looking after the cats when the Hardys were in London.[11] On these occasions, she was sometimes aided by Henry Hardy, who came over from Bockhampton, and who, as a builder, did any house repairs for the Hardys. He was, in fact, now beginning to build his own house, Talbothays, on the land at West Stafford he had inherited from his father.

In what manner and when was Florence introduced into what she called "The Max Gate ménage"? Hardy said she had met Emma at a club in London, a minor resort for artistic ladies, very often of little achievement, but with ambitions to write and to meet writers. This was the Lyceum Club at 128 Piccadilly, fairly near Emma's more fashionable club, the Alexandra, and very close indeed to Hardy's club, the Savile. One does not quite know if Hardy himself engineered this meeting, but the probability is that he did. It is definitely confirmed by Florence's literary executor and trustee, Irene Cooper Willis, who wrote that Florence said she was "1st at Max Gate taken there by Emma who had picked her up at the Lyceum Club and taken a fancy to her".[12] Thus was successfully launched the fiction, sedulously maintained in later years, that Florence was really *Emma's* friend. It was true only in so far as Emma was the means of bringing Florence into the Hardys' home. It ignores the fact that Hardy had met Florence, and had been seeing her in London and elsewhere, ever since summer 1907, apparently without Emma's knowledge, a space of between two or three years in all. Her first visit to Max Gate seems to have been in 1909 or 1910; for writing soon after her death, W. R. Rutland, who had spoken with both Florence and Irene Cooper Willis, stated, "Mrs. Hardy had brought to Max Gate a young woman . . . Florence Emily Dugdale, one of five sisters, [who] was then about thirty."[13] This places her advent roughly in 1909–10.

The situation was complex for Florence. Emma Hardy too, of course, provided personal complexities in abundance. One false impression, however, needs to be corrected. This is that, in what were to prove the last few years of her life, Emma withdrew to an attic in eccentric reclusion. This picture of a Miss Havisham-like existence arises from a misunderstanding of something probably said by Florence to Irene

Cooper Willis. The truth is far different. As long ago as the year 1898, Emma had determined to rival the aristocratic "women in London" of whom she was so jealously contemptuous, by having a set of boudoir apartments of her own, copying the fashion of these emancipated ladies who had often entertained her husband *tête à tête* in such intimate surroundings. Early in 1899, she wrote of "my little apartment where not a sound—even the dinner bell—scarcely reaches me". Two months later, she described this arrangement in ecstatic terms. "I sleep in an *Attic*—or *two*! My boudoir is my sweet refuge and solace—not a sound scarcely penetrates hither. I see the sun and stars and moon rise and the birds come to my bird-table." She wrote with evident enjoyment, though poor spelling, of her "eerie",[14] where she could have her private possessions and her small library, since, she complained, her husband never now allowed her to come into his, or to borrow his books. In 1908, she improved the set of apartments by having a dormer window put in, to widen her view of the beauties of the world from this vantage. The picture handed down of a half-mad creature huddled in a dusty attic could not be farther from the truth, though there was certainly pathos in Emma's bid for an independent life, when resentful disillusion with her distinguished husband set in during the 1890s.

At the same time, from her fainting fit in the summer of 1906, Emma's physical rather than her mental health began to fail. Jacques-Emile Blanche noticed, later that summer, that she seemed bewildered and out-of-place in London society, and allowed, though resentfully, the drawing-room tea-party of her London apartments to be dominated by Lady Grove. From 1900, she had suffered from nervousness in London, and what she called "shyness"; she found it difficult to cross roads in the heavy traffic, and domestic arrangements were too much for her now. In December of this year, 1906, after influenza, she wrote of the difficulties of old age and illness, and her lack of resilience in "getting over the after-weakness".[15] By November 1907[16] her eyes were troubling her—"my ill-disposed eyesight"—and on 20 May 1908 she admitted "strength and sight are fast failing". Sadly, she felt she had "no really *sweet* attentive relatives" to rely upon; "a useful companion", tried in spring 1908, did not satisfy her.[17] Yet her long, well-expressed letter to the *Nation* on the subject of women's suffrage shows she was still enterprising, and though she felt she could not that summer manage the usual seasonal stay in London, she was sufficiently well and capable to go, by herself, that autumn to "France, the country I love most after our own"; she spent several weeks alone in Calais.[18] It was quite a feat for a poor-sighted, shy, elderly English lady of close on sixty-eight, and also quite a shrewd move, since by doing it she left Hardy to deal with the discomforts of builders in the house for the new dormer window. Moreover, she managed on her return to write an article on Calais, which was printed in the *Dorset County Chronicle*; it, too, is a really well-written piece of vivid, descriptive prose.[19]

Yet there were some disquieting developments, not altogether physical. Emma's habitual rampant Protestantism—Hardy had to forward Protestant papers to her in France—was taking an odd turn towards apocalyptic mysticism, such as her 1907 poem *Ten Moons*, which has been quoted.[20] Her horror of Roman Catholics became acute, and she castigated them roundly. She took to distributing "beautiful little booklets . . . of pure Protestantism"; at her bank in Dorchester, the Devon and Cornwall, she pressed these upon an embarrassed junior bank-clerk, who happened to be a Catholic.[21] Then, too, her language about her husband began to show lack of control. Ten years before, for instance, her long letter to Mrs. Kenneth Grahame about the trials and woes of married life, though forceful, was rationally expressed and in many ways true. Now, in 1908, such statements became extreme and idiosyncratic. "My eminent partner", she wrote, "will have a softening of the brain if he goes on as he does and the rest of the world does."[22]

What in fact was happening to Hardy, under these strange and novel circumstances, was a kind of rejuvenation. It was not merely the old story of an elderly man meeting a young woman. For six years, during the writing of *The Dynasts*, he had been "a dead man walking". He had literally expected to die. He had looked, as everyone remarked, like death. George Meredith, whom he visited in 1905, had been depressed by Hardy's "twilight view of life"—just as, to be fair, Hardy had been depressed by Meredith's perennial cheerfulness. Now life had shown a glimmer, and he gratefully responded. When she first met him, Florence said, "his mind was luminous". Some of its new light was certainly borrowed from her, from the sun of her young and devoted admiration.

Hardy, for his part, rewarded Florence with poems to her, which, though few, were of an intensity he had not shown for years. One of these commemorated her advent at Max Gate, and, incidentally, helps to date her arrival there. It was not included in the *Time's Laughing-stocks* collection of 1909, but was first printed in the *Spectator* of 13 August 1910, when it appears to be a freshly-written piece. On that occasion, it did not, of course, have the inscription "To F.E.D.", for it speaks openly of Hardy's overwhelming emotion on seeing her move about the house which had otherwise become such a prison for himself and Emma, like a spirit of new freedom and renewed hope from his ingrown despair.

> Come again to the place
> Where your presence was as a leaf that skims
> Down a drouthy way whose ascent bedims
> The bloom on the farer's face.

> Come again, with the feet
> That were light on the green as a thistledown ball,
> And those mute ministrations to one and to all
> Beyond a man's saying sweet.

Florence's "large luminous living eyes" seemed to him to weigh

> Scarce consciously,
> The eternal question of what Life was,
> And why we were there, and by whose strange laws
> That which mattered most could not be.

Indeed, this year, 1910, during which both Emma and Hardy were seventy, was a crucial time at Max Gate. For one thing, Florence was now there very frequently; by the later months of the year she wrote, "I go there now so often", the implication again being that this was a recent development. On the other hand, Emma, increasingly ill, and in severe pain, was attempting to stage a comeback into society. In mid-April she went up with her husband to London, to try and arrange a flat for "the season". Illness drove her back to Dorchester.

Fortunately for the convenience of meeting Hardy, while he was thus alone in London, Florence this spring secured a small, central flat of her own, in a block near Baker Street. The owner, a friend of hers, had gone abroad and lent her the flat, where she and Hardy were able to see each other without attracting undue public attention. Privately, she was now able to begin introducing him for the first time to her own family. Her elder sister Ethel, who had trained as a teacher at St. Katherine's, Tottenham, from 1897 to 1899, was now married, with a little boy of six. Florence invited her and this nephew to meet the distinguished author at the Baker Street flat. Hardy was relaxed and cheerful, in contrast with his demeanour at Max Gate. Indeed, Florence's sister, Mrs. Richardson, always found him friendly and affectionate. On this occasion, he took her small boy on his knee, and asked him, kindly if conventionally, what he wanted to be when he grew up. The boy, who had just been to Kew watching the gardeners among the bulbs, startled his mother and amused Hardy by answering, "A gardener". So began a situation in which the Dugdale family, one by one, became aware of Hardy's interest in Florence. They accepted in general the idea that she was his "secretary", and even that she was engaged in "research" for him in London, though by this date, his work, which consisted entirely of correcting proofs and writing poems, did not need anything that could be called research.[23]

Meanwhile, at Max Gate without him, Emma poured out her woes in a letter to a new animal-loving friend, Alda, Lady Hoare, of Stourhead in Wiltshire, an advocate of slaughter-house reform. She took the opportunity to ensconce herself in Hardy's study, from which she was now normally banished—"not as formerly"—and to complain of the difficulties of being an author's wife.[24] However, she joined him next month in London, at the flat at 4 Blomfield Court, Maida Vale. The day after she moved in with some of the Max Gate servants, the death of Edward VII placarded the streets.[25] Hardy found fresh encouragement that a new young actress, Lillah McCarthy, wanted to revive the idea of his *Tess* play; but a greater excitement was at hand. On 2 July, Asquith wrote privately to say that the new King wanted to confer on Hardy the Order of Merit.[26]

Two years before, Asquith had offered a knighthood, which Hardy refused. Dorchester gossip, when this leaked out, reckoned this refusal a shame for "dear old Mrs. Hardy", who would have surely loved to be Lady Hardy. Even now, she could not share this triumph. The presentation was fixed for 19 July: but Emma, who had already found the Season too much for her, felt so ill that she went home a week before. With "Miss Dugdale", as he wrote to Emma, to type his acknowledgements of congratulations, Hardy was left alone to receive the honour, and in his own opinion, "failed in the customary formalities".[27] He shared these with another reserved and irritable genius, Sir Edward Elgar. In their complex natures and distrust of the world, the two men were alike, from very much the same cause. Elgar never forgot he had been known locally as the errand boy from his father's Worcester shop; Hardy never forgot his cottage home and charity-child mother. The two struck up an acquaintanceship, which led to desultory correspondence about a possible collaboration; but nothing came of the chance contact of two prickly natures. This was unfortunate since, on the more attractive, creative side, Elgar's music had so much in common with Hardy's poetry—sadness, nostalgia, and deep emotion. What inadequacy Hardy felt at Marlborough House was more than compensated later in the year when Dorchester conferred its freedom on him, and he delivered what was, for him, a remarkably long speech of thanks, in the presence of the borough notables, Emma, Florence, and the poet Henry Newbolt.

His position was now so assured, after the public recognition of the O.M., that he was inundated with literary suggestions and requests. He became, among other things, a mark for forceful approach. Sydney Cockerell, the tireless and shameless director of the Fitzwilliam Museum, Cambridge, wrote outrageously to say that though he had not read any of Hardy's work, he would like some of his MSS for the Museum. Such was Cockerell's powerful and insinuating personality that he not only obtained the manuscripts of *Jude the Obscure* and *Time's Laughingstocks*, but extracted from Hardy permission to distribute his other MSS to various museums, and ultimately got himself the post of Hardy's literary executor, with the right to destroy or preserve as he pleased. Hardy, often curiously innocent, seemed glad to trust a decisive person, who would take the mountainous load of past paper off his hands; and for the rest of his life Cockerell, it was observed, "reckoned himself, Hardy's 'manager' as it were".[28]

"The 'Max Gate ménage'", wrote Florence late in 1910,[29] "always does wear the aspect of comedy to me. Mrs Hardy is good to me . . . I am *intensely* sorry for her, sorry indeed for both." Sometimes the comedy could only be described as black. The summer and autumn of 1910 had seen the arrest, trial, and execution of Dr. Crippen, who murdered his bullying wife, and went off with his secretary, Miss Le Neve. One morning in November, when newspapers were full of photographs of the little murderer with the drooping moustaches, Emma approached Florence "in deadly seriousness" with an idea. Had not Florence noticed how extremely like Crippen Hardy was in personal appearance? It was by no means an unfair observation; but when Emma continued to speculate whether her own body would not be found buried in the Max Gate cellar, Florence left hastily "or she would be asking if I didn't think I resembled Miss Le Neve".[30]

Florence retailed this, and other stories of Emma's eccentricity, to Edward Clodd, who had become yet another of her elderly admirers— he was exactly the same age as Hardy. She phrased her comments in an amused and half-sympathetic way, and in fact, in later conversations with Irene Cooper Willis, she said her early impressions were that Hardy was somewhat unfair to his wife. There was not at this time any of the darker suggestions she came to make continually that Emma was "mad".[31] Nor did she, at this time, ever suggest that Emma came, as Florence put it, "from tainted stock".[32] These seem to have grown through the years, for two reasons. One was to protect Hardy from thinking that Emma had any justification for jealousy against him, by suggesting that these suspicions by Emma were "delusions". The second was her natural reaction to meeting, yet again, by what seemed a gratuitous irony, a situation in which the man she loved had a wife he could not display in public. With Sir Thornley Stoker, the wife was sufficiently *non compos* to be hidden away in the confines of Ely House in Dublin. Just when Florence was laughing at Emma's Crippen fancies, Lady Stoker died; but, worn by the stress of his many years of attempting to conceal her, Stoker himself was beginning to succumb to a fatal disease. Florence might well feel her path was haunted by madwomen, though she had been fond of Lady Stoker, and still liked Emma. In point of fact, Emma would not need to be at all eccentric to make inferences about Hardy's "secretary". In the study at Max Gate, from which Emma was totally excluded, "my secretary", as Hardy called Florence, described how she herself "ramped around", and flippantly criticized phrases in Hardy's poem about "the study cat", Kitsy, which he had just buried.[33] Yet Emma "instead of cooling towards me . . . grows more and more affectionate".

Florence had happy experiences with Mary, Kate, and Henry Hardy, to whom she was introduced this autumn at the Bockhampton cottage, which enchanted her. Returning home for a few days she sent them all postcards of Enfield, apologizing for its dreariness compared with their beautiful surroundings.[34] Hardy now took the step, in December 1910, of introducing her to Florence Henniker as a secretary-help.

The two women, from such different backgrounds, struck up an instant friendship, and Florence was at Mrs. Henniker's house for weeks on end. Mrs. Henniker almost at once wrote a short story about "a modern, emancipated young woman of cities"—Florence—who was, in Hardy's words now, "by far the most interesting type of femininity the world provides for men's eyes".[35]

The "most interesting type of femininity" did not appear at Max Gate so frequently in 1911. Instead, Hardy was more often found with her in London, in spite of his fear of the climate. He came up in mid-winter, and the end of January 1911, and, as Florence wrote, half-satirically, he "has a sore throat because I make him talk in the London streets and then the germs attack him".[36] Most of 1911 was for the Max Gate trio predominantly a year of literary productions, often of a curious and roundabout kind. Hardy's own primary task was a straight-forward one. Macmillan & Co., had become his publishers in 1902, on the expiry of his agreements with Osgood, McIlvain & Co., and Harper & Brothers, reprinting from the former's plates. Now Frederick Mac-millan wished to produce, the following year, in 1912, a new and definitive edition of verse and novels, the Wessex Edition. Hardy's first task was to write a "General Preface to the Novels and Poems", which he completed in October 1911 and which he worked over heavily in the revise proof.[37] It contains his most positive claim to the kinship of his novels to Greek tragedy, even comparing "Wessex" in actual physical size with Attica. As for poetry—"the more individual part of my literary fruitage"—he claimed it was less "circumscribed" than his prose. As if to emphasize this claim, in April 1911 he had printed in the *Fortnightly Review* twelve of the fifteen mordant little short stories in verse he had written the previous year, *Satires of Circumstance*. These were founded on notes made twenty years before, "and then found were more fit for verse than prose".[38]

Other literary doings were less straightforward. In October 1911, Hodder and Stoughton published a book of animal pictures in colour by the young artist E. J. Detmold, intended for children and called *The Book of Baby Beasts*. The pictures had "Descriptions by Florence E. Dugdale", in verse and prose. One poem, *The Calf*, though unsigned, was entirely by Hardy,[39] and is characteristic of him. Another, much neater and more rhythmic than Florence's inept verses, is *The Kitten*. He did more, however, this year than write verses for his "young friend". His January visit to London had been to see the editor of the *Cornhill*; for in the February number there appeared a 3000-word factual story, *Blue Jimmy: The Horse Stealer*, signed F. E. Dugdale. There is no doubt that every word of this story is Hardy's. In style, it is unlike her previous *Cornhill* story, *The Apotheosis of the Minx*, though that itself had shown Hardy's hand in plot and minor detail. It is still more unlike a short article for the *Evening Standard* Florence had recently written on Hardy's seventieth birthday.[40] It is in every way like Hardy in style, and the proof copy is corrected and expanded entirely in Hardy's own hand.[41]

It was Hardy's fate always to be involved with literary ladies; but he had never before passed off his own original work publicly as theirs. One must wonder what Florence felt about such manœuvres. Was her literary ambition greater than her literary pride? Had they made some compact that he would now do everything to launch her? Long after, she wrote in a diary[42] that she remembered Christmas Day 1910 most especially; it may have marked some new stage in their relationship. Certainly the efforts he made for Florence in 1911 were more than he ever made for his wife. Emma had to strike out unaided on her own account. In the previous year, she had disinterred her early story, *The Maid on the Shore*, and asked Florence to type it. Faced with the necessity of saying something about it, Florence did her best[43]—"I do quite *honestly* admire the story. There is a certain charm . . ." Perhaps encouraged, Emma in the quiet isolation of her attic boudoir filled the pages of an exercise book with what she called "Some Recollections". This was an account of her childhood, youth, and family life before her marriage to Hardy, and by the time she had finished, on 4 January 1911, it ran to 15,000 words. It has, without any doubt at all, "a certain charm"; moreover, there is no doubt it is all her own work. Even with the breathless punctuation, spelling, and grammar, it has distinct flashes of real poetic observation and expression; though it had to wait exactly fifty years for publication, it can be read with delight, perhaps most of all for its evocations of the wild North Cornish coast where she had first met Hardy. Nor was this Emma's only bid for literary fame. In December 1911, she persuaded the local publisher-printer, Longman's of Dorchester, to produce her collection of the poems which she had written since 1900. The tiny pamphlet of fifteen poems, enigmatically entitled *Alleys*, concluded with her latest, a rousing antiphon shared by India and Great Britain, *God Save Our Emperor King*.[44] At the same time, she could write a cheerful letter to a relative, making light of the encroachments of age on her and Thomas—"We have both got old, but feel young still."[45]

Yet in spite of such defiant gestures, all was far from well with Emma. Late in 1911, she engaged a fourteen-year-old school-leaver from Piddlehinton to be her personal help.[46] This girl, Dolly Gale, was to carry breakfast and lunch up to Emma's boudoir on the third floor, brush her hair, and be available for help, day or night. She soon found that Emma was in almost constant pain; one of Dolly Gale's chief duties was to massage Emma's back. Gall-stones, or hepatic colic, is characterized by sudden, acute spasms of pain, which radiate over the abdomen and into the back. These may persist for days on end, and a contemporary textbook description of the pain is "agonizing", so extreme that morphia or chloroform were often prescribed.[47] Successful surgery was technically just possible by 1912, but Emma (and Hardy) had a horror of "the Knife". It may seem incredible that Hardy never now, nor at any time, admitted that his wife was in such agony, in the same house. It is true, they only met at dinner, and then did not speak; but now, every Sunday, Trevis the gardener had to push her to St. George's church, Fordington, in a newly-bought bath-chair, which was parked during the service in the Vicarage garden.[48] This was her regular "journey of one day a week" mentioned by Hardy in a later poem. Hardy was, of course, often away from home; on more than one occasion, to "run down" to Aldeburgh "with my young friend", whom he now called "Dear F.D."[49] When at home, he was immured in the study with the immense "drudgery of 20 vols. of proofs" for the Wessex Edition.

The "comedy" Florence had observed at Max Gate was becoming grim tragedy. There were breaks in the darkness. On 24 April, Hardy wrote one of the finest poems he ever composed for a public occasion, his lines on the *Titanic* disaster, *The Convergence of the Twain*, included in a programme of performances for the Disaster Fund in May. On his birthday, 2 June, Newbolt and W. B. Yeats came to Max Gate to present Hardy with the Gold Medal of the Royal Society of Literature; on a sunny day in mid-July, Emma managed to give a garden-party, and nine days later, she took the girls of the parish sewing-guild on an outing to Osmington Mills beach, planning the expedition with entire competence in making all the arrangements for the children. They even took Lilian Gifford, who was with them on a short stay, to a performance at Weymouth of the new comedy, *Bunty Pulls the Strings*. Winter began to close in like a doom upon the household. On a dark day in November, both Hardy and his wife wrote a poem. Hers was pathetic and brief.

> Oh! would I were a dancing child,
> Oh! would I were again
> Dancing in the grass of Spring
> Dancing in the rain

> Leaping with the birds on wing
> Singing with the birds that sing.[50]

Did this now non-speaking couple somehow communicate? For Hardy's poem, far longer and ultimately one of his finest, is permeated with bird-imagery too. *The Bird-Catcher's Boy*, written now, was heavily revised by Hardy a dozen years later for his collection, *Human Shows, Far Phantasies*. These revisions were purely technical and poetic. The poem was originally written in alternate rhyming and non-rhyming lines: Hardy's skilful feat was to make all the lines rhyme, and this revision greatly improved the poem. Yet its story was identical in both versions. The boy, son of a dealer in caged wild birds, protests at his father's inhuman trade. The father orders him roughly to bed. As he climbs the stairs, he runs his fingers along the wires of the bird-cages. That night, he runs away. His father and mother, heart-broken and remorseful, leave the door always unlocked. One night, they again hear his fingers on the cage-wires. They rush to his room. It is still empty. The same night, the body of a ship's boy is washed ashore on the Dorset coast.

Does this haunting poem symbolize Emma's nightly footfall to her attic boudoir after her silent dinners with Hardy? Did he, the husband, unconsciously project his indifference to her feelings, and anticipate his remorse, in the father's roughness? Everybody noticed Emma's almost magical powers with the birds she observed so tenderly from her attic windows. When she called, every kind of bird came fluttering to her, flocking about her, as if she could speak their language, companioning her in their own.[51] This strange, tragic poem is perhaps an allegory of Emma's life and death. It certainly mirrors what Hardy may have felt as he heard her dragging, pain-ridden climb up the stairs each night at Max Gate, when he describes the boy in the poem: how

> . . . without a word
> Bedwise he fares;
> Groping his way is heard
> Seek the dark stairs
>
> Through the long passage, where
> Hang the caged choirs:
> Harp-like his fingers there
> Sweep on the wires . . . .
>
> Hopping there long anon
> Still the birds hung
> Like those in Babylon
> Captive they sung.

9 Hardy and Edward Clodd on the beach at Aldeburgh, circa 1909

10 Hardy and Florence Dugdale on the beach at Aldeburgh, circa 1909

11 Emma on the beach at Worthing with Florence standing behind, circa 1911

12 Florence Dugdale sketched at Max Gate by William Strang, 26 September 1910

13   Gertrude Bugler as Eustacia Vye in *The Return of the Native*, 1920

14 Hardy, Florence, and "Wessex" in Dorchester, 29 October 1924, three
weeks after Florence's return from her operation

15 Cast of the Hardy Players in *Tess of the D'Urbervilles* at Weymouth, 11 December 1924 (*seated left to right*) Gertrude Bugler, Hardy, the Mayor of Weymouth, Florence, the Mayoress of Weymouth

CHAPITRE I

BIOGRAPHIE

Le nom de Thomas Hardy s'est irrévocablement attaché à une seule contrée de l'Angleterre, à cette partie du sud-ouest qui s'étend de la Tamise jusqu'à la mer, du Devonshire à l'ouest jusqu'au Hampshire à l'est, et qui composait jadis le royaume saxon du Wessex. S'imaginer, cependant, avec certains critiques, que son œuvre est seulement le roman de son pays, ce serait par trop la restreindre ; son œuvre, comme celle de tout romancier digne du nom, est une représentation artistique de la vie en général. Le génie de M. Hardy le pousse même vers les plus grands thèmes dramatiques. Émule moderne des tragiques grecs et des dramaturges anglais de l'époque élisabethenne, il cherche à présenter les vieux problèmes " enrichis de vérités nouvelles. " [1] Mais les types qui doivent vivre ces problèmes, comme la scène où ils doivent jouer leur rôle, il les trouve dans la région qu'il connaît le mieux ; là, il est chez lui, il sait interpréter le visage de la nature et l'âme des hommes ; là, il juge sans erreur et, avec les matériaux qu'il recueille, sait nous construire tout un monde en raccourci.

Aussi, pour celui qui a lu les romans de M. Hardy, penser à lui, c'est penser d'abord au Dorsetshire, aux arides étendues de bruyère, aux petites vallées où broutent des troupeaux de vaches, et aux riches vergers où les pommiers laissent

---

[1] Voir *New Review*, Avril 1890 : " *Candour in English Fiction.* "

12

A Satire of Circumstance

EVENTS now moved with horrible swiftness. On 23 November, Emma felt seriously unwell. On the next day, her birthday, she was deeply depressed. On 25 November, there came an event as macabre as any of Hardy's own short stories, or indeed any one of the *Satires of Circumstance* poems he had recently printed. Unannounced, Rebekah Owen, Hardy's egregious elderly American admirer, arrived with her sister from the Lake District. Since they had come from so far, Emma dragged herself downstairs to give the ladies tea. She was obviously very ill, weeping, and in great pain, fearing an operation, and speaking of her dread of "the Knife". Anyone with less of a rhinoceros hide than Miss Owen would have gone away. She refused to budge, intent on seeing her idol, Hardy, ensconced all this time in his study with the Wessex Edition. She seemed to regard Emma's acute physical distress as evidence of mental disturbance, and demanded to see Hardy. When Emma demurred, Miss Owen herself told the maid, Florence Griffin, to go and fetch Hardy. He came, was charming to his flatterers, apparently oblivious to his wife's sufferings, which she cannot possibly have concealed. When the Americans at last left, she went to bed where she stayed all the following day. In the evening of 26 November Hardy went to a dress rehearsal of a stage version of *The Trumpet-Major*. which the Hardy Players were about to present in Dorchester.

The morning after, Emma's little personal maid, Dolly Gale, went to her mistress's boudoir at 8 o'clock. She found her moaning, in great pain, terribly ill and drawn, asking to see Hardy. Dolly Gale rushed to his study with the news. Whether from shock, or from habitual indifference. Hardy stared coldly at the girl, and remarking, "Your collar is crooked", paused to straighten his papers, before going. When he saw how ill Emma was, he was at last shaken. "Em, Em, don't you know me!" he cried. She was too far gone to answer him; her heart, overstrained by months of pain, was failing, and in five minutes she was dead. The little maid stood at the end of the bed, and saw Emma die with Thomas bending over her. It was the first time she had seen death.

This could not be said of Hardy; and the question remains how he could possibly have ignored Emma's sufferings over so long a period. To everyone, he pretended that her death was sudden and unexpected. He softened every aspect of it in the autobiography he wrote a few years

149

later, and excused himself. Even at the time he wrote to Mrs. Henniker, "Emma's death was absolutely unexpected by me, the doctor, and everybody . . . I have reproached myself for not having guessed there might be some internal mischief at work." Yet Dr. Gowring, who had just succeeded Dr. Fisher, signed the death-certificate, without a post-mortem or any apparent hesitation, giving the primary cause of death as impacted gall-stones. Dolly Gale had seen her sufferings for a year. To Rebekah Owen, Emma had spoken of "the Knife", implying that an operation had at least been discussed. The terrible conclusion is that Hardy shut his own eyes to his wife's state, and tried to shut the eyes of others after her death.

One of his very first actions was to send a telegram to Florence Dugdale, who was on her way to attend the performance of *The Trumpet-Major*, from whose stage in Dorchester Emma's death was announced that evening. Within a month she was installed at Max Gate. Dorchester buzzed with gossip. At first the locals thought Hardy would marry his housekeeper-maid, Florence Griffin, but some trial of strength soon took place between the two Florences, and Miss Griffin left. From mid-December to mid-January Emma's niece Lilian made an abortive stay, during which she told Florence that Hardy would never have been a great writer without her aunt. Florence also got rid of her, "Mrs. Hardy in little", as she wrote to Clodd,[1] though not for long. This miniature Emma was to return and subject Florence to the sort of social snubbing, to which she was most sensitive—"I am—so she implies—quite a low sort of person."[2] Florence herself, in fact, fled for a little relief to Enfield, where she had persuaded Edward Clodd to come down and give a lecture to her local literary society. While she was briefly away from Max Gate, she received letters from Hardy, couched in unmistak-able terms. "If I once get you here again", he wrote, "won't I clutch you tight."[3] Of course, this need not mean they were sleeping together, though the maids at Max Gate had no doubt they were.[4] Even more to the point, Hardy had determined, whether or not he slept with her in life, to sleep with her in death. He had taken her on his favourite pilgrimage to Stinsford churchyard, where Emma now lay beside his father and mother. There he would eventually lie himself, and wrote Florence, "a corner, I am told, will be reserved for me".[5] He had, in his mind, already married her in the place most real to him, the grave. Dorchester, of course, had already bedded them, in every sense. Before she arrived, there had been rumours of a mistress in London. Now the tongues were wagging. Florence reported Hardy's warning that[6] "if I am seen walking about in Dorchester with him, or even if it is known I am staying at Max Gate, they will comment unpleasantly".

It was indeed a baptism of fire for the young woman. On the day of Emma's death, she afterwards wrote, she passed from youth "to dreary middle-age". This was an exaggeration; but what cannot be exaggerated is her pitying horror at Hardy's attitude to his late wife. She confessed to Irene Cooper Willis that his instant veneration of the dead woman was a deep shock to her. Though she could say in March, "I have never before realized the depth of his affection and unselfishness as I have done these last three months", his behaviour amazed her.[7] He had found, as well as Emma's "Some Recollections", the twenty years of diary-entries, which were supposedly called "What I think of my Husband"; yet he put down Emma's abuse as "sheer hallucination",[8] and his virtual worship of her memory went on "side by side with the reading of those diabolical diaries", so Florence incredulously wrote.[9] Indeed, he clutched at any sign of Emma's "hallucinations", encouraged by Florence, to save himself from admitting that the diaries represented Emma's real feelings. He had some corroborative evidence for this comforting theory. Shortly before her death, Emma had followed her pamphlet of poems by printing with Longman's of Dorchester an apocalyptic prose vision called *Spaces*, which she had first submitted to Charles Moule, now President of Corpus Christi College. The tactful Cambridge don had advised against publication, on the grounds that the world was not yet ready for Emma's message.[10] However, she ignored his advice, and this remarkable document had appeared over her name. Though Hardy, by January 1913, was actually finding justification, in retrospect, for Emma's extreme evangelical views, and causing these to "weigh heavily on my shoulders", as Florence wrote despondently to Clodd,[11] *Spaces* was too much for him to stomach. It is probably the cause of his writing to both Mrs. Henniker and to Emma's cousin about Emma's recent "delusions".[12] It has certainly all the marks of mild religious mania. Such mental states often attach themselves to whatever is the latest scientific invention. In the 1920s, people with a degree of religious dottiness thought they were receiving divine or demonic messages through wireless waves, just as in the nineteenth century they had similar obsessions about domestic gas.[13] Emma's imagery shows a fixation on the fairly recent phenomenon of electric light. In her description of the Day of Judgement

> Peoples of the world everywhere will prostrate themselves, the electric lights of the world will shine forth again, not *lit* by mortal hands which will have failed to set them aglow . . . They will gleam and burn fiercely with an awful intensity toward their final burning up of the earth . . .

There are other passages, even more extravagant. We may not, however, be as ready as Hardy to put this down to deep-seated hallucination. The jaundice, which frequently supervenes in cases of acute gall-stone trouble, can cause severe delusion, while the standard treatment by morphia might well result in opium dreams, of which poor Emma's "vision" is a not unusual example. Moreover, the contemporary novels by Marie Corelli, of whose work Emma was a reader, though not a whole-hearted admirer,[14] provide almost exact parallels, in style, punctuation, and rhythm: for example,

> Not long now shall we wait for the Divine Pronouncement of the End. Hints of it are in the air—signs and portents of it are about us in our almost terrific discoveries of the invisible forces of Light and Sound.[15]

However oddly expressed Emma's religious visions may seem, one must set against any suggestion of her insanity the businesslike, rational, and practical letters she wrote to the Vicar of Fordington, only a few months before her death, about religious and parish matters.

The swiftest and most striking effect of Emma's death upon Hardy was the sequence of poems he immediately began to write about her. These poems, beginning in December 1912, and actually numbering over fifty in the next two years, have been exhaustively examined by critics. Some of the most austere commentators have judged a few of them to be among the best, or perhaps the only, front-rank poems that Hardy ever wrote.[16] In them, his personal voice is most clear, the emotion most intimately welded to an amazing variety of forms. They seem a totally intimate confession; he himself called them "an expiation"; for most, though not all, are expressions of deep remorse. Yet their full meaning has never been examined, since the circumstances of his last years with Emma have never been fully understood or appreciated. Indeed, on the face of it the remorse, the need for expiation, might well seem a little far-fetched. Hardy's almost necrophiliac habit of loving the dead woman better than the living might seem exaggerated. Yet his guilt was indeed more frightful and more deep than he dared describe in these poems. All he confesses to is a neglect and indifference, of which many husbands could reproach themselves. He has hardly spoken to her, taken little interest in her doings or wishes, has failed to give her holidays in her favourite places, neglected his old loving habits. All this is most movingly expressed at the end of what is perhaps the earliest and best in this series of poems, *The Going*.

> Why, then, latterly did we not speak,
> Did we not think of those days long dead,
> And ere your vanishing strive to seek
> That time's renewal? We might have said
>   'In this bright spring weather
>   We'll visit together
> Those places that once we visited.'
>
> Well, well! All's past amend,
> Unchangeable. It must go.
> I seem but a dead man held on end

To sink down soon . . . O you could not know
That such swift fleeing
No soul foreseeing—
Not even I—would undo me so.

In these stanzas, he reproaches himself for their silent dinner-meetings, for having let love fade, for not taking Emma back to her beloved Devon—though, indeed, a cancelled passage in his autobiography shows they had recently planned an expedition to the West Country.[17] Yet this catalogue of relatively small omissions of sympathy and understanding hardly seems to justify the depth of guilt in the final stanza. For of course the whole truth is not revealed in this apparently all-revealing poem, and its fellows. His full guilt was too horrible to face. He had seen her suffer for months the utmost physical agony, had deliberately turned his eyes away, and pretended not to notice; he even feigned surprise, and underlined with continual guilty insistence the suddenness and unexpectedness of her death, "such swift fleeing". He must now have realized that he had only been able to do this by devoting, for the past five years, all his best care, tenderness, and consideration to another, much younger woman. All this explains the profound remorse which gives these remarkable poems their secret, unspoken intensity and painful inward passion.

They were surely supremely painful also to Florence Dugdale. She was caught up in a situation of guilty connivance. Her extreme sensitivity over gossip about herself and Hardy was noticed by everyone and lasted to the end of her life; she thought biographers "hoped to find something to make into a scandal".[18] His obsession with the dead Emma did not yet check his solicitous concern for Florence. In fact, it was now extended openly to other members of her family. On 4 January 1913, he printed in *The Sphere* the early version of the poem *The Bird-Catcher's Boy*. It had a decorative border designed and signed "C. T. Dugdale"—that is, Constance Taylor Dugdale, Florence's younger sister, art teacher and afterwards headmistress of Enfield Girls School.[19] Yet the spate of poems about Emma was a blow to Florence. She had herself received only a handful of poems in the past five years, the early *On the Departure Platform*, the poem about her at Max Gate, *After the Visit*, and the highly-charged *Had You Wept*, but not much more. These certainly spoke movingly of what seemed their hopeless love. *After the Visit* originally had ended by questioning

what sad strange laws
Made us crave that which could not be!

—that is, the fulfilment of their love while Emma was still alive. Now that Emma was gone, Florence found these wistful, delicate tributes to herself swamped by a succession of passionate poems to the dead woman. Within a month, in December 1912, Hardy had written at least half-a-dozen, *The Going, Your Last Drive, I found her out there, The Prospect, The Voice,* and *The Last Performance.* In January and February, his tone to the dead Emma became even more tender. Though still fingering over in fascinated horror her "diabolical diaries", he was now also reading Emma's artless and evocative "Some Recollections" of her life up to their marriage, including their romantic courtship. On the last day of January, he wrote the poem, *Rain on a Grave,* recalling her love of daisies, mentioned in these recollections. He recalled in *The Change* incidents of their first meeting in Cornwall, and continued the poem to include Emma's arrival in London for their marriage. By the end of February, he had decided to go and visit the places of her upbringing and of their falling-in-love, Plymouth and North Cornwall, a decision embodied in the poem, *A Dream or No.* He wished to be at St. Juliot by 7 March, the exact day he had first met Emma there.

He did not propose to take Florence, nor could she have stood it. His companion was brother Henry, who had been a tower of strength ever since Emma's death; it was even he, not Thomas, who had informed the Registrar of Deaths. Florence was left behind in gloomy cold Max Gate, its walls discoloured with great patches of damp.[20] Isolated and dark, behind its forest of Austrian pines, the house provided a nerve-racking experience for her. She slept with a loaded revolver in her bedroom, and thoughts of Hardy's obsessed expedition for company. Luckily, she had support from his sisters. Mary, as usual, was sympathetic though reticent. Kate, brisk and bluff, blew away the cobwebs of Thomas's pilgrimage. On his stay in Emma's birthplace at Plymouth, she remarked to Florence, "so long as he doesn't pick up another Gifford there, no harm will be done".[21] To his family, who had just moved from the cottage to Talbothays, Henry's new-built house at nearby West Stafford, Hardy had been moaning that "The girl he married died 20 years ago"—that is, at the time of their deep estrangement in the early 1890s. Kate (and the Hardys), who had no cause to love Emma, maintained to Florence "*that* girl never existed". Though Florence herself added, in fairness, "but she did exist to him no doubt", she was heartened, sitting in dark Max Gate with Emma's glaring portrait for sole company, by the forthright attacks of the family on her dead and now all-powerful rival.[22] She permitted herself some sarcasms about Emma and the Gifford family, and was cheered by Kate saying that Hardy "now has his youthful happy laugh".

Meanwhile, Hardy was in Plymouth and St. Juliot, following the track of Emma's "Some Recollections", and inspired as he had never been before. Poems poured from him, at Plymouth *Places* and *The West-of-Wessex Girl,* in Cornwall *After a Journey, Beeny Cliff, At Castle Boterel, The Phantom Horsewoman, St. Launce's Revisited, Looking at a*

Picture on an Anniversary, Under the Waterfall. Many use phrases, incidents, scenes, taken directly from Emma's own written recollections, which he must have carried with him, so close are the likenesses.[23] All tell very much the same tale.

> Summer gave us sweets, but autumn wrought division?
> Things were not lastly as firstly well
> > With us twain, you tell.
> But all's closed now, despite Time's derision . . .

He was creating a myth of their life, and writing out of himself the nagging guilt of reality.

Florence, having to live with the reality, naturally could not stand much more at Max Gate, in spite of the sympathy of the sisters, and, on his return with Hardy, that of Henry, whom she always loved—"true, strong and generous in every thought and deed—Giles Winterborne in the flesh".[24] To relieve her, Hardy took her in April to Mrs. Henniker, who had a house at Southwold in Suffolk. Florence had spent much of the previous year working for Mrs. Henniker on a memorial volume for her husband, the General, who had died on 6 February 1912, and to whose memory Hardy had contributed a poem. Florence felt herself fully at home with the older woman. She and Edward Clodd were among the few who were allowed to know of her existence and her connection with Hardy. "I told her every detail of my life and she entered into it as a sister."[25] After months of gloom, she enjoyed the bustle, the coming and going of distinguished guests at Mrs. Henniker's, who like her father before her, was a prolific entertainer. The sea air revived her.

A revival for Hardy himself at this time, after the ordeals of remorse and retrospective composition, was the offer of a high academic honour. In the middle of April, he was asked to accept the award of an honorary Litt.D. by the University of Cambridge, and on 25 April this was followed by an invitation to become an Honorary Fellow of Magdalene College. The degree, which he went to take at Cambridge early in June, particularly delighted him. He lunched with A. C. Benson, Vice Chancellor elect and Master of Magdalene. To senior members of the university, the self-taught Hardy seemed an intriguing mixture of an old countryman and a pass degree man, with his notebook interest in architecture and literary associations, In his autobiography, a few years later, Hardy claimed that he could have taken a pass degree in the 1860s, but was deterred "mainly owing to his discovery that he could not conscientiously carry out his idea of taking Orders".[26] An unpublished letter of 1866 to his sister Mary, however, gives the reason as being the long time which would have been wasted in complying with the University regulations,[27] studied in a handbook lent him by Horace Moule.

Cambridge in June was full of memories of Horace Moule, the tragic friend whom Hardy had seen for the last time there exactly forty years earlier, a few months before Moule cut his throat in his room in Queens'. The strongest reminder of this man who meant so much to Hardy came, however, from an unexpected source. On 12 June, Hardy's sister Mary, habitually so self-effacing that she would never uncover the slightest hint of emotion, wrote him a letter about the honorary doctorate. It began in what was, for her, a startling manner.[28]

> This is to congratulate you on the honour Cambridge has now conferred on you. It seems as if it came from that dear soul, whose dust, for so many years has been lying in Fordington Churchyard. I came unexpectedly upon an old letter of his yesterday . . .

Hardy himself had described Moule's grave in Fordington churchyard in a poem of deep-felt emotion, *Before My Friend Arrived*, but, with Mary, usually so silent that she would never dream of speaking about any personal matter, the words about Moule are a revelation of the deepest feeling. They strongly suggest—as does the fact that she had kept a letter of his for over forty years—that this withdrawn girl, the model for the hero's sister in *The Hand of Ethelberta* and for Elizabeth-Jane in *The Mayor of Casterbridge*, had been in love with Moule, without perhaps his even being aware of it. If so—and her words make it highly likely—his ruined life and fearful death were her tragedy as well as Hardy's, and had heightened her brother's sense of the universal irony of events.

The final twist to Moule's real-life disaster was that he had been persuaded he was the father of a bastard boy, born to a girl in the lowest quarter of his father's parish of Fordington. This was known to Florence, who could only have learnt it from Hardy. Within a month or so of his sister's reminder about Moule, Hardy wrote a powerful poem which seems based on this story. *The Place on the Map* was printed in the September 1913 number of the *English Review*. This was the magazine which had published Hardy's poem about village abortion, *A Sunday Morning Tragedy*, and which Hardy felt was enlightened enough for narrative poems on frankly sexual topics. The poem is subtitled "A Poor Schoolmaster's Story", and is told in the first person by the schoolmaster.[29] In the schoolroom, he looks at a map showing "a jutting height/Coloured purple, with a margin of blue sea". It is a headland where in "latter summer", he and a girl had walked (or in the manuscript "rode") after having loved there for "weeks and weeks" of "beaming blue, which had lost the art of raining". She tells him she will have a baby—"the thing we found we had to face before the next year's prime". This, which

in realms of reason would have joyed our double soul

Wore a torrid tragic light
Under superstition's hideous control.

Hardy had recently been writing a whole series of poems, in some of which he actually made the speaker of the poem not himself but Emma —for example, *Under the Waterfall, Lost Love,* and *The Haunter.* Now, faced with a reminder of an intense relationship forty or fifty years back, he makes Moule speak in this poem. By a climatic freak, the "latter summer" with "weeks and weeks" of unbroken blue sky late in the season can be dated. For some unexplained reason, the year 1865 was the last time for nearly fifty years that there had been such an abnormal late dry season, remarked on by Hardy in the poem, "hot and dry, Ay, even the waves seemed drying". In September 1865, the rainfall at Weymouth was nil. *The Times* commented on the "extraordinary weather", during which "the sun shone with unmitigated splendour" with temperatures often in the eighties. "The Place" of the poem seems certainly to have been Portland Bill. In Hardy's manuscript, he arranged for it to be followed by *Where the Picnic Was,* which has been plausibly shown[30] to be at a spot on the Ridgeway, overlooking Portland, and in 1914 and again in 1919, he printed the two in conjunction in this way. In 1865, Horace Moule was a schoolmaster; one of seven brothers in a clergy family, ill-paid for his literary journalism, and spending his money on drunken bouts, he was always poor. The bastard child was the crowning blow of his ill-fated life. There seems little doubt that Hardy, painfully recalled to memories of Moule this summer, gave his story in this poem.

Moule also came into Hardy's mind when, in August, he put together "a dozen minor novels", short stories which had never been reprinted, in a volume called *A Changed Man;* for the title story was largely based on the part played in the Dorchester cholera epidemic by Moule's father, which had made him the hero of Fordington. Further, when Hardy in November returned to Cambridge to be installed as Fellow of Magdalene, he revisited the President of Corpus, Charlie Moule, who had actually been in the next room when Horace Moule cut his throat. In the story of *The Changed Man,* the story-telling onlooker, Hardy himself, composes a little uncharacteristic poem about swift and impulsive marriage leading to apparent happiness, though there is a studied ambiguity about the poem, an ingenious exercise in triolet form, called *At a Hasty Wedding.* The question of his own remarriage was now coming up.

What were the thoughts of Thomas and Florence on this subject, at this time? He was still obsessed by Emma and the careless cruelty he had shown her. "I wounded one . . . and now know well I wounded her." Yet criticism, fostered by Florence, Henry, and Kate, was creeping in.

"But, ah, she does not know that she wounded me." The poem, *She Charged Me*, is a chilling indictment of Emma's bullying manner. Besides, the death in September of his childhood sweetheart, Louisa Harding, made him realize that all dead women shared a mysterious attraction for him, though Emma was still "the elect one". The brooding shadow of Emma's ghost between him and Florence was beginning to disperse. For Florence, he still felt some of the tenderness he had shown a few years before. She wrote[31] of his "tender protective affection for me—as a father for a child—a feeling quite apart from passion". She rated it, rather sadly, as something other than love. "He wanted a housekeeper who could be a companion and read to him—etc.—so I came in."[32] Colouring every feeling was the great theme of all his poetry now, that he would anyway die soon. On his seventy-third birthday, he wrote *Exeunt Omnes*, ending

> Folk all fade. And whither
> As I wait alone where the fair was?
> Into the clammy and numbing night-fog
> Whence they entered hither.
> Soon one more goes thither!

Florence's emotions were more complex. She had spent a searing year at Max Gate, where "Life under the conditions that have prevailed for the last twelve months" could no longer be endured by her.[33] Loneliness and humiliation had been her lot. To mitigate the first, she now introduced as companion for herself a dog, a fashionable Caesar terrier, the notorious "Wessex"; but there were more intractable elements in the second. Her year's stay there with Hardy had, in the language of the day, totally compromised her. Modern woman as she was—and also she was now nearly thirty-five—she could not still the storm of tongues in Dorchester, nor most probably the pressures of her own family. At her age, and with this history, no one else would now marry her. Her periodic bad health, too, was a terrible liability. Emotionally, her life had already suffered considerable tragedy. Two years before, on 1 June 1912, she had lost Sir Thornley Stoker.[34] Florence's elderly benefactor had been widowed in November 1910,[35] and in the same year he found himself obliged to retire from his post and governorship at the Richmond Hospital in Dublin. At the age of sixty-five, this energetic and busy surgeon had begun to show signs of arterio-sclerosis and cardiac weakness. He sold his unique collection of antique art, the English and Irish silver, the bronzes and oriental porcelains, which had made Ely House a place of pilgrimage for connoisseurs. A year later, failing still more, he instructed his executors to sell his exquisite old furniture, to add to the personal legacies he intended to leave. When he passed away quietly and gradually in the summer of 1912, Florence was one of the chief beneficiaries under his will. She received £2000, twice as much as his brother Bram, and about one-sixth of the residue of the estate.[36] Typically generous, Florence used some of the income from investing Sir Thornley's legacy in a way that he would have approved, in generosity to her own family. She paid with it the fees for her youngest sister Marjorie to go for three years to a domestic science college. One does not know if, after his wife's death, she had hoped to marry Sir Thornley. Bram Stoker's relatives, irritated at the legacy, were convinced she was Sir Thornley's mistress under the guise of employment at Ely House. It is equally likely that she genuinely had been at some time the junior of Lady Stoker's two attendants, the senior being an Irish nurse called Betty Webb, who benefited even more from the will. Miss Webb's character and reputation are known to have been above reproach. Though fond of Sir Thornley, Florence may have been misjudged.

What, then, caused this romantic young woman, who had been so much attached to one of the most attractive figures of the day, to consider marriage with Hardy, who, for all his fame, could not compete in personal charm and generosity of temperament? It was, one must remember, the heyday of the idea, now healthily almost defunct, that a wife should devote herself to serving a great artist or writer, and to protecting him from the encroachments of the outside world, as if he were some delicate or awkward child. Florence agreed with the self-centred Sydney Cockerell's definition of marriage as providing for a woman "the right to express . . . devotion". She felt towards Hardy "as a mother toward a child with whom things have somehow gone wrong".[38] He confessed to her that "he thought he had never grown up".[39] In this relationship, she could renew Jemima Hardy's role, and at the same time, herself receive the protection of a man at least nominally older in years. For a woman so intellectually alert, there was also an element of ambition. She hoped that the coming year, 1914, would see him receive the Nobel Prize for Literature.[40]

Like many deeply-considered and deeply-felt projects, action was precipitated by casual circumstances. The catalyst was Emma's niece, Lilian. Arriving for Christmas and the New Year, treating Hardy as her "daddy-uncle", she tried to take over her dead aunt's place, and manage Max Gate permanently. To Florence, after the past year of "domestic jars & all sorts of complications",[41] this was the last straw. Florence had made a "compact" with Hardy to care for him, eventually as his wife; but "if it is settled that she [Lilian] stays, I return to my own home, and remain there".[42] Henry and Kate Hardy backed her in refusing to tolerate such a "ménage à trois". Lilian went; but Florence now was convinced "that I should have some position of authority at Max Gate".[43] So the decision was taken.

On 10 February 1914, Florence's father, headmaster of St. Andrew's elementary school, Enfield, entered in his logbook,[44] "The Head Master was absent from duty until 10.45 a.m. owing to the marriage of his daughter with Mr. Thos Hardy O.M., D.C.L. etc., the eminent novelist." The ceremony at Enfield Parish Church took place at eight in the morning "in keeping with the retiring disposition of the well-known author". Apart from her father, who gave her away, the only people present were Florence's youngest sister Marjorie and Henry Hardy. After a wedding breakfast with Mrs. Dugdale at 5 River Front, Mr. Dugdale quietly resumed his school duties, while Florence and Hardy took an early train on their way back to Dorchester. An hour after they had left Enfield, twenty-six reporters knocked at Mr. Dugdale's front door.[45] Hardy's caution had been justified.

Congratulations of friends flowed in. The few who knew of Florence's existence were delighted. To some of them, it seemed that Florence "was so exactly one of your women that it seemed as though you had made her",[46] as, in a sense, he had. The many who did not know of her, such as Edmund Gosse, responded to the news with puzzled warmth, asking for introductions to the new unknown. To them, Hardy's descriptions of Florence ranged from "my long-time secretary" to "a literary woman but not a blue-stocking at all".[47] His official announcement, repeated by the Press, was that Florence had been for many years a close friend of his first wife. He emphasized this in his third-person autobiography, written a few years later. Thus Florence Hardy was, from the first, compelled to be party to a deceit. Only after his death did she rebel over this. She crossed out some sentences in the autobiography (to be printed as her biography of her late husband), and the event stands to this day baldly in the laconic sentence, "In February of the year following [1914] the subject of this memoir married the present writer."

For the time, "there is sunshine within Max Gate", Florence wrote.[48] Hardy, more conservatively, hoped that "the union of two rather melancholy temperaments may result in cheerfulness".[49] Florence at once made her presence felt. "We are having a bedroom enlarged, so that, if T.H. feels equal to it, we may have two or three people together, to amuse one another."[50] She saw herself as a hostess, like her friend Mrs. Henniker, Max Gate full of distinguished literary guests. While the workmen were at it, she and Hardy went off to Cambridge. It was her first public and acknowledged appearance with him, and she revelled in the company, the Cockerells, Quiller-Couch, the Mac-Taggarts, and many others, including Charles Moule, now Hardy's most longstanding friend. Yet there were new-found responsibilities. Henry Hardy had a slight stroke in March, and in May Florence had to take his place as Hardy's companion in yet another expedition to the Gifford tombs at Plymouth. "The whole process was melancholy", she wrote, and wished Henry could be there instead of her. In June, a living Gifford took up the irritating reminder. Emma's nephew Gordon, an L.C.C. architect, invited himself to Max Gate. To Florence's indignation, he informed her that Emma had said he should inherit the house on Hardy's death.[51] There were other problems in marriage. Just before Emma died, Florence had produced another set of "descriptions" for the artist Detmold, entitled *The Book of Baby Birds*, once more with unacknowledged verse-contributions by Hardy. Shortly after her marriage, the publisher asked her to do a similar illustrated book about dogs, prompted by the photograph of her and "Wessex", which had appeared in the press. For Hardy's sake, she refused; but she was perturbed. "Ought I—in fairness to my husband—to give up my scribbling? . . . I have a feeling, deep within me, that my husband rather dislikes my being a scribbling woman. Personally", she added, pathetically, "I *love* writing."[52] Happily for her she managed to quiet her conscience towards him, and *The Book of Baby Pets*, with Detmold's pictures, appeared during the following year.

On 4 August, such personal problems were temporarily blotted out by the huge tragedy of Europe. Hardy and she were "both almost paralysed with horror", Hardy regarded it as mankind's final rejection of all hope and sanity. In a month after the outbreak of war, he seemed to age ten years.[53] The horror obsessed him; in addition, he was convinced the Germans would land on the Dorset coast. He could not bear Florence to leave him for a single night. He would not have ended *The Dynasts* on its final brief note of hope had he ever foreseen this. In desperate gloom, he shut himself in his study, revising and working over a new collection of poems. In the twilight days just before war, he had already written his personal epilogue[54] to the volume.

> Whatever the message his to tell,
> Two thoughtful women loved him well.
> Stand and say that amid the dim:
> It will be praise enough for him.

Satires of Circumstance appeared on 17 November. Its title, taken from the group of story-poems printed in the *Fortnightly Review* for April 1911, and new expanded, was his publisher's choice, not Hardy's.[55] He himself had expressed grave doubts about reprinting this sardonic section, since it contrasted so sharply with the new-found tenderness of his more recent poems. "The scales had not fallen from my eyes when I wrote them, and when I reprinted them they had."[56] The Emma poems too caused him doubts. Were they too intimate to publish? He questioned Benson at Magdalene in November 1913, and Gosse as late as 28 June 1914. He knew, though, that they contained some of the finest poetry he had so far written. This finally decided him.

Yet the book as a whole by no means depends on the section "Poems of 1912–13", with its Virgilian motto *Veteris vestigia flammae*—"ashes of an old flame". For one thing, it contains many other poems to and about Emma. It also has poems of great power from Hardy's past work, some previously printed, *Beyond the Last Lamp, The Convergence of the Twain, The Place on the Map, Channel Firing, The Schreckhorn*, others appearing for the first time, *Wessex Heights* and *A Thunderstorm in Town*. The actual *Satires of Circumstance* sequence, does, in fact, as Hardy had feared, clash with many of these other poems, most especially in quality. Some reviewers suggested rightly that they would have made better short stories, as Hardy had originally conceived them.

The quality of most of the rest is remarkable, and in many ways new. It is not only that deep feeling has given Hardy a deeper style of utterance; it is also a matter of technical mastery. One feature is his echo and use of folk-tune for dramatic effect. In *Beyond the Last Lamp*, the monotonous movement of two lovers in the rainy evening is given a haunting dance-like quality by the refrain in mid-stanza "Walking slowly, walking sadly" and its variants. It was a folk-dance memory he was to use later in *Voices from Things Growing in a Churchyard*, where it became "All day cheerily, All night eerily." The lilting rhythm of *The Voice*, which opens, "Woman much missed, how you call to me, call to me", is suddenly and totally broken, as if by a fiddler double-stopping to indicate the approaching finish of the dance, by the last four lines:

> Thus I; faltering forward,
> Leaves around me falling,
> Wind oozing thin through the thorn from norward,
> And the woman calling.

Again and again, Hardy almost lulls one with rhythm, to effect a sudden and dramatic musical break, such as this.

Another remarkable point is the realistic conversational quality. In no less than three very different poems, a piece of scene-setting leads to the story-teller's interjection "Well", followed by a climax. In *The Going*

> Well, well! All's past amend,
> Unchangeable. It must go

The Convergence of the Twain

> Well, while was fashioning
> This creature of cleaving wing,

and in *Wessex Heights*

> Yet my love for her in its fulness she herself even did not know;
> Well, time cures hearts of tenderness, and now I can let her go.

This conversational style, allied often with the utmost metrical and rhythmic ingenuity, is one reason why Hardy commends himself so much as a model to poets in the second half of our century.

The *Satires of Circumstance* volume, one suspects, is the most read and most quoted book of Hardy's poems today. It did not seem particularly notable in its own day. Most of the reviewers were puzzled or at best lukewarm. They seem to have preferred the recent short-story collection, *A Changed Man,* and found most of these poems merely painful and gloomy. This feeling, by what is perhaps the greatest satire of circumstance, was one shared by Hardy's wife, Florence herself.

13

Deaths and Visions

HARDY's book of poems gave Florence great pain. She had put off a full reading in order to rush up to London to Harley Granville-Barker's patriotic adaptation of scenes from *The Dynasts* on 25 November. In spite of having been given an uneatable dinner at Max Gate[1]—Florence always had trouble with her cooks—Granville Barker had done a neat job of stage craftsmanship, and produced a piece in key with the highly emotional feeling of the times. Hardy cynically commented that "the good Barker's abridgement" made the original author seem "as orthodox as a churchwarden"; but it was a huge success, and did much to ensure that, throughout the 1914–18 War, *The Dynasts* became a tract for the times.[2] Henry Ainley spoke the special epilogue, and then led the entire audience at the Kingsway Theatre in speaking in unison the words of God Save the King. Florence was deeply moved (Hardy himself was absent with a cold), and was proud to receive praise from such people as H. G. Wells and John Masefield.[3] Now as she sat poring over her husband's poems, her changeable temperament swung to the other extreme. She seemed to herself an utter failure for her husband to produce "such a *sad, sad* book". She was full of self-blame. Yet her feelings were more complicated. After all, she had accepted apparently with pleasure a much more gloomy collection of poems five years before, *Time's Laughingstocks*, which Edmund Gosse had found to be "poignantly sad". The fact was that *Satires of Circumstance* contained about thirty poems connected with Emma, and only a tenth of that number to herself. This was why she felt she should have been "a different sort of woman".[4] The "crucifixion" that Emma herself had felt in 1898 over Hardy's published poems to so many other women was now repeated in Florence's bitter experience over this book. The poem in which she was bracketed with Emma was not improved, in her eyes, by the two being called "bright-souled" rather than "thoughtful".

Hardy had, as he had told her, never outgrown adolescence. He had, like an adolescent, not the slightest inkling of the pain he was causing. With age, too, his more generous earlier sympathies were hardening. Scrooge-like, he thought that as a social reformer Dickens was "a humbug", only writing for popularity. He privately dismissed the Georgian poets as "The Tibbalds' Row school of rhymeless youngsters". When British and German soldiers fraternized in No Man's Land at

Christmas 1914, Hardy strongly disapproved, and even praised a German lieutenant who stopped his men "hobnobbing".[5] He found "the attitude of Labour" over compulsory conscription "a very ugly one". He said that the mistake of the English over Ireland lay in not "crushing utterly" the 1916 rebellion.[6] Life with him was also hardening Florence. She castigated women who "use him to their own advancement", forgetful that she herself had passed off work written by him as her own. A course of philosophy he gave himself early in the New Year, G. E. Moore and Bergson, did not make him any the more approachable on a human scale, though he admired the latter for his poetical, intuitive, and human side. Florence's physical weaknesses, which once seemed to hold such tender attraction for Hardy, now only exposed her to his intractable temperament. In March she suffered a whole month of sciatica; he would not take her (as he had taken his father) to Bath for a cure because he was absorbed in writing, while he made it clear that if she went alone he would be miserable.[7] In May, her health forced just such a separation. Recurrent nose and throat infections demanded a nasal operation. Hardy strangely dismissed it as "a slight external operation".[8] It was certainly not "external" or "slight"; it put Florence in a London nursing-home for several days, during which he did not visit her, followed by convalescence in Welbeck Street with Mary Jeune.

While Florence was absent, a Hardy family conference took place at Max Gate. It was a peasant discussion about money. Hardy was probably the richest author in England, but he liked to pretend the war might ruin him. "I suppose if the worst came to the worst we would be given a pension", he told Florence. She had asked for a settlement on their marriage, "but it seemed to annoy my husband, so I desisted".[9] He gave her instead a housekeeping allowance so small that she had to rob her own dress allowance, something she hated. Brother Henry and sister Kate, however, were not impressed by Thomas's protestations of poverty. They knew there was money, and were determined it should not go to Florence. It must be left to "a Hardy born". They picked on a remote cousin, descended from Hardy's uncle James, the jobbing mason at Higher Bockhampton.[10] Hardy was not persuaded; but the astounding fact remains that the wealthy author made absolutely no attempt to pay his wife's London surgeon, the nursing-home fees, nor anything to do with her operation. This came out of Florence's own private income and savings, £70 in all, the whole of her annual income from Sir Thornley's legacy, nearly £1000 in modern terms.[11] Six years before, no trouble had been too much for him to protect her health. He had worried continually about her wrapping up at night, had arranged innumerable visits to the seaside, had shown her constant tenderness. There was only one conclusion she could draw. Self-absorbed to a degree she had never anticipated, Hardy clearly no longer loved her in

any real sense. His attitude was like the half-hearted obligatory gestures of consideration he had previously shown towards Emma. He
talked vaguely of taking Florence "to the western coast when she had
got over it, to pick up". In practice, all she got was one night in an
Exeter hotel after a day's long, hot, tiring, and dusty drive along the
Devon coast.[12] Hermann Lea, who now lived in the Bockhampton
cottage, drove them on one or two small local picnic outings but "T.
says he has had enough motoring for the present"[13]—he had to pay
Lea for the petrol.

Though Florence was still painstakingly loyal to him, from this time
onward a note of complaint and criticism enters into much that she
writes about Hardy. In particular, after years of restraint and trying
to be fair, she unloosed her tongue about Emma and the Giffords. She
repeated with relish a story Mary Jeune had told her. Years earlier
Mary had invited Archdeacon Gifford to one of her distinguished
dinner parties, so large that the hostess did not really know everyone
who was there. She asked the Archdeacon to take Mrs. Thomas Hardy
down to dinner, and stirred by subconscious memory had said, "I think
she is a relative of yours." He replied, "Mrs. Thomas Hardy is my niece,
and she is the most horrible woman in the world." Florence commented how "keen and understanding" Mary Jeune was,[14] and added
some ironical news about Emma's nephew, Gordon Gifford. The self-
styled "heir" to Max Gate had blotted his copybook for good by getting
married to a waitress in a teashop. "T. seems very quiet about it."
Wickedly, Florence saw this as a chance to get rid of the oppressive
Gifford property at Max Gate. Why not give Gordon the overpowering
clock, the gloomy furniture, the Gifford family portraits left in the
house by Emma? "I could spare them well enough," she remarked
and hinted so to Hardy. Hardy replied shortly to her teasing that he
himself had paid good money for them to Emma's family, and they
were now his.[15] Florence's sarcasm did not stop there. In summer 1915,
after a year of war, hopes of a quick settlement were over. The long
slog of trench warfare would require huge armies. Voluntary recruiting
would not be enough. Conscription was in the air, though unpopular;
some politicians were suggesting it should be confined to single men.
Florence said that Gordon was marrying his "tea-shop girl" only to
avoid being called up, and her shrewd conjecture was confirmed when
Gordon's sister naïvely let the cat out of the bag. At all events, she
ensured that he was never asked to Max Gate again; yet her open resentment of the Gifford family continued. She maintained that if her
own name were Gifford, Hardy would have provided her with holidays,
more money, new furniture, stays with her mother's relatives in
Brighton, invitations for her own friends and relatives to Max Gate.[16]
The only way to get him to take her anywhere, she wrote, would be if

she promised to go and "hunt up Giffords—and I really cannot stand more of that".[17]

The name Gifford, in fact, was a safety valve for Florence. Resentment directed at her husband would have left her plunged into remorse at criticizing one so old and so distinguished. Yet one criticism, though unspoken to him, was fundamental, and she was quick to define it. "His liking for people seems quite apart from any sense of obligation to them."[18] He would accept hospitality, help, advice, kindnesses from his friends, but feel absolutely no necessity to do anything for them in return. Florence, with her spontaneous if erratic generosity, was pained and embarrassed for them both, but particularly on her own account, since people, she found, suspected she was the cause. As she said, her own instinct would be "to make this a second home for the people I like, and who have been good to me".[19] Instead, she found her husband determined to be increasingly "a recluse", though she might have been warned, since from the moment of her marriage "it was impressed upon me that I must *keep off* people".[20] She had hardly reckoned this would include the affectionate friends of both Hardy and herself.

More happily, there was one subject on which her generous instincts and his inclinations could work together. This was the topic of "the heir" to Max Gate, who would inherit the house and a large number of Hardy's family possessions, and also be "a strong arm" to Hardy in his last years, like an adopted son.[21] They had discussed this ever since they were married, and made plans. This fact, incidentally, disposes of the idea, sometimes debated, that they hoped for any child of their own marriage; and obviously, such an idea[22] had equally never entered into the calculations of either Gordon Gifford or of Hardy's own immediate family. Florence acted tactfully. Realizing that Hardy, like his own relatives, would not tolerate anyone who was not "a Hardy born", she pressed the claims of someone whom Hardy already knew and liked, and who had the right qualification. Frank William George was, on the face of it, only a remote cousin; but he had an impressive array of Hardys in his ancestry. His great-grandfather, John, was a young brother of Hardy's grandfather, Thomas; his grandfather was William Jenkins Hardy, and his mother was Angelina Hardy. All these male Hardys were Puddletown bricklayers and masons, like Hardy's own direct ancestors.[23] Angelina Hardy had married, in 1878, William George, who kept the Royal Oak Inn at Bere Regis. Their son, Frank William George, was born at Bere on 5 December 1880, and was therefore nearly two years younger than Florence. He grew up tall and extremely good-looking. What was more, he managed to enter one of the gentlemanly professions, so all-important to Hardy. He was a barrister and a member of Gray's Inn. He was called to the Bar on 17 November

1913, shortly after Hardy had enlisted his old legal friend, Sir Frederick Pollock, on his behalf. This put him apart from all Hardy's other relatives. Florence had met one of the sons of Nat Sparks, Hardy's carpenter cousin at Bristol. Both Nat's sons, James and Nathaniel junior, were artists of considerable achievement, but to Florence the Sparks cousin she met was "a perfect young cad . . . the sort of man one would not care to have as chauffeur". Her attitudes in such matters were, unfortunately, increasingly those of Hardy, who left out of his family tree everyone who did not have gentlemanly pretensions, or professional qualifications. Frank George seemed to both of them the ideal selection, "the only decent relation". It is fair to say that their dislike of the other relatives was returned in kind by the Sparks cousin, who referred pointedly to Hardy as *"Mr.* Thomas".[24]

The choice of heir was dogged by the Hardyesque irony and fatality that affected all his most cherished concerns. On 22 August 1915, Frank George, who had joined the 5th Dorsetshire Regiment as a second-lieutenant, was killed at Gallipoli. Within only a few more months, disaster again assailed Hardy. His beloved sister Mary, his second self, had suffered lately from her chest. A year before, Dr. Gowring had diagnosed this as asthma.[25] It was a wrong diagnosis, but Gowring, a competent physician, did not deserve the scorn poured on him by Hardy and Florence afterwards.[26] In the early stages, it is often difficult to distinguish asthma, marked by inability to expand the lungs, from its opposite, emphysema, or inability to contract them. Mary died of this on 24 November,[27] her last days painfully distressing as she struggled for breath. Even more distressing, in another way, were the scenes before her funeral. Mary, reticent to the last, failed to make a will, and it was known she had a modest fortune, which Thomas would have to administer.[28] The Hardys were suspicious. To Florence, the shy withdrawn woman had been a "dearest sister". Would Thomas let Florence have some money? How would the estate be shared? Tempers were uncontrolled. To Florence's horror, the cheerful, friendly Henry shouted at his famous brother, Kate was sulky and difficult, and quarrels continued on the day of the funeral itself. Even worse for Florence was the old country custom of continually going into the death-chamber to kiss the corpse. Morbidly conscious of infection, from her own nose and throat troubles, Florence was sickened by this peasant crudity. For the first time, she began to realize some of the difficulties Emma had encountered.[29]

For Hardy, however, his sister's death was a profound and momentous experience. Nearest to him in age, temperament, and tastes, she had been his closest companion all through his life. He regarded their relationship as a spiritual marriage. In the poem *Conjecture*, he spoke of her literally as a third wife.

> If there were in my Kalendar
> No Emma, Florence, Mary,
> What would be my existence now—
> A hermit's? Wanderer's weary?—

Her innocent pride in him had been his greatest inspiration from their earliest days. It was maintained in their old age. In March 1912, she wrote[30] to a relative about the Latin inscription chosen by Hardy for the family memorial at Stinsford,

> I would rather it had been an English inscription and no Latin, and I daresay you would also, but you know how fond Tom is of books and languages and I think he could not feel satisfied unless there was some show of learning in this.

On her scanty holidays, she wrote careful postcards to him about places connected with books and authors.[31] That he and she had, as now seems likely, both loved the same man, Horace Moule, was a double bond. The dead woman seemed present everywhere with him, even at her own funeral service. "As Mr. Cowley read the words of the psalm . . . they reminded me of her nature, particularly when she was young: 'I held my tongue and spoke nothing: I kept silence, yea, even from good words.' That was my poor Mary exactly." Even after ten years, he wrote of her with deep feeling, "She came into the world . . . and went out . . . and the world is just the same . . . not a ripple on the surface left."[32] He was immediately moved to recreate her in poems, just as he still recalled Emma. He wrote of their happy youth, climbing trees together.

> My fellow-climber rises dim
> From her chilly grave—
> Just as she was, her foot near mine on the bending limb,
> Laughing, her young brown hand awave.

He even recalled, in new poems, the ideas of poems he had written to Mary fifty years before. In *The Musing Maiden* (1866) he had imagined her in Dorset, himself in London, both looking at the moon, so that

> Up there our eyesights touch at will

Molly Gone (1916), one of his most beautiful poems, carried the identical thought.

> Thinking thus, there's a many-flamed star in the air
> That tosses a sign.
> That her glance is regarding its face from her home so that there
> Her eyes may have meetings with mine.

Many poems to Mary, written in this effort to revive their past, have been mistaken for poems to Emma. "You were the sort that men forget" is obviously Mary—Emma, for good or ill, was hardly the sort one would forget—and *The Man with a Past*, written shortly after Mary's death, seems a picture of brother and sister.

> Innocent was she,
> Innocent was I,
> Too simple we!

This mysterious poem of menace speaks of three blows "which she dumbly endured". Again, "dumbly" is hardly a credible picture of the voluble Emma, remembered by Hugh Walpole as talking incessantly; but it is a faithful one of Mary.

Mary's death at the end of 1915 signalled a fundamental change in Hardy's life. Not only was he thrown back on the past as he had been at Emma's death three years before; the past now almost wholly absorbed him. His "recluse" element took possession from the beginning of 1916. He retired to his study and shut out the present. It was a self-protective retirement. For one thing, it was becoming impossible for him to think about the progress of the war. "He says he keeps from brooding over present affairs by concentrating his mind on the poems he is writing."[33] Present affairs, in the years 1916–17, were indeed practically unthinkable. The huge slaughter of the Somme in one year, and of Passchendaele in the other, made the war seem mankind's final madness. As a culmination of the general tragedy, Hardy heard on Christmas Eve 1917 that one of his most sympathetic friends, Alda, Lady Hoare, had lost her only son, the heir of Stourhead.[34] Hardy might well live only for the past and for poetry. With some minor exceptions this was the pattern of the dozen years of life that now remained to him. The young poets and writers who shortly began to visit him, Robert Graves, Walter de la Mare, Virginia Woolf, Siegfried Sassoon, recorded their common impressions of the benevolent, ancient, and smiling English Man of Letters, who came down for his tea and twinkled mildly at them. Only Sassoon commented that the real Hardy was not there with them, in a poem of rare insight, called *Max Gate*.

> Old Mr. Hardy, upright in his chair,
> Courteous to visiting acquaintances chatted
> With unaloof alertness while he patted
> The sheepdog whose society he preferred.
> He wore an air of never having heard
> That there was much that needed putting right.
> Hardy, the Wessex wizard, wasn't there.
> Good care was taken to keep him out of sight . . .

Up in Hardy's study, it was a different matter. Not only was his world peopled by his parents, Emma, Mary, Horace Moule, and hosts of others from the past; Hardy was evolving, in poem after poem, a new personal poetic mythology. He rejected, apart from a few sad instances of nostalgia, the Biblical mythology of his youthful verse. He rejected his hard-won classical mythology. He rejected any easy Wordsworthian pantheistic myth-making. His own mythology, private to the outside world, was built upon the lives, events, and associations of those he had known deeply and closely. With a set of personal symbols, he freed his poetry for supreme expression. The key to some of these symbols is lost; many are crystal-clear. The month of March stands for adventure and new life, instead of the poetically-conventional April, because in March he had first met Emma. September stands for fulfilled happiness, since then he married her. November symbolizes disaster and death, being the death-month of both Emma and now Mary. The words "My friend" nearly always symbolize wisdom unable to save or guide itself, though able to guide others, drawn from Horace Moule. The love of his mother's peasant fireside represents a wealth of superstition, which is somehow nearer the truth than either rational thought or religion, as in his poem, *The Oxen*, written shortly after Mary's death, and based on a country legend from their mother, telling how at twelve on Christmas Eve, the oxen knelt in their stalls, and how, in his words,

> So fair a fancy few would weave
> In these years! Yet, I feel,
> If someone said on Christmas Eve,
> "Come; see the oxen kneel

> "In the lonely barton by yonder coomb
> Our childhood used to know,"
> I should go with him in the gloom,
> Hoping it might be so.

With a mythology totally explicable to himself, though not always to others, Hardy could write with a freedom greater than ever before. Often Nature provides symbols, which are connected with places and persons in his life. Sometimes these may be identified, more often not. A sunny stream represents happiness, though often happiness of an impermanent kind, because Hardy's "two years idyll" with Emma was spent overlooking the millstream at Sturminster Newton. We cannot tell the origin of its opposite symbol for unhappiness, a pond on a heath, often reflecting moonlight, always an image of coldness and parting. The flight of a heron from trees beside the pond always means some final loss. We do not need to know or guess what experience with what girl gave Hardy this heartfelt symbol. It is enshrined in his mythology as an image of uttermost despair and deprivation.

The two years, 1916 and 1917, saw Hardy creating poems of intense meaning and feeling through this highly personal mythology. Shut up in his study, he evolved a tender and tragic world from the past. For

Florence, who had to live below in the present, these two years were a terrible experience. In December 1917, she wrote of them, "I have had home worries, of a kind sufficient to break down any woman's nerve, I think", and in the same month, after a rare visit to the theatre to see Barrie's *Dear Brutus*, she did break down and wept uncontrollably.[35] By "home worries',' she meant both her responsibilities at Max Gate, and those connected with the Dugdale family. The first incident was a tragi-comedy of guilty conscience by the Max Gate pair. In January 1916, both still dazed by influenza, Thomas and Florence heard with horror, accompanied by self-centred indignation, that Edward Clodd was going to publish his reminiscences. There was panic at Max Gate, as they thought of their stays together at Aldeburgh before marriage, well before Emma's death. They had considered Clodd "perfectly safe". Now it transpired, "he has been keeping a record of all conversations etc." Florence impulsively wrote one of her furious letters to Clodd, threatening that Thomas would expose him in the Press.[36] What she meant by these threats is not clear, but her letter is unfortunately only the first of a number of examples of her wild fluctuations of personal feeling. Siegfried Sassoon wrote, "She had very little judgment about people, was easily prejudiced."[37] The most striking example is the see-saw of her feelings in this same year, 1916, about Sydney Cockerell. She began by judging Cockerell "a wonderfully fine man".[38] During the year he was a regular visitor, and by October Florence found "a hateful expression" on his face.[39] Yet by 14 December, she wrote, "I want to retract anything I may have said . . . All badness must have been in myself."[40] In this case her fluctuations correspond with the contradictions of Cockerell's own tortuous character, and he himself ungenerously was to dismiss Florence as "an inferior woman with a suburban mind". Yet these rash judgements were more unfortunate when Florence applied them to many other friends, servants, and even relations. On the downswing of a temporary mood, she would not only attack in letters, but would write, in letters to a third party, the most harmful and unjust opinions and stories. Examining Florence's large series of letters to Rebekah Owen, which started in 1913, Beatrix Potter (Mrs. Healis) burnt many of the most indiscreet letters, including "several that seemed positively libellous".[41] Such letters afterwards caused her intense shame, and her correspondence is punctuated with sudden implorings to destroy letters, and even more, to return and forgive letters in which she has attacked the friends or acquaintances to whom she has taken a sudden, unreasoning dislike. Her letter to Clodd naturally blighted one of Hardy's longest and most sympathetic friendships. Clodd, who had largely educated himself, like Hardy, with evening reading, including classes at Birkbeck College, was a real ally, as Thomas and Florence had found. The break not only deprived Hardy of profitable financial advice, which Clodd, a banker, dispensed over his investments. It alienated and disillusioned his friend and exact contemporary, and although Clodd patched the quarrel up in the 1920s, when both were eighty, things were never the same. Clodd, who had a reputation for generosity and loyalty, outlived Hardy by some two years and wrote that he "was a great author: he was not a great man; there was no largeness of soul".[42] The whole exercise was ridiculously unnecessary; when Florence read Clodd's *Memories* later that year, she found it "so *dull*", and in it, in fact, Clodd explicitly rejected the idea of "prying" into private lives. However, it intensified the Max Gate suspicions of the outside world. Much of 1916 was taken up with Florence's alternate admiration and horror over Sydney Cockerell. Her wide-eyed reverence for one who had personally known both "Tolstoi and Ouida" makes pathetic reading; yet she was shrewd enough to feel there was something wrong or even sinister about this assiduous and rather unpleasant name-dropper. Besides—another horror—he too "takes notes of conversations here".[43]

Everywhere at Max Gate was the shadow of Emma. "I may not alter the shape of a garden bed, or cut down or move the smallest bush, any more than I may alter the position of an article of furniture."[44] Sarcastically quoting Milton, she wrote of Thomas's "late espoused saint",[45] and spoke of his wish to visit Plymouth, "to gaze, once again, I suppose, at the house where SHE was born."[46] She herself was frequently ill. In spite of operation, the nose infection seemed ready to spread to the ear, and threaten mastoid. She had two series of expensive inoculations, and the surgeon Yearsley advised a long holiday.[47] Florence's ironic prophecy came true. The only way for her to have a holiday was to agree to go with Thomas "to hunt up Giffords", alive and dead. In September 1916, they went to see Emma's cousins, the Giffords of Launceston, whom Hardy had never known, and then on to St. Juliot to see the memorial to Emma he had designed and paid to be put up there. As Florence wrote, it was an effort of self-control on her part. "One has to go through a sort of mental hoodwinking and blind one's self to the past."[48] Not that the present, at bathless Max Gate, was very desirable for an often-ill woman. "I have to bath in a puddle—a quart or three pints of hot water in a smallish hip bath."[49]

Dugdale family affairs were a constant strain. Her strong, self-reliant father, who added to his life-saving tally by successfully rescuing two children from drowning, had a complete, though fortunately not permanent, nervous collapse. Her mother was always delicate, her sister Eva, a nurse, had difficulties with her jobs. Her youngest sister Marjorie, whom Florence had seen through college on a three-year domestic science course, became engaged and married a young airman with no money. Florence for once defied her husband,

and had the penniless bridal pair to spend their honeymoon at Max Gate. Kate Hardy, who had no illusions about her famous brother, applauded Florence for this. "Bravo F!!!!!", she wrote in her diary with multiple exclamation marks.

By the end of 1916, Florence herself wrote, "Sometimes I feel *eighty*", older than her husband, who seemed well and cheerful, "in spite of his gloomy poems". These, of course, so far as they concerned Emma, were still a thorn in the flesh to Florence. At the end of 1916, "strangers must imagine that his only wish is to die & be in the grave with the only woman who ever gave him any happiness".[50] At the end of 1917, "the idea of the general reader will be that T.H.'s second marriage is a most disastrous one and that his sole wish is to find refuge in the grave with her with whom alone he found happiness". For on 30 November 1917, "the general reader" was given a chance to see what Hardy had achieved in this concentrated, solitary life of poetry over the past few years. On that date, *Moments of Vision* was published, his largest collection, and in many instances his finest. He had already tested the public demand, just over a year before, with a carefully-chosen *Selected Poems*, in which nine of his latest were included. The enthusiastic response demanded a second impression within a month. In this selection, he had also made a belated gesture to Florence. Three out of the first four reprinted poems were poems addressed to her; he also signed a presentation copy for her married, older sister.[51]

The *Moments of Vision* collection of 1917 differs in many important ways from all Hardy's previous or subsequent collections. It dates from one recent period of composition; a mere handful of poems gives evidence of earlier work. Instead of a rag-bag effect, as in all other volumes, there is an impressive unity. If Hardy felt need of justification for his self-imposed, self-centred "recluse" life, it is here. The work is different in outlook from poems written before the war. The confident self-righteousness of the fourteen *Poems of War and Patriotism* had been badly shaken by a visit in 1916 to a Dorchester prison-camp. There is a new, human tone. Briefly, where before Hardy had always blamed man's troubled affairs on a First Cause or Immanent Will, often in poems of turgid, versified philosophy, he now saw Man himself as a creature of weakness and unreason, and even included his own failings in this criticism. His philosophic correspondence with Galsworthy, in the spring of 1916,[52] shows Hardy far less dogmatic and confident as a prophet, seer, and reasoner—"a miserable reasoner", he confesses. *Moments of Vision* is wholly on a human scale, the scale, too, of Hardy's own personal mythology. In no other volume has he followed so closely Sir Philip Sidney's advice, "Look in thy heart and write." Though Hardy said of these poems "they mortify the human sense of self-importance", their concern for human failing celebrates true humanity.

As in *Satires of Circumstance*, there were about thirty poems connected with Emma, but these show a new aspect of memory. Several poems are directly inspired by Emma's own words in her manuscript of early "recollections" which Hardy was now re-reading, the disturbing "diabolical diary" having been at last consigned to the flames. Some of his finest poems draw on Emma's phrases. *During Wind and Rain* describes her two childhood houses at Plymouth in detail; even its title and theme echo the storm on the day she left Plymouth, as if it washed away her happy past. *The Interloper* begins with her descriptions of the Cornish coast, *The Five Students*, with its refrain of "dark she, fair she", echoes exactly Emma's words about herself and her sister, "she dark, I fair", though her sister is not included in the "students" of the poem. The poem, *Near Lanivet, 1872*, describes an actual incident in their courtship. Poems about a still older past are concerned with his sister Mary, and set in the Bockhampton cottage. An admiration for "a *very* good-looking girl", young Mrs. Hanbury of Kingston Maurward, noted by Florence was wistfully responsible for a pathetic poem about the great house, entitled *In her precincts*, to which Hardy himself added the words "Mrs. H..bury".[53]

Another source of inspiration from the past is the rhythm of folk-tune refrains from Hardy's own childhood. An unusually high proportion of poems have this folk-song pattern. The "Ah, no; the years, oh!" of *During Wind and Rain* is the best known; a poem to his sister Mary, written at the same time, *Logs on the Hearth*, had the refrain, "That time, oh!", which was removed in later printings. Other poems have a folk-song story-pattern, the scheme, for instance, of the traditional song, *Ten Green Bottles*, in which each verse subtracts one. Such are *The Five Students*, where the students diminish stanza by stanza, or *Looking Across*, where the Hardy family one by one—father, mother, daughter-in-law, daughter—go "across" to live in Stinsford Churchyard, leaving Hardy alone "looking". The events of his life with Emma are charted in simple, folk-tale succession: the persistent image of sun on a stream always takes its place as their brief, early happiness. In *The Five Students* similarly, the death of the "dark and fair he, dark and fair she" are chronological, though the "students" never, in fact, met in any place but in Hardy's mind. They are probably Horace Moule (died 1873), Tryphena Sparks (1890), Moule's brother Henry (1904), and Emma (1912). A cancelled last stanza identifies "the course" that all (Hardy being the fifth) followed. It is Love, "Heaven's central star", in the stanza's Shelleyan phrase. Like so many in *Moments of Vision*, this poem is a celebration of the ideal of Love.

So Hardy, neglecting the present-day world around him, delved into the deep past for evidences of love. He was perhaps only dimly conscious of neglecting those nearest to him now, especially the much-tried Florence, with her almost overwhelming problems. Perhaps some of the tenderness drawn from the past did at last spill over into the present, and to her. Though he had been able to ignore his first wife's physical suffering, something of his second wife's mental suffering seems belatedly to have struck him. When he received the first copy of *Moments of Vision* from the printers late in November, he inscribed it "this first copy of the first edition, to the first of women Florence Hardy".[54] It was some compensation for the pain she inevitably received from many of the poems within. Moreover, earlier in this same year 1917, he and she had concocted a scheme which would at least bring them into closer touch, and allow her, even though in a most curious way, some literary work at last.

14

Late and Early

Moments of Vision was a critical success. The Georgian poets Hardy had privately disparaged were generous in praises.[1] At the age of seventy-seven-and-a-half, the great achievement of *Moments of Vision* seemed to Hardy his final word in verse. He had indicated this by ending the collection with the famous, personal poem about his own death, *Afterwards*. He had now, he wrote to Gosse in a letter[2] whose arithmetic seems difficult to confirm, spent fractionally more of his life in producing verse than in producing prose. This constituted a fitting resting place for his reputation. In *Afterwards*, too, he most significantly reversed a process of his youth. In the 1860s, finding no magazine would accept his poems, he "prosed" them into early novels: a passage in *Desperate Remedies* paraphrases completely a youthful sonnet. *Afterwards* begins by turning two passages from a novel into poetry.

> When the Present has latched its postern behind my tremulous stay,
>   And the May month flaps its glad green leaves like wings,
> Delicate-filmed as new-spun silk, will the neighbours say,
>   "He was a man who used to notice such things"?
>
> If it be in the dusk when, like an eyelid's soundless blink,
>   The dewfall-hawk comes crossing the shades to alight
> Upon the wind-warped upland thorn, a gazer may think,
>   "To him this must have been a familiar sight."

In the novel *The Return of the Native*, there are "new leaves, delicate as butterflies' wings"—there is a similar passage in *The Woodlanders*—and on "the isolated and stunted thorns . . . a night-hawk revealed his presence . . . flapping his wings . . . alighting". The images of the novel have been cannibalized for the poem. Hardy was making what seemed to him his final statement that he was, and always had been, essentially a poet.

Yet what of himself as a man? What would, in literal fact, "the neighbours say" about him? What picture would the world get? To one so morbidly self-conscious and secretive, this question was supremely important. Should he write an autobiography as many of his friends suggested? "My reminiscences; no, never!" he exclaimed in a letter[3] to Sir George Douglas in December 1915: but the supposed threat of

Clodd's reminiscences just a month later made him think again. He could hardly go on prohibiting all his friends to write about him. Besides, Clodd's published *Memories* showed Hardy the dangers of attempting to enforce such suppression. It seemed suspicious to any intelligent reader, who knew the long friendship, similar tastes and background of the two men, that Clodd wrote separate sections on several less close friends, such as Sir Henry Thompson, yet none on Hardy, although the book was dotted with anecdotes revealing him as a principal guest at Clodd's Aldeburgh home for many years. From as early as 1894, a couplet of a fellow-guest, Grant Allen, was quoted,[4] describing a Whitsun week spent at Aldeburgh.

> How late we tarried, slow and tardy,
> Yet loth to lose one tale from Hardy!

Hardy, to the end of his days, never quite realized that omission and silence aroused more suspicions than they allayed; but *Memories* must have made him think again about the wisdom of further prohibitions.

If he wrote an autobiography, it would have to disguise more than his comparatively recent indiscretions with Florence. The process would stretch back to the beginnings of his life, and even beyond. From quite early in his years of fame, he had sedulously built up a fictitious history of his past life and ancestry. He had abandoned as unbecoming to a great author his own family's humble origins and struggles. He never breathed to anyone, for instance, that his mother was one of seven children brought up on parish charity; that close relatives, like his uncle John Hardy, were labourers; that several were disreputable or drunk; that his mother, and both his grandmothers, had been pregnant well before their marriages; and that the women in his family, with few exceptions, were domestic servants. He had shoals of living cousins, one of whom, Augustus Hardy, who had just died, was a prison warder at Portland Gaol. He wrote to them on business only, if at all. With who knows what damage to his own integrity and personality, he had cut himself off from his native roots. Yet he still lived a life where this past might uncomfortably break in. Though he was genuinely fond, for instance, of his brother and surviving sister, Henry and Kate, and saw them frequently, it is clear from the latter's diary that these two, simple-mannered and speaking broad Dorset, were hustled out of the way if they happened to coincide at Max Gate with their brother's more distinguished callers.[5] He himself was morbidly conscious that his own education had been nothing like that of these visitors. He had spent a year or so at a "National" village school, some few more at a Nonconformist school of the British and Foreign Bible Society in Dorchester. When the master of this school set up a small fee-paying school of his own in the town, Thomas's parents had paid the guinea a term for him to continue there;[6] but at sixteen he had left to be articled to a local architect. A great deal of Thomas's considerable learning had been self-acquired and self-taught, though aided and to some extent inspired by the ill-fated son of the Dorchester clergy family, his older friend Horace Moule. Two terms of elementary French in his twenties, when he was an architectural assistant in Town, and went to evening classes at King's College, London, completed the tally of his formal education. In a sense, the Order of Merit at seventy, and the Cambridge doctorate and college fellowship at seventy-three, had come too late, either to restore his personal confidence over this lack, or to lift the obsession about it that had been gathering over the years.

It is easy to condemn Hardy for snobbery, both intellectual and social. He was certainly more culpable here than his first wife, who has always been blamed for such tendencies; it was, after all, he not she who inserted into his entry in *Who's Who* the information, unique in that publication, that his wife was the niece of an archdeacon. Yet the simple label of snobbery misses the deep wound in his nature, which caused his extraordinary manœuvres of concealment. The rigid class divisions of Victorian society were nowhere in the British Isles so fixed as in Dorset. In Scotland, for instance, where self-education was recognized and indeed honoured, Hardy's close contemporary, Sir James Murray, could proceed from obscurity to social acclaim and the learned achievement of the *Oxford English Dictionary*. Hardy felt his own achievement continually threatened by the past, from which he had broken with such pains, and particularly by any fancied hint of contempt at his educational and social origins. The tragedy was that any such contempt was largely self-created by his own suspicious imagination.

What then was to be done, to sum up his life in prose as, he felt, his last book, with the last poem in it, had done in poetry? How should he produce what would seem an authoritative version, which would not be subject to contradictions nor risk the appearance of bias? One natural solution suggested itself. He was, after all, now married to a self-styled "scribbling woman", and one, unlike poor Emma, whose spelling, grammar, and arrangement of sentences were generally above reproach. Yet difficulties at once presented themselves. Florence's unaided style and experience might not be up to the work. Her half-dozen or so short tales for children and her brief natural history "descriptions" gave no guarantee of capability for an adult work of such scope. True, she had kept her hand in, after marriage, by reviewing novels; but this ephemeral, mechanical work gave no sign of anything but routine competence.

However, sometime in 1917, they made a start; Hardy would give

Florence factual notes, which she would write up and expand. She began to type what she called "Notes of Thomas Hardy's Life . . . (taken down in conversations etc.)".[7] These fragmentary typescript notes soon proved unsatisfactory. For one thing, Florence was a self-taught and not particularly accurate typist. When rushed or bothered, she could produce distinct errors, even mis-typing the titles of poems.[8] Several obvious mistakes creep into even the opening pages of these notes, and some over-eager modern scholarship has produced biographical conjectures out of what are simple mis-types. One of these mistakes, in fact, shows when these notes were being taken down. Page 14 of the typescript reaches the point, in the middle of April 1862, when Hardy first seeks work as an architectural assistant in London. At this juncture, it is clear that Florence was distracted from the typescript. She was having more than usual difficulty over servants in mid-1917. At a tactless remark of hers, the cook had "bristled up and said 'Please, m'm, I think I'd better leave'."[9] When she returned from domestic discord to continue her notes about Hardy in April 1862, she headed the next section, "Last week in April 1917". This method was clearly not going to work. The typescript in fact peters out half-a-dozen pages later.

A new and very natural idea now succeeded this abortive beginning. It would be more efficient than the haphazard taking-down and writing-up of notes, and would satisfy Hardy's imperative need to furnish the world with a flattering portrait of his life. It arose from two stories which had appeared some years before over Florence's maiden name in the pages of the *Cornhill*, the highlights for her of serious literature. Yet neither was really her work. The first, *The Apotheosis of the Minx*, shows signs, in plot, construction, and actual words, of Hardy's hand; the second, *Blue Jimmy*, was entirely written by him, and passed off as hers. No one had apparently recognized the deception. It was natural for the two to believe that if Hardy wrote his own autobiography, in the third person throughout, it could be passed off, after his death, as a biography written by Florence.

Once again, one must wonder how she could acquiesce in such a literary deception. One answer is that the idea coincided with a revival of her ambitions to be known as a writer. In the summer of 1917 a new personal attachment gave a fresh impetus, in the midst of "home worries", to her natural zest for life. She found a friend who lightened the burden. In London again for inoculations under the supervision of Macleod Yearsley, Florence was taken home to meet his wife. Louisa Yearsley, herself the daughter of a physician, was lively, interesting, and sympathetic. She divined how nervous and uncertain Florence was, how repressed by the régime at Max Gate, and she drew her out and made much of her. Florence responded to Louisa, younger than herself, with the warmth and gratitude of one who has been starved. With habitual self-criticism, she at first felt she had chattered absurdly. Louisa reassured her, seeing how terrified Florence was, even of her kindly surgeon husband. "I am afraid of all these things," Florence confessed.[10] Louisa, to shake her out of the gloom of Max Gate, invited her often to their cheerful London house. "What pleasure it was to be in such a happy and delightful home," wrote Florence, unconsciously comparing the two households.[11] Louisa took her to London stores, for Florence to dream among furniture and clothes. "Max Gate furniture looks very mid-Victorian and ugly after the wonderful things we saw at Heals," Florence sighed.[12] Louisa directed Florence's unaccustomed dress-shopping; at Jaeger's, "I should have chosen an absurd golf-coat had you not been there to advise."[13] Above all, persuading her to leave Hardy for a night or so, in the care of Kate from Talbothays, the Yearsleys took her to London theatres and cinemas. "Going to a play two days in succession was a wonderful occurrence for me," wrote Florence, ruefully adding, "not likely to happen again for many years."[14] These experiences made her feel a person again; the vision of herself as a writer flamed up freshly in this new breath of pleasure. "I want to plunge anew into a literary career. I want to write a play." Yet the vision of Hardy and dog "Wessex" waiting for her on Dorchester station-platform stilled such hopes. "Of course I never shall."[15]

Florence was therefore ripe for this curious literary imposture, however strangely and dishonestly it would bring her name before an eventual public. To another friend she wrote, mysteriously, "I have a tremendous job in hand—literary."[16] The stage-management of a system, to conceal the true process of authorship, was worked out with Hardy's usual minute care and secrecy. Diaries and notebooks were used, excerpts selected to be introduced into the text and originals destroyed, with almost no exception. Letters were sorted into some kind of order, mostly by Florence, and many of these also ultimately destroyed. Hardy wrote, page by page, and this was typed by Florence. When each section of typescript was completed, his original manuscript, like the diaries, notebooks, and letters, on which it was based, was destroyed too. Alterations and additions to Florence's typescript were made by Hardy, and sometimes by Florence, in a typographical hand, possibly as an attempt at disguise.[17] Naturally, Hardy wrote throughout, and described all his doings in the third person, sometimes with deliberate vagueness, particularly when associating poems and other works with actual events and persons, as if Florence had been uncertain of the true facts. Whether even Florence was allowed to see every source is doubtful. Hardy's life up to the age of thirty is specially sparse in its quotation of letters, only a very few to his sister Mary being admitted. The originals, kept by Kate, show that even these had passages omitted. Florence was spared having to read and copy love-letters to and from Hardy and Emma during their wooing. At some tempestuous time during Hardy's first marriage, Emma not only burnt Hardy's love-letters to her, but had demanded back her letters to him, and burnt them too.[18] When Florence reached this period in his life, Hardy produced for her an edited version of sections of Emma's "Some Recollections". Luckily Emma's manuscript did not share the fate of others, and it can be seen today, with Hardy's own somewhat officious and often clumsy attempts to improve Emma's spelling, grammar, and punctuation, together with his instructions to Florence how to dovetail the pages together.

Not unnaturally, the work produced by such curious means, over the next decade, is itself a curiosity. For one thing, the extracts from Hardy's notebooks, diaries, and letters, printed as they stand, were written anything up to fifty-five years earlier. They therefore often have the freshness, interest, excitement, and thought of a comparatively young man. The linking narrative, however, is naturally that of a very old man. Moreover, it is that of a man who had not written prose for over twenty years, since the publication of his last novel. It is stiff, awkward, without trace of fire and enthusiasm, a pedestrian jog from one fact to another, often with extraordinary and clumsy circumlocutions. Among many examples, when Hardy wishes to say that he and Emma avoided the Diamond Jubilee of 1897 by choosing to go abroad, he writes,

> All the world, including the people of fashion habitually abroad, was in London or arriving there, and the charm of a lonely Continent impressed the twain much.

When such circumlocutions become most extravagant, one suspects, often rightly, that some embarrassing fact is being concealed. Above all, such a style in itself defeats the fiction that the book is written by Florence. Its allusions and idioms are all of a generation far older than her own.

The extreme contrast between the pedestrian narrative and the vivid diary and notebook entries has at any rate the effect of making the latter memorable. Remarks on poetry, painting, philosophy, nature, folklore, shine out like lumps of quartz embedded in common-place clay. Among them runs one distinct vein which is highly indivi-dual to Hardy. Like Keats, but without his exuberant gusto, Hardy had an appetite for the grotesque, verging on the morbid. One of the few critics who has really studied this autobiography,[19] says it affords "an astonishing anthology or necrology of mortuary occasions". Hardy is shown, in Devon, "a bridge over which bastards were thrown and drowned": he recalls lovingly famous murders and hangings, and the exploits of hangmen. Grotesque country tales are recalled. A village girl bore a bastard to a squinting man, and trained the baby to squint likewise by hanging a bobbin between its eyes. This fondness for grotesque was noted by Hardy himself. He cannot go to Paris on holiday but "As was the case with Hardy almost always, a strange bizarre effect was noticed by him at the Moulin Rouge."[20] In church, he speculates on "the bizarre world of thoughts" in the minds of the congregation. Skeletons, coffins, portents, and apparitions crop up everywhere. This is to say, Hardy remains a traditional, complete countryman. The autobiography has all the virtues and vices of village gossip, admirable in human interest, but avid to chronicle disaster. It is the epitome of what Emma called "his peasant origins".

Hardy also loved to chronicle obsessively the doings of the great and famous in high society, and his own success in entering that society. He wrote long lists of fellow-guests at dinners, country houses, and dances. Even Florence found this excessive, though she copied them; in the brief months between his death and the book's publication, she curtailed many such catalogues. With Hardy, it was more than a countryman's need to gossip about the great, notorious, or beautiful. He wished to make claims for his own family. Hence arose his obsession, like that of his own John Durbeyfield in *Tess*, that the Hardys had once been important, but had come down in the world. The extraordinary effect of this was that it led him to belittle, in these pages of the autobiography, his own attractive father. Thomas Hardy senior was one of six children (four never mentioned by Hardy), whose share of cash to start a career was just over £14 each.[21] In fifty-five years, he increased this to £850, plus the considerable goodwill of a thriving business, and some valuable real estate. Yet Hardy, in order to pretend to past glories for the Hardy family, represents his father as an amiable idler, who "had not the tradesman's soul",[22] neglected his business and lost money. It is the most astonishing result of what may be called Hardy's own d'Urberville complex.

So Hardy and Florence became in several ways the prisoners of this deception they had deliberately started. The long-drawn process proved a strain on both participants. Hardy found that to read the mass of personal letters from the past thirty or forty years, before destroying them, was a searing experience. "They raise ghosts", he wrote to Sir George Douglas in May 1919, and again, in a similar vein, the following autumn. Until now, his memory had been able to select past themes for poems: now the past forced itself upon him. Yet there were, for Hardy, compensations. In the wads of paper, there were sketches and drafts of early poems themselves, which he had forgotten. These often seemed worth rescuing and revising. From now onward, many of his published poems have a note "from an old copy" or "Rewritten from an old draft". Besides, however painful, memories kept alive the poetry in him. To his surprise, he found himself, after saying farewell in 1917, actually accumulating enough verse, new and old, for a fresh book. This, appropriately called *Late Lyrics and Earlier*, gradually began to grow.

Its growth was sometimes strangely subject to the needs and demands of the course set by Hardy's mind in the autobiography. What if an experience, recorded truly in a poem, conflicted with the half-truth or concealment he had adopted in his prose account? There is a startling example of how Hardy now had to tailor even a poem to fit the story of the autobiography. As he progressed to the fateful year 1912, his version of his life laid more and more stress on how unforeseen Emma's death in that year had been: how up to the last days, he had no inkling. Yet he found a draft of a poem, written under the shock of her death, where the final stanza began in a way that showed Emma far from well in her last days.

> And that calm evening when you climbed the stair,
> After a languid rising from your chair,

Her last pain-ridden climb, night after night, up the Max Gate stairs could not be admitted by the husband, who had now produced his prose version of a wife relatively pain-free and healthy to the last. Dictated by the story he had now told in the autobiography, he completely altered the lines.

> And that calm eve when you walked up the stair,
> After a gaiety prolonged and rare,

The fact that Emma was half-weeping with pain during that last evening, on which she tried to entertain her guests, had at all costs to be denied. Even "climbed", suggesting difficulty, had to go, and the independent "walked up" substituted; while the entirely fictional "gaiety prolonged and rare" was introduced to exonerate the guilty Hardy from his neglect, so that the poem could conclude

> No thought soever
> That you might never
> Walk down again, struck me as I stood there.

Florence became even more a close prisoner and sufferer under the task she had undertaken. Reminders of Emma were everywhere. From a notebook of 1896, she found Hardy had taken Emma more than once to Brighton. Florence was morbidly sensitive on this point, since Hardy consistently refused to take her to Brighton to see her own relations— "and not poor relations, either".[23] There were worse and more wounding shocks. Her life was becoming a series of frustrating ironies, as if she were some character in Chekhov, whose stories she had just discovered, "the best thing in literature I have come across lately".[24] In Hardy's diaries, she read and copied his lament that, in their late thirties, he and Emma had no child. Florence was now in her own late thirties; she had no hope of a child herself. In May 1918, her friend, Louisa Yearsley, had a baby son. In November, Florence's own sister Marjorie had one also. Florence's thoughts were resigned and sombre. "There is nothing like having a child I am convinced. It gives purpose and dignity to life; it should make middle-age and old-age beautiful and contented."[25] Such beauty and content were not for her, while there were even more ominous reminders of her own coming middle-age. In 1919, Lilian Gifford, a year younger than Florence, had a severe menopausal breakdown. Though she ultimately recovered, it confined her for over a year in a London asylum, where Florence had to visit her for Hardy.[26] The strain of copy-typing his book, in intervals of house-keeping, was increased by his ever-increasing correspondence. On his eightieth birthday in 1920, there were 200 telegrams of congratulation for Florence to answer. She burst out to St. John Ervine in 1921 that during the last seven years she had only been away from Max Gate for one clear week, and that, in 1915, spent in a nursing-home. "I begin to feel the strain mentally."[27] It was an understatement.

There were, of course, compensations and light relief. In the excitement of writing to a rich Middle-West book-collector, with a well-appointed house in Ohio, Florence determined, early in 1919, to get something done about the main inconvenience of Max Gate. This was the water, pumped from a well, heated in saucepans and kettles over the kitchen fire, and poured into hip-baths—"no bathroom even. I expect this is the only house of this size in Dorchester without."[28] She got to work on Hardy, and, though moving slowly, by October he was consulting brother Henry about hot water systems.[29] In August 1920, "a bathroom with a glorious big bath and lots of very hot water" delighted Florence, who added, "I tremble to think what T.H. will say when he has to pay the bill."[30] He had been partly persuaded by hopes of a Nobel Prize that year. The *Daily Mail* had advocated his claims in an article entitled "Our Greatest", and Florence, who had just bought bacon from Selfridge's through the Yearsleys, commented, "If he does get the Nobel Prize . . . we shall be able to have bacon from Selfridge's for breakfast every day."[31] Though the award to Knut Hamsun disappointed their hopes, there were other tributes pleasing to Hardy. The praises on his eightieth birthday were universal and included a special deputation from the Society of Authors, though Hardy probably enjoyed best "a really most elegant speech of congratulation" by the postman.[32] The year before, he received a tribute, organized by Siegfried Sassoon, of a volume of holograph poems by nearly fifty living poets. The year after, 1921, he received a birthday address from 106 younger writers, together with a first edition of the 1820 volume of

Keats, whom he himself celebrated shortly afterwards in two haunting poems.

In 1919, his publishers arranged for his *Collected Poems* in two volumes and in 1919–20 for a *de luxe* printing of all his works, poetry and prose, the Mellstock Edition, on paper watermarked with Hardy's initials.[33] In 1920, Oxford gave him an honorary D.Lit., and the O.U.D.S. performed *The Dynasts* on the same occasion, while he and Florence were there.

Florence consoled herself for her husband's difficult temperament by realizing that it was remarkable for him still to be writing at the age of nearly eighty.[34] She paid tribute to his qualities by having her baby nephew named Thomas after Hardy, "whom I hope he may resemble in as many ways as possible".[35] Everyone was impressed by him. At seventy-five, in 1915, Galsworthy found him "a nice alert old fellow".[36] At nearly eighty, in 1920, the undergraduate manager of O.U.D.S., Charles Morgan, saw him as "sprightly, alert, birdlike".[37] Only along two lines did he show the effects of age, or any sign of senile obsession. The first, common enough in the old, and part of his native temperament, was excessive closeness over money. His refusal, in 1915, to pay Florence's surgeon, was only a start. In 1917, her London inoculations cost her £100, though "If I were a Gifford of course all this would be paid for me."[38] In 1918, this trait developed into a resentful suspicion that other people might make money out of his works. Hearing that dealers and collectors were profiting from signed copies, he refused to autograph books, even for close friends. He actually prepared for the unfortunate Florence a formal letter of refusal to autograph books except for charities, whom he would alone wish to benefit, "and he has alas, nothing to spare in cash". Sending such a statement for her rich husband at once put Florence into difficulty, especially as he was not even consistent. He autographed many books for Paul Lemperly, the wealthy American collector, in return for presents of sugar, candies, chocolate, and sugar wafers for his own sweet tooth, skilfully begged by Florence.[39]

Hardy's other out-of-hand obsession was his impatience over literary criticism. Visiting him at Max Gate, just after going down from Oxford, Charles Morgan was embarrassed at his complaints about contemporary critics. "I could not understand what general reason he had to complain of them."[40] About the same time, Florence found him talking to himself, "and I heard a few sentences about critics—of what nature you may guess".[41] He was now so childishly touchy that she had the unenviable task of preventing his seeing even the mildest printed criticism. "As it was in the [London] Mercury I naturally thought it would be at least a just estimate," she lamented when one such article slipped through her net.[42] E. M. Forster at this time considered Hardy "very vain" to take magazine criticism so badly. Hardy was particularly enraged when criticism was mixed with attempted biography. Once more, as his concocted autobiography progressed, he was the prisoner of his own invented life-story, and had to stick to it at all costs, even at the cost of truth. Florence began to catch her husband's vituperative style. When Llewelyn Powys, returned from five years in Africa, wrote a quite innocent account of a conversation with Hardy, Florence commented,[43] "We were told he was a lion hunter from Central Africa, and he proved to be a lion hunter of another type"; she sent an angry letter to the unfortunate Powys.

This, in the summer of 1922, coincided with the most violent outburst of Hardy's obsession. Fifteen years before, a young scholar, F. A. Hedgcock, who was preparing a thesis in French for the University of Paris, wrote for information to help with his study, *Thomas Hardy, Penseur et Artiste*. He asked questions which, though expressed with diffidence, were innocently tactless. "Is it possible to enquire what your studies at King's College comprised?" was natural enough, for a French thesis; but an honest answer would have revealed the elementary nature of Hardy's French classes there. After three years, Hedgcock obtained an interview through Gosse, assuring Hardy, "I shall bring none of the aggressiveness of the interviewer";[44] and indeed he found Hardy very uncommunicative on personal matters. His published thesis arrived in 1911; Hardy pencilled in it, "Biographical details . . . mostly wrong", and forgot this apparently minor work in a foreign language.

On 22 June 1922, however, a somewhat casual letter arrived at Max Gate from Vere Collins, a director of the Oxford University Press, on holiday in Skye. Collins proposed the Press should issue an English version of Hedgcock's book, which Collins himself would translate. Hardy at once sent a telegram disapproving of "publication in English as it stands", and a series of letters, five in three weeks, followed. Hardy heavily annotated Hedgcock's early biographical chapters. He enlarged, to fit his own version, the Bockhampton birthplace, "seven-roomed . . . and rambling . . . with a paddock and till lately stablings"; he exaggerated his own education, "Greek & Latin", he denied that the Dorset dialect was "spoken in his mother's house". He was furious at the quite unmistakable likeness in early novels between his architect-heroes and himself—"impertinent and unmannerly in its personalities". Hedgcock was told, through Florence, at Hardy's dictation, that a translation could not appear unless all personal details "be omitted except those authenticated by Mr. Hardy". He replied, with dignity, that "far from seeking to pry into private matters", his book was a serious philosophic study, an example of "criticism à la Taine, into which ancestry, environment, all enter as determining factors". He withdrew, but stipulated, reasonably, that all Hardy's notes about his "inaccuracies" should be destroyed as damaging to his own professional reputation.[45]

Instantly, a similar incident occurred. Professor Samuel Chew, of Bryn Mawr, had visited the Hardys in 1921, and in 1922 they received his monograph on Hardy. In September he asked for comments for revision, and received more than he bargained for, pages of typescript notes from Florence, on the exact lines of Hardy's annotations to Hedgcock. The Bockhampton cottage had now grown even larger, "House and premises . . . with two gardens, horse-paddock, sand and gravel pits . . . and outbuildings." The Hardys became a "landed" family. Any resemblance between Hardy and his heroes is false. "Jude was a working man, not at all in Hardy's position . . . there is not one word of autobiography." Hardy was deeply stung by one commonplace criticism, his inability to portray Society. "Eveline 5th Countess of Portsmouth obtained an introduction to the author because this novel [*The Hand of Ethelberta*] was the *only* one she had lately met with which 'showed society people as they really were'." Poor Chew was made to pay for his innocent request.[46] "Is this banal fact worth stating?" was the mildest of Hardy's comments on what the author doubtless considered a complimentary book.

Some of this may be explained, though hardly excused, by the fact that a few months earlier, in January and February, 1922, Hardy had a recurrence of his chronic inflammation of the bladder. At his age it was serious, and two doctors and Florence's sister, the nurse, Eva Dugdale, were called in. Hardy, even more in character, spent his time in bed writing a long introduction to the new book of poems he had just sent to the publishers. It was in the main yet another swingeing attack on critics. "Some of his friends"— probably Gosse and Cockerell, whom he consulted—"regretted this preface, thinking it betrayed an over-sensitiveness to criticism." Hardy brazened it out by claiming that, as a poet, he had a right to be sensitive.[47]

The deepest root of these obsessions lay in the fear that his poetry would not be appreciated as much as his novels. Florence commented later that year, "He thinks it impossible for any book to be good that treats only of his novels";[48] the well-meaning Chew was told that his sympathetic treatment of the poems "would bear lengthening" to do justice to what "the best critics acknowledge" as Hardy's finest work. Rejoicing in his self-made miracle that he was still writing poems in his eighties, he determined that the world should recognize it. For all the often-told story of his enclosing a stamped addressed envelope with poetry for magazines, he was the opposite of modest about his verse. He had much justification. Though *Late Lyrics and Earlier* is not as satisfying a volume as *Moments of Vision*, it is an astonishing collection for a man in his eighties, and shows all sides of him. As usual, the narrative poems are least happy. There were about half-a-dozen of these, mostly about fictional women, all somewhat oddities. The longest, so much in the style of Browning as to risk parody, is about a woman organist, dismissed for her immoral life, who commits suicide in the organ loft; another is about the ghost of a prostitute, who died in the Lock Hospital for Venereal Diseases, while a third was a Gothic fantasy, written fifteen years before, about a widow haunted by the memorial brass in which she vowed not to wed again. In contrast with these laboured efforts, the lyrics, old and new, are among Hardy's best. The Bockhampton cottage was now so full of memories, that he found it painful to visit, especially after having to break into it with Barrie one day in May 1921.[49] Yet it provided him with a perfect lyric of a place where wild life always stood at the lonely threshold, peering in, *The Fallow Deer at the Lonely House*.

> One without looks in tonight
> Through the curtain-chink
> From the sheet of glistening white;
> One without looks in tonight
> As we sit and think
> By the fender-brink
>
> We do not discern those eyes
> Watching in the snow;
> Lit by lamps of rosy dyes
> We do not discern those eyes
> Wondering, aglow,
> Fourfooted, tiptoe.

The lyric background to the birthplace, the rhythms of folk-songs from his mother and father, pervade this collection. One West Country folk tune, which he had already used for a poem in the early months of the war,[50] provided the basis for two more poems here, *Meditations on a Holiday* and *The Colour*. The same folk-rhythm that had been heard in *Beyond the Last Lamp* was heard again in *Voices from Things Growing in a Churchyard*; the poem itself was an offshoot of "his favourite walk" to the Stinsford family graves, where Florence found it "so depressing to go and look at the tomb under which I shall probably lie some day— very soon I think".[51] Her own trials were, of course, augmented by the usual large quota of poems concerned with Emma, about thirty in all. There was some comfort that these did not idealize the first marriage so whole-heartedly; its early years were now poignantly summarized as

> A preface without any book,
> A trumpet uplipped, but no call;

Florence was allowed one of his rare tributes to herself in a moving and beautiful lyric, ending

> . . . For one did care,
> And, spiriting into my house, to, fro
> Like wind on the stair,
> Cares still, heeds all, and will, even though
> I may despair.

Hardy, for all the tortuous deceptions of his outward life, was seldom anything but honest in poetry. Stress of poetic utterance forced the truth from him. As he approached the final pages of the book, he faced the problem of which poem to put last. In *Moments of Vision*, the poem *Afterwards* was intended to be his personal summary of a long life. Now that life had prolonged itself for five more unexpected years, what self-portrait should he now give? Mean or even uncharitable as many of his recent actions were, he had not lost the penetrating power of self-knowledge, or self-criticism. He could realize in poetry what he would not admit in life. In a mood only approached by W. B. Yeats, in his own old age, Hardy faced himself and his betrayals. He used an image centred on the cottage fireside, now more real to him than any other scene. He recalled his mother's saying, as the green and wet wood sighed and muttered in the flames, that it was his own voice talking to him. The primitive fancy, together with that other childhood echo, the resounding texts from the New Testament, mingled into a message of humility that spanned his experience, as he comprehended it in the title of the poem, *Surview*.

> A cry from the green-grained sticks of the fire
> Made me gaze where it seemed to be:
> 'Twas my own voice talking therefrom to me
> On how I had walked when my sun was higher—
> My heart in its arrogancy.
>
> "*You held not to whatsoever was true,*"
> Said my own voice talking to me:
> "*Whatsoever was just you were slack to see;*
> *Kept not things lovely and pure in view,*"
> Said my own voice talking to me.
>
> "*You slighted her that endureth all,*"
> Said my own voice talking to me;
> "*Vaunteth not, trusteth hopefully;*
> *That suffereth long and is kind withal,*"
> Said my own voice talking to me.
>
> "*You taught not that which you set about,*"
> Said my own voice talking to me;
> "*That the greatest of things is charity . . .*"
> —And the sticks burnt low, and the fire went out,
> And my voice ceased talking to me.

15

A Human Show

FOR a man well into his eighties, Hardy continued to show remarkable activity and freshness of mind and body. There were, of course, his twin obsessions, money and the imbecility of critics, which could still rouse him to malevolent grumbles. There was also, and again naturally, an elderly conviction that the country was going to the dogs. With post-war freedoms, and bright young manifestations in the arts and in society, the 1920s was a great decade for gloomy and moralistic prophets of doom. Dean Inge's *Outspoken Essays*, that cleric's profitable ventures into popular journalism, were favoured reading with Hardy, and, indeed, with Florence also.[1] Hardy himself could contribute suitable warnings of disaster. "England and Europe", he wrote to Galsworthy in 1921, "do not look particularly attractive in their political aspects."[2] He added the conviction, historically unjustified though heard in various guises during this century, that books would decay, and the only form of writing would be "for football and boxing journals", and for the cinema. He spoke of a new "dark age".

In spite of such pessimistic judgements, Hardy was in fact as much involved in the demands of literature as he had been in the busiest periods of his life. He corrected with keen attention the proofs of his *Collected Poems* and of the Mellstock edition of his works. Proof-correction with him meant meticulous revision, and he did not spare himself. "He allows nothing to interfere with his morning's work," wrote Florence,[3] rather ruefully, since all the extraneous chores of an author, such as answering letters, and dealing with requests and permissions, now fell on her. The task was sometimes less than amusing. She found herself faced by communications such as that of the exasperated correspondent, who wrote, "Dear Sir, I am wondering why the devil you don't answer letters!"[4]

Nor was Hardy's literary work by any means solely revision. In spite of eye trouble, his only physical defect, and one to which the dim oil-lamps at Max Gate must have added, he was actually in his eighty-fourth year producing new work. This proved, of all things, to be a play. *The Famous Tragedy of the Queen of Cornwall* is both a literary and dramatic curiosity, and, on its own terms, a very considerable achievement. The Tristram and Iseult story had, of course, an immense

191

attraction for Hardy since his own Cornish wooing fifty years before, renewed by his revisitings there with the reluctant Florence. Indeed his dedication of the printed version shows how, when obsessed, he could be unconsciously cruel. The play is inscribed to Emma, her sister, her brother-in-law, and Florence, "those with whom I formerly spent many hours at the scene of the tradition, who have now all passed away save one". He seemed oblivious that the "many hours" spent by the survivor, Florence, had meant her acquiescence in what she considered a lie about the past, while he eulogized "an Iseult of my own", Emma. Apart from such considerations, there was an ironic compression in the writing; much of this stemmed from the construction of the play. Hardy decided to maintain the unities of time and place as, he remembered, he had done with *The Return of the Native*. His one hour of events, from Tristram's return to the death of the lovers, was composed in strict Greek tragedy form, with Chorus. Wishing "to avoid turning the rude personages of, say, the fifth century, into respectable Victorians, as was done by Tennyson, Swinburne, Arnold etc.",[5] Hardy used a style of verse which was classically laconic, but whose convoluted brevity was more in the manner of Browning, "intricate oddity", as one critic remarked.[6] It was certainly too difficult for the local players, who were entrusted with first performance in Dorchester in November 1923, and in London early next year. Yet the dramatic power, even in awkward phrases, was unmistakable. Florence, whatever her feelings over the dedication, judged the play itself, *"really* good".[7] Granville-Barker flirted with the idea of a professional production, while Rutland Boughton found the brief text ideal for the libretto of an opera, which he composed, and which was successfully performed at the Glastonbury Music Festival.

The creative vitality of Hardy's life was due in large measure to his lifelong self-discipline in reading and note-taking. This had continued steadily since he first started in the 1860s. In the 1890s when he began to turn from prose to poetry, his main reading naturally took the same direction. There was always a steady interest in philosophy, and extracts from Schopenhauer, Haeckel, and Von Hartmann are prominent; but the emphasis gradually changes to poetry and to theories of how to write poems. He copied many paragraphs, at various times, from a periodical called *Literature*, and from the *Quarterly Review* on "English Prosody". The last, in July 1911, is notable in that half his extract is copied for him in Florence's hand, showing that over a year before Emma's death, she had taken Emma's place as notebook amanuensis. Appreciation of modern poetry, in his notebooks, was disappointingly small. He was still suspicious of the "Georgians", and seems not to have heard of the Imagists. It is true that he copied two long extracts from "Prufrock"; but he got these at second-hand from a publication by S. P. B. Mais called *From Shelley to O. Henry*, and annotated them merely as an example of the work of "T. S. Eliot—a poet of the vers libre school".[8]

He was, however, keenly alive to all forms of twentieth-century thought. In January 1920, he extracted from the *Quarterly Review* A. S. Eddington's article on Einstein, and on 21 June 1921, Florence wrote that he "ponders over Einstein's Theory of Relativity in the night".[9] He referred to Einstein in poems and other notebooks, and was clearly fascinated by the implications of the idea of relativity. Though, as always, politics found little place in his life and thought, he extracted from *The Times* long reviews of books on scientific humanism, and notably one about Spengler's *The Decline of the West*.

His intellectual life seemed to burn brighter as his body grew feebler. Not that his physical energies showed much of the flagging one would expect from a man of his age. Only a few months after his severe illness of February 1922, the summer found him bicycling, at the age of eighty-two, over to Talbothays to see Kate and Henry. Nor did he, as he got older, shy off from social occasions as much as he had done in the war years. London society, of course, was now too much, but his London ladies, such as Florence Henniker and Agnes Grove, were welcome guests still. He had even more noteworthy callers. On 20 July 1923, Hardy achieved one of the highest of those social distinctions so dear to him. Edward, Prince of Wales, drove through the streets of Dorchester with him, and afterwards lunched at Max Gate. True, there were Hardyesque ironies even in this event. The Prince was late coming downstairs for lunch, and Florence, hovering anxiously, heard a violent quarrel between him and the equerry. The Max Gate staff was inadequate for their needs, and the gardener, having opened the gate, nipped round to the back door, and did double duty serving the meal. "The eldest son of the sovereign has never before, I think, paid such a compliment to literature," Florence proudly meditated;[10] but Max Beerbohm's amusing parody of the occasion probably comes nearer the truth. Nor was it without strain. Kate Hardy found Tom and Florence "very highly strung" after it.[11]

For Florence generally, life was very much a mingled yarn of dark and light threads. Intellectually, she was gaining confidence through increasing responsibility, however exhausting this might be. The floods of letters to be answered, from his eightieth birthday onward, might be "a nightmare", "an avalanche". The mechanical tasks of the autobiography were hers too. By 1919, she had only brought her arrangement and sorting of Hardy's correspondence up to 1900—"nineteen years more to do". Yet her work was now more than secretarial, and involved a considerable amount of trust. It also gave her experience in handling literary matters, which her past history of little books for

children had hardly provided. One literary venture, with which she was
entrusted, was the printing in pamphlet form of small separate works
by Hardy, mostly poems. This originated oddly in competition with
Clement Shorter, the editor of *The Sphere*, who had at one time given
her employment. Shorter between 1914 and 1916 had printed half-a-
dozen such pamphlets himself in a series called "A Bookman's Hobby".
These printings were irksome to Hardy, and Cockerell advised that
Hardy or his wife should prevent them by producing their own. Florence was allowed this welcome task, and from 1916 to Hardy's death,
several appeared at irregular intervals under her supervision; though
details were also overseen by Cockerell himself, it gave her more of a
stake in Hardy's work than she had hitherto been allowed.[12]

Intellectually, she also began to gain confidence from welcome
literary visitors. Max Gate was not so isolated as she was apt to complain in moments of depression—"I feel rather covered with blue
mould."[13] Sassoon, de la Mare, E. M. Forster, Galsworthy, T. E.
Lawrence were favoured guests, Barrie a frequent one. She entertained
Charlotte Mew, and felt great fondness for her, and admiration for her
work—"She has genius, I think".[14] It was a far cry from the children's
stories in the *Enfield Gazette*, for Florence to be in such literary company.
Her judgements became clearer, though too often tinged with personal
feeling. She distrusted Edward Clodd's account of Meredith, largely
because she knew Clodd had the key to some of her own secrets. Yet
stimulating company made her grow as a person. She took her place
locally, though always remembering how Hardy had criticized Emma
for running after local people, and agreeing with him. "The local clergy
are the greatest sinners. They want to make T.H. a spectacle."[15] There
was even a visit from a bishop—"It does get a bit stifling at times".
In February 1924, she became a Borough Magistrate,[16] a position
Hardy himself had held to the end of the war, yet repudiated the idea
of having too close Dorset connections. "I do not think I could ever
bring myself to live at a place called Puddletown",[17] where numerous
Hardy relations still lived. She openly preferred the local aristocracy,
like the Ilchesters, and felt herself of their world.

Nor were her preoccupations exclusively intellectual and literary.
Thanks mainly to kind friends, like the Yearsleys, she made periodic,
though brief escapes from the Max Gate atmosphere to more frivolous
pursuits. A few months before the crushing duties of her husband's
eightieth birthday, she spent her last two hours of one such visit to
London having alterations made to "a quite delightful little evening
gown—a very full skirt of petunia coloured charmeuse . . . the bodice
entirely of gold lace". Even over this pleasure hung the shadow of
missing the train back to Dorchester, with Hardy waiting. Another
pleasure was the installation at Max Gate of a telephone, so that,

Hardy grumbled, she could talk to her friends in London, though he himself regarded the instrument with obstinate suspicion.

On the other hand, Florence had a heavy load of nervous and physical problems, quite apart from the nightmare of managing a house totally unfitted for domestic comfort. On the physical side, Hardy's life and her own were becoming like some terrible fairy tale. He threw off illnesses, even the serious one of February 1922, and seemed to become in some ways more spry and active as his years mounted, while she continually worsened in health, as if his incredible life was feeding on the failing vitality of hers. In 1920, in spite of the many inoculations two years before, Florence was, she wrote to Louisa Yearsley,[18] "feeling all anyhow", and was *"afraid"* she would have to see the surgeon again. On 29 October 1922, the local doctor, Gowring, advised the removal of a gland from Florence's neck.[19] At the beginning of the following year, Florence had her neck X-rayed. One trouble was Hardy's peasant unwillingness to allow surgery. On 7 June 1923, he himself wrote to Macleod Yearsley asking whether the gland in Florence's neck really needed an operation.[20] He ended typically, "I rather wish it could be dispensed with altogether, if you think no further harm would arise beyond the slight disfigurement it causes, which we do not mind." One wonders whether "we" really included Florence. Photographs round about this time showed her strained expression. The thistledown lightness Hardy once praised had changed to a watchful, anxious look. In spite of physical stress, she could still manage a joke. On one of her rare visits to London, late in 1923, she wrote, "I stayed the night at Barrie's flat, and whether it was the effect of my presence there . . . he was taken to a nursing home the next day."[21] Nine months later, Florence herself was in a London nursing-home. Though Yearsley had at first agreed with Hardy not to touch the gland, the operation for its removal now appeared urgent. She entered the Fitzroy House Nursing Home on 29 September 1924, and the operation took place the next day.

Florence returned from her ten days in the Fitzroy House Nursing Home, in a hired car, driven by Henry Hardy and the Dorchester garage hand, Voss.[22] Weak, nervous, and run-down, so much aged that, though only forty-five, she looked almost an old woman, she soon found herself facing one of the worst trials in her whole life. Whether or not this was largely a figment of weakness and illness, allied with her own uncertain temperament, it is necessary to go back, at this point, over the past seventeen years.

In 1908, the year Part III of *The Dynasts* was published, the Dorchester Debating, Literary and Dramatic Society was addressed by one of its members on Napoleon's threatened invasion of England. Another member, A. H. Evans, had the idea that a dramatized scene from

Hardy's *The Trumpet-Major* would help to illustrate the lecture. From this arose the project that the Society, instead of Shakespeare, Goldsmith or Sheridan, should perform a full dramatic adaptation of Hardy's novel. Evans, father of the famous actor Maurice Evans, made an episodic version of scenes, stressing the comedy. He persuaded Hardy to agree to this, to write additional dialogue himself, and actually to suggest and sanction a happy ending, instead of the dark final curtain of the book. Otherwise, fidelity to detail was fanatical. Genuine old pikes and firelocks were used, uniforms copied from those still existing in family attics. On 18 November, the play attracted not only a local audience but many London critics to the improvised theatre in Dorchester Corn Exchange. So began an annual custom of presenting a Hardy play at about that date, to which was added a London performance each December at the Cripplegate Institute and elsewhere to an audience of the Society of Dorset Men in London. These ritual performances were taken over by a Dorchester builder, T. H. Tilley, and continued, to a limited extent, through the war, during which the Wessex scenes from *The Dynasts* and some love-scenes from *Far From the Madding Crowd* were given. Hardy showed a great interest in all rehearsals, and in 1910 for *The Mellstock Quire*, a version of *Under the Greenwood Tree*, he supplied old carols; at one rehearsal, though seventy, he nimbly stepped forward to demonstrate one of the old country-dances.[23]

In 1913, the chosen play was an adaptation of *The Woodlanders*. Hardy, this time, insisted on the tragic ending of the novel, with Marty South's poignant speech at Giles's grave. The words were spoken by a seventeen-year-old girl, Gertrude Bugler, daughter of a South Street, Dorchester, confectioner. Her performance moved even the London critics, and on 20 November, her picture in costume appeared in the *Daily Mail*.[24] She was a natural actress, slender, with expressive eyes and very dark hair. When the plays were fully revived in 1920, she was an obvious choice for Eustacia Vye in *The Return of the Native*, which she performed brilliantly, particularly in the scene where Eustacia joins the Christmas Mummers. The happy idea was conceived that the Players should perform the mumming play at Max Gate. When they did, Gertrude Bugler charmed not only Hardy but also Florence, who wrote, "She is a beautiful creature, only 24, and really nice and refined." At the same time, there was a puzzle. "She tells everyone she is taking my advice *not* to go on the stage and I am puzzled as to *when* I did give that advice." She concluded that the advice must have been Hardy's, and joked about Hardy's partiality for Miss Bugler, whom she herself greatly liked.[25] Florence had, as a matter of fact, already discussed the idea of a stage career with Gertrude Bugler, but offered no advice.

No play was produced in 1921. The play for 1922 was *A Desperate Remedy*, a version, with slightly altered title, of Hardy's first published novel. Gertrude Bugler was cast; but in 1921, she had married a farming cousin, also named Bugler, and by May 1922 she was pregnant. She told the society's secretary she must resign the part. Hardy was disappointed, and a message reached her that he would like her to call at Max Gate for one of his books, which he had inscribed for her. Early in June, she called, and was received by Florence with a total absence of her former friendliness. She returned, puzzled, to Beaminster, where she now lived, to be followed on 13 June by a letter of violent complaint from Florence, rebuking her for her call. "It is simply 'not done' in our station of life for any lady to call on a gentleman . . . I am regarded and treated as hostess."[26] One wonders that Florence's two grandfathers, one in his butcher's shop, the other in his smithy, did not cross her mind as she wrote of "our station in life"; but she had by now adopted Hardy's own facility for adjusting the past to fit the present. Mrs. Bugler, so far as she could understand the drift of Florence's letter, wrote back with spirit and common sense; and there the matter rested. Unhappily, Mrs. Bugler's child died at birth about the time of the November play performance.

These stage productions had stimulated Hardy's desire, never far below the surface, though he often denied it, to write in dramatic form. A talented amateur actress was also a stimulus, and *The Queen of Cornwall* was created, with the leading part intended for Mrs. Bugler. The players assembled at Max Gate to read through the difficult verse-speeches. Mrs. Bugler was a fine verse-speaker, among her other accomplishments, but once more she was not to play the part. Another baby, happily to be safely delivered, was found to be on the way, and again she had to resign. She managed, however, a long and friendly talk with Florence, and affairs seemed to be on the old footing.

It was an ambition among some of the Hardy Players, as they had come to be called, to stage *Tess of the d'Urbervilles*, though there was a certain nervousness about how Dorchester would take a work still thought to be immoral. However, in 1924, Hardy resurrected for them his own dramatic version, made in the 1890s, and never performed on any stage, since Stoddard had rewritten it so drastically for production in New York. Hardy's original version was being rehearsed by the Players when Florence returned from her operation early in October. Gertrude Bugler was to play Tess, in spite of the responsibility of a very young child at home. Quite apart from the recent operation, Florence had many things on her mind. In June, she had written to the sympathetic Louisa Yearsley,[27] "I do wish you were nearer so that we could discuss all sort of things that one cannot write about." As well as these unmentioned problems, Florence added that the difficulty of housekeeping, unrealized by Hardy, "is almost enough to drive anyone into an asylum".[28]

The first night of *Tess* took place on 26 November. Hardy did not attend, being terrified of strangers at first nights, one of whom had actually *"asked him questions*, a thing he hates".[29] At the dress rehearsal and other performances, however, he was wildly excited, and, as one eye-witness noticed, more often in the wings than in the auditorium. The four nights and a matinee in Dorchester were followed by two performances at the Pavilion Theatre, Weymouth. The Mayor of Weymouth gave a dinner to the company, and Gertrude Bugler sat at Hardy's right hand. Florence was noticeably irritable and nervous during these days. Early in December, Mrs. Bugler, back in Beaminster, received an extraordinary letter from Florence, strained and angry, but impossible to understand; nor could her husband interpret it when she handed it to him. Almost immediately, on 9 December, there followed a telegram and another letter. This letter was in a style familiar to many people who had received violent epistles from Florence. Her first letter, Florence now wrote, had been written when she was "completely unstrung and utterly miserable". She mentioned her operation, only two months ago. She hoped that Mrs. Bugler had burnt the letter. In fact, Mrs. Bugler kept it, but returned it after Hardy's death. Its exact contents have escaped Mrs. Bugler's memory.

There was quiet for a month; but Gertrude Bugler's superb performance with its "reserve, pathos, and charm" had won appreciation in other places than Dorchester. On 8 January 1925, Frederick Harrison, who managed the Haymarket in London, wrote to ask if Gertrude Bugler would play Tess with a professional cast at his theatre. The scheme was to stage in April or May a series of matinees, while John Barrymore was appearing in a six weeks' season as Hamlet. If the matinees caught on, *Tess* would go into evening performance, after Barrymore returned to America. Hardy had written a new prologue-scene at Harrison's suggestion, and fresh lines for a later scene. Mrs. Bugler went to Max Gate to discuss these with Harrison and Hardy. Salary and rehearsal-times were agreed upon.[30] Florence was helpful and kind, suggesting where Mrs. Bugler might stay in London, and reassuring her that other actresses with husband and child had managed their careers successfully.

Mrs. Bugler returned to Beaminster, and began to learn her new lines; but one day, in the second half of January, came another telegram from Florence, followed almost immediately by Florence herself, announcing that she was there without Hardy's knowledge. She had come to implore Mrs. Bugler to give up the idea of playing in London. Hardy was in an excited state; he would want to go to London, and might damage his health. Florence herself spoke wildly of a poem written by Hardy about an elopement, which she had burnt. Mrs. Bugler found this an alarming interview. She did not at once agree, though Florence followed up with a letter written on 25 January, saying that it would be "a tragedy to go to London". Early in February, Mrs. Bugler wrote to both Harrison and Hardy, renouncing the part. A happier, though long delayed sequel, came in the year after Hardy's death. The two women met again as friends, and Florence invited Mrs. Bugler to play in a revival, which Philip Ridgeway was staging at the Duke of York's. She played with great success, with her name in lights as "Thomas Hardy's Own Tess". One of the company paid her the tribute of praising her performance "with that huge part surrounded by a lot of hard-baked professionals".[31]

Mrs. Bugler remembered Hardy as a man of the generation of her own grandfather—he had died in 1918—who had been kind to her, and who had said, as he walked with her down the Max Gate drive, after the meeting there with Frederick Harrison, "if anyone asks you if you knew Thomas Hardy, say, 'Yes, he was my friend'." That afternoon, on 12 January 1925, the assiduous Sydney Cockerell was also present. Nearly forty years later in February 1964, long after Florence's death, Mrs. Bugler received a rough draft of the chapter by Cockerell's biographer entitled "Thomas and Florence Hardy". Florence had been right when she wrote, as far back as October 1916, that Cockerell "takes notes of conversations here". Cockerell recorded in his diary for 10, 11, and 12 January that there was "a cloud" over Max Gate, and gave Florence's words. She had said Hardy was absorbed in Mrs. Bugler. He was off-hand with Florence, spoke roughly to her, showed her she was in the way, and forgot her birthday (the 12th)—as, incidentally, Florence always said he had done with Emma's. Florence had felt in the night she would go mad, and wondered if it were her time of life; she was now forty-five. As late as the following August, she returned, on a walk with Cockerell, to the topic of what Cockerell called Hardy's "infatuation" with Mrs. Bugler. Hearing of all this for the first time, Mrs. Bugler wrote a calm and sensible letter, much as she had done after Florence's first outburst in 1922, and it is printed in Cockerell's biography.[32]

It is virtually impossible to make any final judgement on what these occurrences meant, but there are a few certain points. Florence certainly hinted to Gertrude Bugler that Hardy was easily carried away when talking to a young woman, though it is not sure what incidents in his past she had in mind. Mrs. Bugler believed, as was suggested by Hardy's inscriptions in books to her, that he saw in her the heroines of some of his most deeply-felt novels come to life through her performances. It is also certain that only a few days after Mrs. Bugler renounced the part, in February 1925, Florence sent a violent and hurtful letter to the elderly Rebekah Owen. Almost immediately, on 16 February, she followed with another letter to Miss Owen of contrition and appeal. "Please burn it, and forgive and forget." She added, "I have had a rather bad nervous illness and am still feeling unwell."[33] People noticed that at this time she had a nervous tic, a habit of pursing or twisting her mouth when talking, particularly at the beginning of a conversation.[34]

Also, within the next few weeks, Florence took a more than usually angry and unbalanced part over yet another book which aroused Hardy's indignation. A young American graduate, Ernest Brennecke, junior, of Columbia University, had brought out in 1924 a short critical study, *Thomas Hardy's Universe*. This was intended as only the first part of his doctoral dissertation, and early in 1925 he produced a biographical part, *The Life of Thomas Hardy*, virtually the first independent attempt at biography. He had visited Max Gate, and been given lunch. Unluckily, Brennecke, as many more distinguished overseas enquirers were to do, had made a muddle of his notes when writing them up, and his mistakes, trival in themselves, roused Florence's extreme wrath. To her disproportionate anger, he had described the Max Gate lunch wrongly. "We loathe plum tart and custard," wrote Florence, and surmised he had confused this with some hotel meal in Dorchester. He had committed the solecism of showing the non-smoking Hardy with a cigarette between his lips. Worst of all, he had reproduced the "most revolting" photograph of Florence in motoring costume, taken at Oxford in 1920, which she had been lamenting to her friends ever since. Her tone was vindictive to a degree, verging on paranoia. "I disliked the man when I first saw him, and he must have realised this, which accounts for the way in which he writes of me."[35] Not that Hardy was far behind, sending a cable of protest to Brennecke's New York publishers, repudiating the book through Macmillan, and threatening an injunction for breach of copyright.[36] Such anger over an innocuous book, with its foolish but harmless statements, was excessive; but Brennecke had fallen over the perpetual stumbling-block in mentioning Hardy's lack of formal education.

One luckier American visitor, who got away with a whole skin this summer, was a nephew of Mark Twain, Cyril Clemens. He indeed claimed later that Hardy confided to him the process by which he and Florence were constructing the concealed autobiography, now very nearly up to date. Though he probably embroidered and expanded this from other sources, such as J. M. Barrie's reminiscences, there is no cause to doubt him, as other overseas visitors later in the field have done. The same information also slipped out to an English writer, Lascelles Abercrombie, who in his *Encyclopedia Britannica* bibliography of Hardy in 1929, mentioned a "Memoir" or autobiography in Hardy's Works, and got castigated by other bibliographers for his pains.

For, amazingly, considering Hardy's age, Florence's trials, and all other distractions, the work of collecting, examining, editing, and shaping the past still went on. So did its greatest by-product, the finding and reviving of old poems, the reliving of old themes to provide new poetry. Some memories lay too deep. The death in April 1923 of Mrs. Henniker "after a friendship of 30 years", produced only a laconic note in the autobiography,[37] and no poems. Yet steadily the poems, revised, restored, and newly written, grew to a book of the same size as *Late Lyrics and Earlier*, and by summer 1925 it was ready for the press, under its first title of *Poems Imaginative and Incidental*, soon changed to *Human Shows, Far Phantasies* as being, Hardy wrote, "not quite so commonplace". In spite of the change of title, the collection still verges on the commonplace when compared with some of Hardy's others. Many of the early rescued and revised poems, *Retty's Phases*, for instance, seem trivial, and only interesting when, as in this instance, there is an original manuscript—as early as 1868—to show that Hardy's shaping hand, even in old age, had not lost its skill. The technical improvements to *The Birdcatcher's Boy*, now first collected here, have been mentioned. Yet, in spite of one long narrative poem, and one in dramatic or at least dialogue form, the impression left by the book is thin. As usual, memories of past loves and affections have the most quality. Emma, Louisa Harding, Rosamund Tomson, Tryphena Sparks (possibly), and Horace Moule (notably) stir Hardy's lines to lyric intensities. Florence has no part; but a poem dated on the day in 1924 when she left the London nursing-home after her operation, *Nobody Comes*, shows the bleak loneliness at Max Gate, with Hardy waiting for the car to draw up there. His anxieties and disappointments emerge more movingly than in any direct love-poem. It is also a poem as "modern" as anything by the younger generation.

> Tree-leaves labour up and down,
>> And through them the fainting light
>> Succumbs to the crawl of night.
> Outside in the road the telegraph wire
>> To the town from the darkening land
> Intones to travellers like a spectral lyre
>> Swept by a spectral hand.
>
> A car comes up, with lamps full-glare,
>> That flash upon a tree:
>> It has nothing to do with me,
> And whangs along in a world of its own,
>> Leaving a blacker air;

And mute by the gate I stand again alone,
And nobody pulls up there.

Hardy could not say there was any public lack of appreciation of him as a poet over this book. An edition of 5000 copies, published on 20 November, was practically sold out the day before publication.[38] The book went on selling and was well noticed. One critic, Edward Shanks, commended Hardy's technical dexterity by naming him "the most fertile inventor of stanza-forms in all English literature".[39] The gist of its reception was that Hardy, far from being an outmoded poet, was perhaps more truly of the twentieth century than many of its younger poets. He was now recognized as the spiritual parent of the whole generation of modern poets.

16

Winter's Last Word

WRITING in the *Nation and Athenaeum*, early in December 1925, Leonard Woolf saw Hardy as one of the spiritual parents of the modern generation of poets. For all his eighty-five years, his "queer, original personality" seemed as individual and modern as anything they were trying to express. Young writers, as essentially different as Woolf's wife, Virginia, Robert Graves, Siegfried Sassoon, and J. C. Squire, were all ready to recognize and to learn from him. Partly, too, in a mellower old age than had once seemed likely, he seemed equally ready to learn from them. He had seen signs of genius in Charlotte Mew, and acknowledged them by catching an echo of her "queer original" voice. The feeling and diction of his own *Nobody Comes* has strong resemblance to some lines in the moving final stanza of her finest poem, *The Quiet House.*

> Tonight I heard a bell again—
> Outside it was the same mist of fine rain,
> The lamps just lighted down the long, dim street,
> No one for me . . .

He accepted new experience with youthful if cautious enthusiasm. Though he took Florence's advice and did not venture to London for the professional production of his dramatization of *Tess*, he was eager about it. Kate Hardy found her brother "highly-strung" about the outcome.[1] Thanks to an enterprising new manager, Philip Ridgeway, and a brilliant young actress, Gwen Ffrangcon-Davies, it was a success. After its 100th performance on 25 November 1925, attended by Florence on his behalf, a plot was hatched. On 6 December, the company arrived at Max Gate to give a drawing-room performance of the play. Hardy was delighted, chatted happily with the young actors and actresses, and charmed them all with his innocent appreciation of their work. He was surprised to find himself liking "a job I quite disbelieve in—a dramatised novel".[2]

Tess was performed in the cramped Max Gate drawing-room, with the London cast sitting literally at Hardy's feet. In these last years, many young poets and writers came to the house to sit metaphorically in the same position. One of the foremost was Siegfried Sassoon. This tall, handsome yet strangley uneasy member of an exotic, oriental family, who had somehow become more English than the English, was capable both of feeling and inspiring extravagant affection. Wilfred Owen addressed him as "Keats + Christ + Elijah + my Colonel + my father-confessor + Amenophis IV in profile."[3] For Hardy, according to Florence, he was his "adored Siegfried Sassoon", and it is clear he attracted her too. On his part, Sassoon could see no wrong in Hardy, though he was secretly and somewhat meanly critical of Florence, who admittedly reported his charms in terms of almost schoolgirl gush. When Sassoon toured the United States in 1920, reading his own poetry, he would pause in his hesitant and embarrassed recital to substitute a favourite poem by Hardy.[4] Edmund Blunden flitted in and out of Max Gate, with his perennial topics of the past war, Christ's Hospital, cricket, and Keats; he won from Hardy the valued though hardly correct opinion that he had an air of Keats himself. De la Mare was another constant and approved guest, while T. E. Lawrence, now settled in Dorset as Private Shaw, "utterly captivated" Hardy[5] by a life and personality that had been so unlike Hardy's own. All of them, in their turn, were fascinated by Hardy. To them he seemed a living link with an incredible past of English letters, a Victorian who had achieved his reputation before the Queen died, now creating work that was as much of the twentieth century as their own. He was one with the monolithic past, when there were giants in literature, Tennyson, Browning, Swinburne, Dickens. In a world of the 1920s, whose growth seemed to have been cut away by the great scythe of the war, he was a symbol of continuity.

Some young writers used their visits frankly as copy for their impressions of the great man. Robert Graves, who claimed to have "kept a record" of his talk with Hardy, managed to get the highest possible score of mistakes into a few pages.[6] He caused Florence pain by writing that Hardy criticized Gosse for imitating Hardy's "old friend Henry James" drinking soup. Since Gosse, not James, was the "old friend", and it was Florence, not Hardy, who had given—to her everlasting regret—an account of the soup-drinking imitation,[7] there is little need to believe the rest of Graves's "record". Virginia Woolf also gave a Bloomsbury-eye view of the Max Gate ménage, new style, and commented how much Florence talked about and addressed the dog.[8] Since meeting Virginia Woolf could be a nerve-racking experience, Florence was understandably taking refuge. She had been brave enough at the uncanny advent of T. F. Powys. On his notoriously weird approach, Hardy jumped in the air in alarm, but Florence calmly carried off the situation.[9] One importunate admirer and visitor was John Middleton Murry. He spun such a tale—though indeed a true one—of his financial difficulties, with a second wife, like his first, dying of tuberculosis, that Hardy obtained, through Gosse, £250 for him,[10] from the Prime Minister, Stanley Baldwin. Florence, too, pitied the handsome Murry's predicaments and godmothered one of his children.

The respect, not to say veneration, in which Hardy was held by these young writers, was a constant pleasure to Florence. In spite of continued disappointments over the Nobel Prize, she felt this was immortality, and a justification of her faith in his universal greatness. It brought her into contact with people of her own age, or even younger. She could feel, however small her own literary efforts, some sort of kinship. Max Gate was more populous than during the lonely, early years of her marriage; she could now, because he was less solitary, poke fun at Hardy's indifference to company, and report dialogues such as this.[11]

F.H. It's twelve days since you spoke to anyone outside the house.
T.H. (triumphantly) I have spoken to someone.
F.H. (surprised) Who was it?
T.H. The man who drove the manure cart.
F.H. (much impressed) What did you say?
T.H. 'Good morning'.

Yet Hardy in company could sometimes be a liability and anxiety for Florence. With extreme age, his mind and his tongue reverted to some of the less seemly obsessional topics of his youth. One was the hanging and public execution of women, originating when he was sixteen from the Dorchester execution of Martha Brown, sublimated in middle-age into the execution of Tess, but always morbidly present. In 1919, with Lady Ilchester and daughter, he recounted the terrible details, told him by an ancestor, of the burning of Mary Channing, the murderess—"I tried in vain to stop him, for the daughter turned quite white—she is only fifteen."[12] In 1925, after a visit to Lady Pinney, "he was bustled into the car"[13] by Florence, to stop him talking about Martha, while, when the Galsworthys visited him in 1927, he insisted on discussing a sensational murder which he remembered his parents talking about when he was a boy.[14]

Generally, however, the picture was one of twinkling benevolence, or the dignified, ageless ancient of the Augustus John portrait in 1923, and Florence could breathe freely. He learned at last to accept honours and tributes gracefully. On 15 July 1925, a deputation from Bristol University arrived by appointment at Max Gate, to confer the degree of Hon. D.Litt. from that young academic body, joining the honours bestowed on him by the older universities, Cambridge, Oxford, Aberdeen, and St. Andrew's. It was suggested about this time that there should be a Thomas Hardy Chair of Literature at a future University of Wessex, a project which has never materialized. Hardy even overcame his dislike of displaying himself in public. When John Drinkwater's stage adaptation of *The Mayor of Casterbridge* was performed at

Weymouth, on 20 September 1926, Hardy accepted the invitation to attend, and received an ovation in the packed theatre. On 21 July 1927, he consented to lay the foundation stone of the new Dorchester Grammar School, and managed a vigorous speech in the teeth of a strong wind. Characteristically, he half-suggested a relationship between his namesake, the Elizabethan local philanthropist, and himself, though he must have been aware there was no evidence for its existence. Ironically, he partly owed the reputation he had now acquired in his home town to the Prince of Wales's visit in 1923. After he was seen driving with the Prince, and tales began to circulate about the royal lunch at Max Gate, the majority of Dorchester's citizens realized that he was a famous man. Indeed, on the day itself, the final hopeful chorus from *The Dynasts* was sung in the Prince's honour by the choir of Holy Trinity, Dorchester, in a setting by their organist, Edgar A. Lane.[15]

By sheer endurance and longevity, he had established a position for himself everywhere, a living miracle. There was the further miracle of his continuing poetry. Lyrics still poured from him, some of them as moving and accomplished as anything he had written in all his long life. As always, the death of a woman he had loved in the past provided the most potent inspiration. On 7 December 1926, Agnes Grove died. Two-and-a-half years before, after receiving birthday greetings from her, he sent her a note saying he often thought of her, and of their dancing together in 1895 at the Larmer Tree festivities. Like her compatriot at that far-off time in Hardy's affections, Florence Henniker, Agnes had fallen on evil days. For ladies of their class, depending on dividends, the war was a crippling blow. Florence Henniker's will showed her unable to make the generous bequests she wished: Agnes, before her death, was confined by comparative poverty to her country home. A journey into Shaftesbury to buy cheap meat in the market had to be made in a rickety motor-cycle and side-car[16], a sad comedown for one of the dashing Stanleys.

Hardy, deeply affected by the loss of this impetuous, domineering, but warm-hearted companion of his difficult middle-age, wrote her into history in his briefly-titled poem *Concerning Agnes*. The dancing, the summer setting, their holding hands, all "That old Romance" were contrasted with the woman now dead, as he imagined her, "white, straight, features marble-keen". The final stanza was classically noble, like some threnody of those Athenian poets to whom he felt his work akin.

> There she may rest like some vague goddess, shaped
>   As out of snow;
> Say Aphrodite sleeping; or bedraped
>   Like Kalupso;
> Or Amphitrite stretched on the Mid-sea swell,
> Or one of the Nine grown stiff from thought. I cannot tell!

Not all Hardy's memorial verses were of such quality, or inspired by a subject which could equally pluck at a reader's heart. Less than three weeks later, Hardy suffered another loss, though not a human one. The notorious dog, Wessex, whom Florence had brought to Max Gate in 1913, died. The childless Hardy was a doting master. He excited the dog to frenzied naughtiness with tit-bits of cheese-rind. At Christmas, he made Wessex ill with goose and plum-pudding. The indulged dog was a menace to all guests, dominating the lunch table. According to Cynthia Asquith, it "contested" every forkful on the way to her mouth. With less respect than Florence for the local aristocracy, it insisted on eating dinner with the Ilchesters when the Hardys visited Melbury House. Distinguished guests were savaged and even bitten. The respectable trousers of both John Galsworthy and the surgeon, Sir Frederick Treves, were reduced to tatters. The dog was yet another of Florence's constant anxieties. Her dread that something would happen at Max Gate, during one of her infrequent absences, was caused as much by Wessex as by the elderly Hardy. She was afraid that the dog might bite someone so badly that the police would destroy it before she could return to plead for reprieve. The sight of a policeman standing at the front door of Max Gate, on some quite innocuous errand, brought the instant reaction, "Oh, not Wessie again!" She and Hardy justified the dog in all its anti-social actions. Servants seemed stupidly alarmed; Florence felt they should realize that Wessex only "flew at" them, and did not mean to bite. She was genuinely indignant when a postman, not realizing such fine distinctions, kicked out a couple of Wessex's teeth in self-defence. Only T. E. Lawrence of Arabia, perhaps by some esoteric desert magic, managed to remain unscathed. Yet there is a pathetic insight into the emptiness of Florence's life at Max Gate in her lament over the dog's death. "He was only a dog, and not a good dog always but *thousands* (actually thousands) of afternoons and evenings I would have been alone but for him."[17] Wessex was laid to rest in the pets' cemetery to the left of the front door, with the graves of numerous cats, and with Moss, the old, quiet dog of long ago, who had gained no such dubious notoriety.

The dog Wessex also claimed like Agnes Grove a memorial poem, *Dead 'Wessex' the Dog to the Household*, though hardly one of the same quality. Yet the standard of the new collection accumulating in Hardy's study was astounding. *Winter Words*, though not his finest volume, represents almost every manner of Hardy's verse, lyric, narrative, reflective, humorous, love-poems, nature-poems, epigrams, dialogue, and philosophic pieces. Nothing like it had been produced by a man of his age since Goethe. All his themes are represented. If any one dominates, it is tragic love.

> Love is a terrible thing; sweet for a space,
> And then all mourning, mourning.

Deep-laid family history raises its perennial ghosts, in haunting folk-melody.

> Three picture-drawn people stepped out of their frames—
> The blast how it blew!
> And the white-shrouded candles flapped smoke-headed flames
> —Three picture-drawn people came down from their frames
> And dumbly in lippings they told me their names . . .

Hardy does not tell us, though these "Family Portraits" are surely of the generation of the real Tess, and belong, as he says, to "my blood's tendance". Another candlelit portrait is named, as the man speaks.

> This candle-wax is shaping to a shroud
> To-night. (They call it that, as you may know)—
> By touching it the claimant is avowed,
> And hence I press it with my finger—so.
>
> Tonight . . .

The initials H.M.M.—Horace Moseley Moule—introduce the speaker. Though many of the conjectures about the "story" of *Standing by the Mantelpiece* are as mysterious as the poem itself,[18] perhaps the most simple and the most likely has been overlooked. Horace Moule cut his throat in his bedroom at Queens' College, Cambridge. In the outer keeping-room was his brother, Charles Moule, also a close friend of Hardy, part-original of Angel Clare. The brothers, according to Charles's evidence at the inquest, had argued all afternoon about some distressing, unknown matter. It would be like the literal method of Hardy's habitual composition to make Horace address his own brother in this enigmatic poem, the subject of their discussion still an unsolved mystery—

> And let the candle-wax thus mould a shape
> Whose meaning now, if hid before, you know,
> And how by touch one present claims its drape,
> And that it's I who press my finger—so.

It was not the first time Hardy had written a poem in the person of his own youth's tragic mentor.[19]

Yet, in astonishing variety, Hardy's protean verse is comic too. *Liddell and Scott*, a tongue-in-cheek account of the great lexicon, is in Hardy's best style of learned humour. One of its most sprightly Browning-like couplets was actually added in the last few months of Hardy's life, rhyming the name of Donnegan, an earlier lexicographer, with "con again". Love, of course, especially lost love, is the most persistent theme. Emma, Louisa Harding, Tryphena Sparks (perhaps), Agnes

Grove, are joined by several unidentified loves, such as the girl rescued from a poem dated 1884, ten years after Hardy's first marriage. The most striking, the girl of *The Mound*, is surely the one on whom Sue in *Jude* is based, for the poem is parallel to Sue's confession, in Jude's lodging, of her past life.

> . . . saying she'd not be bound
> For life to one man, young, ripe-yeared, or old,
> Left me—an innocent simpleton to her viewing;
> For, though my accompt of years outscored her own,
> Hers had more hotly flown.

The revisions to the manuscript show that this poem was at first even more direct and personal; Hardy drew a simple self-portrait.

> I was an innocent simpleton to her viewing.

His account of the girl's previous sexual experience had "feverishly flown" and "fervidly flown" before settling for the less explicit "hotly flown". Identification, as with so many of Hardy's love-poems, is both unnecessary and impossible; but it seems we are here in the presence of that mysterious "H.A.", the advanced girl of the innocent Hardy's first London days in the 1860s, from whose encounters he returned shattered to his native Dorset, with a store of emotional experience to last him literally a whole lifetime as a poet.

A lifetime of poetry was what *Winter Words* was meant to summarize. Hardy wrote for it an introduction, which started with a bold but true claim.

> So far as I am aware I happen to be the only English poet who has brought out a new volume of his verse on his . . . . . . birthday.

Landor, the only other English poet with a comparable length of life, produced no new volume in his last twenty-five years. Unfortunately, Hardy's ruling obsession about the critics occupied more than half of a short statement which one would hope to have the dignity and maturity of much of the poetry itself. Hardy was to do even worse than this, and produce a mean-minded attack on critics while actually lying on his death-bed. Nor unfortunately, could the adjective "eighty-eighth", which Hardy had probably intended, be inserted in the blank and dotted space; for 2 June 1928 was a date which Hardy never lived to see.

Thursday 24 November 1927 was the twelfth anniversary of the death of Mary Hardy; Sunday 27 November was the fifteenth anniversary of the death of Emma. Florence had a superstitious feeling that the double occasion portended some fate for Hardy. Hardy was equally prone to superstition, especially over anniversaries. For two or three days, he wore "a very shabby little black hat he must have had for

twenty years"[20] and carried Emma's black walking-stick. "Very pathetic," commented Florence, "all the more when one remembers what
their married life was like."[21] He was still revising poems for *Winter
Words*, and on that Sunday, he wrote a new and good poem, *An Unkindly
May*, with its typical later-Hardy couplet.

> 'Nature, you're not commendable to-day!'
> I think. 'Better to-morrow!' she seems to say.

As so often, Nature was wrong, and Hardy right, at least about his own
immediate future. On 11 December, he took to his bed. He felt immensely tired, though alert enough mentally to talk theology with Florence,
both agreeing that "there was not a single grain of evidence that the
gospel story is true". His physical weakness alarmed Florence. Though
she asserted to herself, "this may be the beginning of the end, but I do
not think so", she sent for Eva Dugdale, who had nursed Hardy through
the kidney attack of 1922. Dr. Gowring, when asked what was wrong,
now merely said, "old age". On Christmas Day, Hardy said he would
never have a drawing-room tea-party again. His mind was still intensely
clear, and seeing likenesses between the present and the remote past.
He observed that the youthful aesthete, Stephen Tennant, was the only
other man he had ever met who walked like Swinburne,[22] an instance
of his century-bridging which so fascinated the young.

Among ominous arrivals during the New Year was Sydney Cockerell.
The Cambridge reputation of the Director of the Fitzwilliam Museum
was that when he appeared at a distinguished bedside, no doctor's
skill could save the patient. Barrie also came down for a night. Outside
the weather was bitterly cold with deep snow-drifts. Hardy had occasional rallies in the first ten days of the year and a specialist, called in
from Bournemouth, said that his arteries were those of a man of sixty.[23]
On 10 January, he insisted on signing a cheque subscribing to the
Pension Fund of the Society of Authors, which still preserves it. In the
evening he asked Florence to read him the whole of Browning's *Rabbi
Ben Ezra*. The next morning, his mind had reverted to his earliest
cottage days at Bockhampton, in the little mudwall home, of which he
had written a loving description only a few months before.[24] He asked
the parlour-maid, Nellie Titterington, to prepare him the sort of
breakfast his mother gave him long ago. This was kettle-broth—
parsley, onions, and bread boiled up in water—and a rasher of bacon,
cooked in front of him in the flame of his bedroom fire. Thus, as the
aristocracy of literature began to whisper about Westminster Abbey,
Hardy enacted the part of the rough carpenter in *The Hand of Ethelberta*,
who instructs the Marquis's brother how to grill his rasher on the bars.
Eva Dugdale, Florence, and Nellie Titterington took turns in watching
him. As it grew dusk, he asked Florence to read him a verse from

The Rubaiyat of Omar Khayyam. It was the first book, outside his own
work, that he had given her as a love-token in the summer of 1907. She
read to him.

> Oh, Thou, who Man of baser earth didst make,
> And ev'n with Paradise devise the snake:
> For all the Sin wherewith the Face of Man
> Is blackened—Man's forgiveness give—and take!

He motioned her to read no more. It was his last gesture towards the
Prime Mover. Just before nine in the evening, Nellie Titterington heard
him call out to Florence's sister, "Eva, Eva, what is this?" The doctor
was fetched and joined Florence at the bedside, but Hardy, though
conscious almost to the end, spoke no more.

It was over. The delicate child, who one day, with his abnormally
quick ears, overheard his own parents say that they did not expect him
to live, had lasted more than eighty-seven years, and left an achievement of work that challenged any other English writer. They dressed
him in his scarlet doctoral robes, in state at Max Gate, a symbol of
success; yet sister Kate, coming to view the body, saw only the likeness
to his own local kin—"the same triumphant look on his face that all the
others bore—but without the smile".[25] For the tokens of the hard-won
struggle from obscurity to status were to continue even after his body
was at last cold.

Even before, when his brain for the first time had begun to cloud, an
incident had demonstrated his strange division of nature. Beckoning to
Florence, in the stillness of his last days, he had dictated two virulent,
inept, and unworthy satirical jingles on two most hated critics, George
Moore and G. K. Chesterton. Such were the great author's very last
literary works, justifying the genial Clodd's reluctant verdict, "There
was no largeness of soul". The events of the next few days—to say
nothing of the next decade—somehow typify the tragi-comic contrast
between mean and noble that had haunted his living days. More especially, they ranged his humble beginning against his exalted ending
in conflicts that would have been laughable if they had not more often
been matters for weeping. Hence the "bitter humiliations", which
Florence, two months later, confessed that these days brought her,[26]
and which she never forgot to the end of her own life.

The immediate cause was her co-executor and trustee. As a relative
at another family funeral complained, "Cockerell took charge and
ordered everybody about."[27] Ignoring the wishes of Hardy, Florence,
Kate, and Henry, whom he dismissed as "a rough kind of man with no
literary leanings",[28] Cockerell rang up Barrie asking him to fix a Westminster Abbey funeral with the Dean; Barrie wrote by return to say
all was arranged.[29] Yet Florence knew Hardy had specifically willed he

should lie at Stinsford "out there" with his parents, his sister, and Emma. To Kate, the decision was "a staggering blow".[30] Florence was caught between two fires, "the nation" (as interpreted by Cockerell) and the village. In distress, she consulted the Vicar, with whom Hardy had grimly joked about his burial. He suggested a gruesome though historic compromise. Let Hardy's heart be buried at Stinsford, his ashes in the Abbey. Florence allowed herself to be persuaded, only to find that to Kate this was "another staggering blow", disgusting for Hardy's intimate friends, such as Clodd, who found it "repellent". The whole operation caused local cynicism mixed with ribaldry. "Almighty, 'e'll say; ''Ere be 'eart, but where be rest of 'e?' " Irony persisted in every detail. At the solemn early-morning moment, when the heart-casket was brought out of Max Gate to the waiting hearse, the siren from Eddison's steam-roller factory, against which Hardy had vainly protested, hooted derision at his death. In London, the Abbey service, hastily organized by Hardy's publishers, was a chaos of wrong invitations and uninvited gate-crashers, "a sick horror" for years to Florence.[31] The Dean of Westminster, too, had been assailed by complaints, one from "the head of a great religious body" throwing doubt on Hardy's Christianity, morals, and general suitability for the Abbey. He even privately consulted the Vicar of Fordington, whose aid Emma had enlisted twenty years before "to try & make Tom more religious."[32]

Worse was to come. Florence was too dazed to understand much of what was said in Barrie's flat after the ceremony; but shortly, she found Cockerell claiming that she had consented to a memorial in Dorset to match the huge seventy-foot stone column on Blackdown commemorating the other Hardy, Nelson's captain. A bare six weeks after Hardy's death, she and his other trustee were at open war. By July, sick of the whole business, she tried to resign her own trusteeship, but was dissuaded by Sir Daniel Macmillan.[33] Henry Hardy added a family note to the quarrel by offering to build a tower at his own expense, provided "he could have it done by himself and according to his own ideas".[34] Meanwhile, the one thing on which she and Cockerell agreed was that much of Hardy's remote past should be destroyed. Funeral pyres of burnt letters, especially those from the early part of his life, darkened the garden at Max Gate. Year by year, the ironies deepened. In November 1930, local subscription provided for a stained-glass memorial window in Stinsford Church. Florence was naturally asked to unveil it, and would have accepted; but earlier that year, William Heinemann had published Somerset Maugham's *Cakes and Ale*. The germ of the story, in Maugham's words, lay in a great novelist marrying as second wife "his secretary, who guards him and makes him into a figure". The publisher's advertisement spoke of this character as "exploiting" her husband's fame "before and after death". To Florence, always guiltily sensitive, this seemed "A barely-veiled attack on me".[35] Maugham disingenuously denied his book was based on the Hardys, and, indeed, his Rosie, the first wife, was the very opposite of Emma; but there were certainly strong hints of Florence in the second Mrs. Driffield. These were enough, anyway, for Florence's feeling that "to unveil the window might give colour to that accusation". Similar untoward events marred other attempts at memorial. A. E. Newton, the American book collector, put up a ten-foot granite column opposite the Bockhampton cottage, and enraged Cockerell. Kate objected to a site in Dorchester because it had been a public lavatory. Eventually, in September 1931, Eric Kennington's small-headed statue was unveiled at the top of High West Street by Sir James Barrie, with a whimsical speech.

Hardy had died on the very eve of Florence's forty-ninth birthday. The ten years of Florence's survival were almost totally sad. New furniture, a car, a visit to Italy—all things she had longed for—did not lift the gloom. The year of her husband's death saw the death of his cousin Theresa, who, Florence was horrified to find, died in poverty, and of his brother Henry, Florence's one true local ally—"The kindest soul imaginable" . . . "a great loss to me".[36] The first volume of her so-called *Life* of Hardy was produced with suspicious speed on 2 November of that year. Florence had only time to remove firmly nearly every complimentary reference to Emma, to her courage, her decision, her encouragement, her successful London lunch-parties, above all, any suggestion that she and Florence had been friends.[37] The book, in all its oddity, with an inaccurate index reprinted to this day, had a disappointing press, as Florence gloomily reported; yet it was followed in 1930 by its sequel, *The Later Years*, equally unsatisfactory, for obvious reasons only known to Florence and to some friends such as Barrie. More satisfying were her work as J.P., and in the Mill Road Building Association scheme to clear the slums of "Mixen Lane".[38] Her personal life, lacking its centre, had unhappy aberrations. She wrote some violent and terrible letters, notably to H. M. Tomlinson and to other people who, she thought, belittled life at Max Gate in the last years.[39] Her repentance, after such outbursts, was pathetic. She was more than half in love with Sassoon, and her letter on his marriage[40] in 1933 is tragically humble. "I have made many mistakes in the past and no doubt have forfeited your friendship." Relations with the overbearing Cockerell were increasingly stormy, and after he attacked her in the *Times Literary Supplement*, "to the amazement of even his own friends",[41] she took the sole trusteeship, with the assistance of Irene Cooper Willis. By then, in the spring of 1937, she was herself a dying woman; many of the utterances she is said to have made to eager researchers may owe their provable inaccuracy to her alleviants for pain. The enemy she had dreaded in her many operations on ear, nose, and throat, attacked her elsewhere. She died on 17 October 1937 of cancer of the rectum.[42]

Max Gate, and some of the Hardy wealth, though not, of course, his copyrights, "my most prized possession", as Florence called them,[43] devolved on Kate. She also became the last repository of the Hardy family secrets. Returning to Talbothays from the opening, on 10 May 1939, of the reconstruction of Hardy's study in the Dorset County Museum, Kate threw down her bonnet on the sofa, laughed heartily, and referring to the complimentary speakers, exclaimed, "If they only knew!"[44] The last "Hardy born", she too was about to take his secrets to the grave. On 7 August 1939, her diary recorded[45] bravely, "Another break down . . . Brain seems spent but I've got to carry on." In 1940 she marked the hundredth anniversary of his birth by her own death. It was a coincidence Hardy himself would have appreciated.

Abbreviations Used in the Notes

Bailey: J. O. Bailey, *The Poetry of Thomas Hardy: A Handbook and Commentary*, Chapel Hill, 1970.

Beatty: C. J. P. Beatty (ed.), *The Architectural Notebook of Thomas Hardy*, Dorchester, 1966.

Björk: Lennart A. Björk (ed.), *The Literary Notes of Thomas Hardy*, 2 vols., Gothenburg Studies in English, No. 29, Gothenburg, Sweden, 1974.

"Dearest Emmie": C. J. Weber (ed.), *'Dearest Emmie', Thomas Hardy's Letters to his First Wife*, London, 1963.

DCC: *Dorset County Chronicle*.

DCL: Dorset County Library.

DCM: Dorset County Museum.

DCRO: Dorset County Record Office.

Gerber and Davis: Helmut E. Gerber and W. Eugene Davis (eds.), *Thomas Hardy: An Annotated Bibliography of Writings about Him*, Northern Illinois, 1973.

Hawkins: Desmond Hawkins, *Hardy, Novelist and Poet*, Newton Abbot, 1976.

LTH: F. E. Hardy, *Life of Thomas Hardy*, 1 vol., London, 1962.

MTH: *Materials for the Study of the Life, Times and Works of Thomas Hardy*, 72 monographs, St. Peter Port, Guernsey. Various dates from 1962.

Millgate: M. Millgate, *Thomas Hardy: His Career as a Novelist*, London, 1971.

ORFW: E. Hardy and F. B. Pinion (eds.), *One Rare Fair Woman: Thomas Hardy's Letters to Florence Henniker, 1893–1922*, London, 1972.

Orel: Harold Orel (ed.), *Thomas Hardy's Personal Writings*, London, 1967.

Purdy: R. L. Purdy, *Thomas Hardy, A Bibliographical Study*, Oxford, repr. 1968.

Rutland: W. R. Rutland, *Thomas Hardy: A Study of His Writings and Their Background*, repr. New York, 1962.

SREH: E. Hardy and R. Gittings (eds.), *Some Recollections by Emma Hardy ...*, Oxford, 1961; repr. New York, 1973.

THN: E. Hardy (ed.), *Thomas Hardy's Notebooks*, London, 1955.

TLS: *Times Literary Supplement*.

YTH: Robert Gittings, *Young Thomas Hardy*, London, 1975.

Notes

1: THE IDYLL, pp. 1–12

1. Gerber and Davis, 26–27.
2. ibid., 23–24.
3. Both in DCM.
4. Gosse to Emma Hardy, 9 May 1907, DCM.
5. In DCM.
6. Björk, 208–243.
7. ibid., xxxv, though some later notes are in Emma's hand.
8. Emma Hardy, *Diary*, DCM.
9. LTH, 110–111.
10. David B. Green, " 'The Eve of St. Agnes' and *A Pair of Blue Eyes*", *Notes & Queries*, N.S. IV (1957), 153.
11. Björk, 36.
12. ibid., 95–103.
13. YTH, 94–95.
14. YTH, 204.
15. Emma Hardy's Diary, DCM.
16. I. C. Willis, notebook, DCM.
17. LTH, 112–113.
18. D. F. Barber (ed.), *Concerning Thomas Hardy*, 126.
19. MTH, No. 25.
20. As, for example, the reasons for the tragedy of Horace Moule.
21. Millgate, 140 et seq., for good discussion of the novel.
22. Though Hardy had intended to use this in his earliest and unpublished novel, *The Poor Man and the Lady*, YTH, 102.
23. Björk, 253.
24. ibid., 322.
25. Millgate, 124, and National Library of Scotland.
26. Millgate, 118.
27. Purdy, 27.
28. J. Henry Harper, *I Remember*, 166, quoted C. J. Weber, *Hardy of Wessex*, 108.
29. LTH, 118.
30. LTH, 118–120.
31. LTH, 115–116.

2: THE THEATRE OF LIFE, pp. 13–24

1. Harold P. Clunn, *The Face of London*, 495.
2. The year is incised on the houses.
3. See the poem, *A January Night, 1879*.
4. LTH, 147.
5. Harold P. Clunn, *The Face of London*, 487.
6. Charles Morgan, *The House of Macmillan*, 66.
7. *The Thomas Hardy Year Book 1972–1973*.
8. LTH, 121–122.
9. F. Mabel Robinson to Irene Cooper Willis, 17 December 1939, DCM.
10. See illustration, No. 1.
11. LTH, 124–125.
12. *Athenaeum*, No. 2666, 30 November 1878. Reprinted in Orel.
13. Mary Hardy to Mary Antell, 8 October 1908, postcard, Eton School Library.
14. LTH, 124.

15. Purdy, 34.
16. Millgate, 160, shows parallels between *The Trumpet-Major* and *Vanity Fair*.
17. LTH, 125–126, 129; THN, 52.
18. LTH, 126; THN, 53.
19. Personal information, Benjamin Bishop.
20. See, for example, *The Times* for 5 December 1878.
21. Though, as a purely human influence, Hardy partly had the veteran Anne Procter in mind. Hardy to Sir George Forrest, 21 March 1925, Sotheby's Sale Catalogue, 9 July 1968.
22. Harold Scott, *The Early Doors*, 35, n. 1.
23. Orel, 95.
24. THN, 54; but so mistranscribed as to be meaningless.
25. See illustration, No. 2.
26. *The Era*, 4 July 1881.
27. G. Atherton, *Adventures of a Novelist*, 263.
28. LTH, 129. Hardy's prose notes and the poem are similar in description.
29. C. J. Weber, *Hardy of Wessex*, 116–122, gives the best summary of these events.
30. LTH, 137–139; Purdy, 38–39.
31. P.O. London Directory, London Suburbs (South), 1880.
32. Hardy to Gosse, 14 February 1922.
33. Kegan Paul to Hardy, 24 February 1881, DCM.
34. LTH, 146.
35. Björk, 327–329.
36. C. J. Weber, *Hardy of Wessex*, 126.
37. YTH, 139–140.
38. Millgate, 165.
39. Mary Hardy to Emma Hardy, 28 January 1881, DCM.

3: WIMBORNE, pp. 25–35

1. Clive Holland, *Thomas Hardy, O.M.*, 99.
2. LTH, 151–152.
3. C. J. Weber, *Hardy of Wessex*, 127.
4. *Thomas Hardy: The Critical Heritage*, 89.
5. LTH, 44–45.
6. St. Helier, *Memories of Fifty years*, 195.
7. *The Lancet*, 1904, i, 1163–1167; *British Medical Journal*, 1904, i, 991–993.
8. St. Helier, op.cit., 196.
9. LTH, 149.
10. Denys Kay-Robinson, *Hardy's Wessex Re-appraised*, 97–99.
11. THN, 61–62.
12. LTH, 150–151.
13. Millgate, 148.
14. LTH, 134, 136, and 126.
15. Thomas Hardy to Emma Hardy, 13 April 1891, DCM.
16. J. M, Barrie to Florence Hardy, 3 February 1928, quoted Millgate, 203.
17. St. Helier, *Memories of Fifty Years*, 2 and 188.
18. THN, 57.
19. B. and P. Russell (eds.), *The Amberley Papers* I, 24, 87, 349.
20. St. Helier, *Memories of Fifty Years*, 295–296.
21. LTH, 251.
22. Millgate, 187–188.
23. Preface to new edition, July 1895.
24. Rutland, 194–195.
25. Orel, 242 and 17.
26. See J. C. Maxwell, "Mrs. Grundy and 'Two on a Tower' ", *Thomas Hardy Year Book 1971*, 45–46 on Hardy's "impish sense of humour".
27. See above, p. 18.

28. Tindal Atkinson to Hardy, 31 December 1881, DCM.
29. D. F. Barber (ed.), *Concerning Thomas Hardy*, 141.
30. Purdy, 28–30, gives the best account, though it obscures the shortness of Hardy's *London* run.
31. Barry Duncan, *The St. James's Theatre*, 207–208.
32. Most of what follows is contained in various sources in the Theatre Museum, Victoria and Albert Museum.
33. DCM.
34. Purdy, 296, who does not, however, see the contemporary bearing of the verse.
35. ibid., 78–80.
36. *Thomas Hardy: The Critical Heritage*, 118–132.
37. LTH, 180.

4: DORSET HOME, pp. 35–49

1. Gerber and Davis, No. 1902.
2. ibid., No. 2318.
3. Millgate, 200 and 204.
4. LTH, 157.
5. C. J. Weber, *Hardy and the Lady from Madison Square*, 130.
6. LTH, 155.
7. THN, 62–63.
8. DCM.
9. DCM.
10. MTH, No. 22.
11. Bodleian Library, MS. Eng. Misc., d. 530, f. 93.
12. Camille Honig, "In Search of Thomas Hardy", *New Statesman*, 10 June 1944.
13. As suggested, but not developed, by Millgate, 233.
14. LTH, 167.
15. DCRO.
16. Edward Sampson, "Thomas Hardy—Justice of the Peace" (unpublished).
17. Millgate, 237–248.
18. Barbara Kerr, *Bound to the Soil: A Social History of Dorset*, Chapter X, "Dorchester: The Sovereign Seekers".
19. Personal information, Mrs. L. Largent.
20. Björk, 151.
21. *Kelly's Directory*, Dorchester, 1885; Kate Hardy's Teachers' Certificate, DCL.
22. LTH, 371.
23. LTH, 176.
24. St. Helier, *Memories of Fifty Years*, 240.
25. J.-E. Blanche, *Mes Modèles* (trans. Jo Manton).
26. LTH, 199.
27. Millgate, 198–199.
28. Philip Gosse, *A Naturalist Goes to War*, 78 (Penguin edition).
29. Letters to Hardy from Morley and Alexander Macmillan, DCM, contradict Hardy's own memory (LTH, 168), which is followed by Purdy, 56.
30. S. L. Bensusan, quoted Blunden, *Thomas Hardy*, 173.
31. W. R. Rutland, *Thomas Hardy*, 87.
32. Accounts, Overseers of the Poor, Melbury Osmond, DCRO.
33. Hardy to Gosse, 3 and 5 April, 1887.
34. DCM.
35. Barbara Kerr, *Bound to the Soil: A Social History of Dorset*, Chapter VII "Thornford: The Clay and Coppice People".
36. LTH, 153.
37. LTH, 185.
38. As pointed out by Evelyn Hardy, "Thomas Hardy and Turner", *London Magazine*, June/July 1975.
39. William Rothenstein, *Men and Memories*, 302.

40. Hardy to Gosse, 24 December 1886.
41. E. Charteris, *Life of Edmund Gosse*, 157.
42. Henry Gifford, "Thomas Hardy and Emma", *Essays and Studies* (1966), 113.
43. C. J. Weber, *Hardy and the Lady from Madison Square*, 131.

5: THE ORIGINAL TESS, pp. 50–62

1. L. Edel (ed.), *The Diary of Alice James*, 93.
2. F. Mabel Robinson to Irene Cooper Willis, 17 December 1939, DCM.
3. LTH, 187.
4. Hardy to Gosse, 3 April 1887.
5. LTH, 189.
6. LTH, 188.
7. Hardy to Gosse, 3 April 1887.
8. Typescript of *Life* (Mrs. Hardy's copy), DCM. Cancelled passage.
9. Emma Hardy's Italian Diary, 1887, DCM.
10. LTH, 190–196.
11. Emma Hardy's Italian Diary, 1887, DCM.
12. Simon Nowell-Smith (ed.), *Letters to Macmillan*, 130–131.
13. Purdy, 72.
14. Gosse to J. A. Symonds, 24 February 1890, University of Bristol, quoted Phyllis Grosskurth, *John Addington Symonds*, 280–281.
15. Hardy to Gosse, 11 November 1886.
16. Gosse to Hardy, 28 August 1887, DCM.
17. LTH, 200, 201, 203.
18. LTH, 207–208.
19. LTH, 202.
20. LTH, 153. Other facets of this unnamed character anticipate Alec d'Urberville.
21. *Victoria County History*, Berkshire, Fawley and Chaddleworth, P.O. Directory.
22. Fawley parish registers.
23. ibid.
24. Puddletown parish registers.
25. LTH, 282.
26. Register of baptisms, St. Mary's, Reading.
27. Calendar of prisoners in the County Bridewell, QSR/253, Berkshire County Record Office; Court Order Book, ibid.
28. L. Radzinowitz, *A History of English Criminal Law and its Administration from 1750*, 144, n. 23, 578, 670, 703, Appendix II.
29. QSR/253, Berkshire County Record Office.
30. MTH, No. 20.
31. DCM.
32. Christ's Hospital Records, Guildhall.
33. LTH, 201.
34. LTH, 207.
35. LTH, 210.
36. By Evelyn Hardy, "Thomas Hardy and Turner", *London Magazine* June/July 1975, 23–25.
37. Personal information, Norman Atkins.
38. LTH, 209–212.
39. I owe my knowledge of this story to Professor Norman Page. It was fully reported in *The Times*.
40. J. T. Laird, *The Shaping of "Tess of the d'Urbervilles"*, which gives an admirably full account of the various forms *Tess* took.
41. Warneford Hospital, Case Book VI. Class No. WV/7/vi.
42. SREH, 28.
43. Personal comment, Dr. Richard Hunter.
44. Florence Hardy to Rebekah Owen, 24 October 1915.

6: TESS AND JUDE, pp. 63–78

1. T. P. O'Connor, reporting, perhaps not trustworthily, a remark to his wife. Repr. MTH, No. 54.
2. Emma Hardy to the Editor, *Daily Chronicle*, 5 September 1891, DCM.
3. Maggs Sale Catalogue, 1938, No. 664, item 197.
4. DCM.
5. Quoted Millgate, 302.
6. LTH, 224.
7. ORFW, 15, 82.
8. J. T. Laird, *The Shaping of "Tess of the d'Urbervilles"*, 5.
9. Millgate, 263, offers an excellent summary of some of these activities.
10. LTH, 220.
11. Theatre Museum, Victoria and Albert Museum.
12. LTH, 224.
13. Information, John Antell.
14. Kelly's P.O. Directory, 1890, 1895, 1900. Hardy also bought 51 High West Street.
15. By Melvyn Bragg. See below, p. 85.
16. YTH, 215–216; Millgate, 401, n. 11. See also above, Chapter 5, p. 57.
17. See Millgate, 265, for many similar examples.
18. Björk, 11, 404, 405.
19. J. A. Symonds to Hardy, 9 April 1889 and 7 January 1892, DCM.
20. Katherine Adams to Sydney Cockerell, 4 August 1920, *The Best of friends*, 24–25.
21. Sir Henry Thompson to Hardy, 22 October 1890, DCM.
22. Edward Clodd, *Memories*, 161–162.
23. *Speaker* (London) IV, 26 December 1891.
24. Millgate, 300–302.
25. Beatty, 33.
26. LTH, 254.
27. J. Pope-Hennessey, *Lord Crewe*, 3–5, 14–15, 19, 38, 40.
28. Raymond Blathwayt, "The Hon. Mrs. Arthur Henniker", *The Woman at Home*, 1895.
29. ORFW, 14–15.
30. ORFW, 3.
31. ORFW, 15.
32. ORFW, 20.
33. ORFW, 29.
34. ORFW, 33.
35. ORFW, 31.
36. YTH, illustration 14b.
37. Purdy, 345.
38. Anna Winchcombe, "Four Letters from Tryphena", *Dorset*.
39. G. K. Chesterton, *Autobiography*, 277.
40. (Unsigned) *Illustrated London News*, 18 August 1894, p. 195.
41. LTH, 433.
42. YTH, Chapter 9.
43. J.-E. Blanche, *Mes Modèles*, 84 (trans. Jo Manton).
44. Rosamund Tomson to Hardy, [1889], DCM.

7: PROSE TO POETRY, pp. 79–92

1. ORFW, 46.
2. Hawkins, 147.
3. ORFW, 47.
4. Hawkins, 147.
5. *Weekly Sun*, repr. in DCC, 20 June 1895.
6. ORFW, 48.
7. Millgate, 325.

8. Hardy to Gosse, 14 July 1909.
9. Emma Hardy to Rebekah Owen, 24 April 1899.
10. TLS, 1 January 1940.
11. DCM.
12. Richard M. Ludwig (ed.), *Letters of Ford Madox Ford* viii.
13. Ford Madox Ford *Mightier Than the Sword*, 128–130. Copied and adapted, without discrimination or acknowledgement, three years later by Carl J. Weber in his *Hardy of Wessex* (1st ed., 1940) which began the legend.
14. Emma Hardy to Rebekah Owen, 17 February 1897.
15. Hardy to Gosse.
16. Emma Hardy to Edward Clodd, 29 March 1897, Brotherton Library.
17. Hardy to the Editor, *Temple Bar*, 9 March 1896, Eton School Library.
18. D. Hawkins, "Concerning Agnes", *Encounter*, February 1977.
19. William Rothenstein, *Men and Memories*, I, 303.
20. Hardy to Edward Clodd, 17 January 1907, Ashley 5723, f. 2, British Library.
21. LTH, 281.
22. "*Dearest Emmie*", 37.
23. ORFW, 53–54.
24. LTH, 285.
25. Quoted Blunden, *Thomas Hardy*, 112.
26. ORFW, 44.
27. As suggested by Melvyn Bragg in his Royal Society of Literature lecture, May 1975.
28. ORFW, 58.
29. J. Hillis Miller (ed.) provides useful details of both versions (New Wessex edition).
30. Stourhead Collection, Wiltshire County Archives.
31. MS. version; altered in printed version to end "it near".
32. Florence Hardy to Louise Yearsley, 18 April 1923.
33. Not 1904, as all biographies repeat; but see below, Chapter 9.
34. Florence Hardy to Winifred Thomson, 29 August 1928, Bodleian MS. Eng. Misc., d. 534, f. 132.
35. LTH, 250–251.
36. "*Dearest Emmie*", 39–40.
37. A. E. Filmer, quoted Blunden, *Thomas Hardy*, 170–171.
38. ORFW, 66.
39. LTH, 285.
40. LTH, 293.
41. ORFW, 65–66; LTH, 295.
42. ORFW, 71.
43. ORFW, 72.

8: WAR AT HOME AND ABROAD, pp. 93–105

1. Hardy to Gosse, 27 December 1898.
2. Alfred Pretor to Emma Hardy, December 1898, DCM. See also Phyllis Grosskurth, *John Addington Symonds*, 33, 35–36.
3. Quoted Bailey, 21.
4. Newman Flower, *Just As It Happened*, 96.
5. Bodleian MS. Eng. Misc., d. 530, ff. 93–96.
6. ibid., 89.
7. Quoted YTH, 148.
8. See above, p. 38.
9. No. 775, Sotheby's Sale Catalogue, 9 July 1968.
10. Emma Hardy to Rebekah Owen, 27 December 1899.
11. Dr. Roger Fiske, personal communication.
12. DCM.
13. Gerber and Davis, No. 1229.
14. LTH, 303.
15. *Daily Chronicle*, 8 September 1899.

16. Quoted Blunden, *Thomas Hardy*, 106 and 109.
17. Carl J. Weber, *Hardy and the Lady from Madison Square*, 134.
18. Emma Hardy to Rebekah Owen, 19 February 1897.
19. Emma Hardy to Rebekah Owen, May 1900.
20. Emma Hardy to Rebekah Owen, 24 April 1899.
21. Bertha Newcome to Mrs. Gosse, 8 March, Brotherton Library.
22. Emma Hardy to Rebekah Owen, 24 April 1899.
23. Emma Hardy to Rebekah Owen, 27 December 1899.
24. LTH, 302.
25. THN, 68.
26. ORFW, 76.
27. See Bailey, 191–192.
28. Emma Hardy to Rebekah Owen, 27 February 1899, quoted Bailey, 114.
29. Emma Hardy to Rebekah Owen, 31 December 1900.
30. ORFW, 88.
31. Hardy to Gosse, 6 March 1899.
32. LTH, 304.
33. LTH, 328.
34. Orel, 201–203.
35. *"Dearest Emmie"*, 43.
36. ORFW, 89.
37. Quoted Carl J. Weber, *Hardy and the Lady from Madison Square*, 132.
38. No. 775, Sotheby's Sale Catalogue, 9 July 1968.
39. *"Dearest Emmie"*, 41.
40. ibid.
41. Walter Gifford to Emma, 7 September 1898, DCM.
42. *"Dearest Emmie"*, 43–45, though confused by the editor, C. J. Weber's assumptions, such as the idea that Emma's sister was still living in Cornwall, which she had left years before.
43. Emma Hardy to Rebekah Owen, 4 March 1902.
44. "Wives in the Sere", *The Tatler*, 31 July 1901.

9: DYNASTS AND DESTINIES, pp. 106–121

1. Warneford Hospital, Case Book VII, W.V./7/vii, 1 March 1900.
2. Hardy to Gosse, 31 January 1904, 28 February 1906, 5 March 1908.
3. H. W. Nevinson, *Changes and Chances*, 307–308, quoted Blunden, *Thomas Hardy*, 110.
4. J.-E. Blanche, *Mes Modèles*, 82 (trans. Jo Manton).
5. Gerber and Davis, Nos. 305, 1427, 1731.
6. E. Smyth, *As Time Went On*, 205.
7. A. C. Benson, *The Diary of Arthur Christopher Benson*, 81–82.
8. Elizabeth Cathcart Hickson, *The Versification of Thomas Hardy*.
9. LTH, 114.
10. LTH, 145 and Preface to *The Dynasts*.
11. LTH, 148.
12. LTH, 152.
13. LTH, 177.
14. LTH, 203.
15. LTH, 221.
16. LTH, 225.
17. LTH, 247.
18. LTH, 284.
19. See above, p. 32.
20. A. E. Filmer to Edmund Blunden, quoted Blunden, *Thomas Hardy*, 170–171.
21. Orel, 145.
22. *Thomas Hardy: The Critical Heritage*, 344.
23. Walter F. Wright, *The Shaping of "The Dynasts"*, 304–305.
24. ibid., 37.

25. ibid., 38–53 & 53 n.
26. *Wilfred Owen: Collected Letters*, ed. Owen and Bell, 355, 487, 547–8.
27. J.-E. Blanche, *Mes Modèles*, 81, 83, 84, 87–88 (trans. Jo Manton).
28. ibid., 83.
29. In *Portraits of a Lifetime*, a so-called translation of *Mes Modèles* by Walter Clement, 179.
30. Agnes Grove, *The Social Fetich*, 14.
31. *"Dearest Emmie"*, 54–62.
32. Hardy to Gosse, 3 January 1905.
33. Bodleian, MS. Eng. Misc., d. 177, ff. 314–317.
34. Orel, 66–72.
35. Personal information, John Antell.
36. Warneford Hospital, Case Book VI, W.V./7/vi, 1897–1899.
37. LTH, 333; Roger Fulford, *Votes for Women*, 137; Thomas Hardy to Millicent Fawcett, 30 November 1906, Fawcett Library. Emma "marched" in a carriage.
38. LTH, 326.
39. Florence Hardy to Louise Yearsley, 10 April 1923, and Mrs. Henniker to Hardy, 20 March 1914, DCM.
40. ORFW, 19 and note 62.

10: FLORENCE AND THE DUGDALES, pp. 122–136

1. Birth certificate, Edward Dugdale, General Registry.
2. Langton Matravers, parish records, DCRO.
3. Census, 1851, Portsmouth.
4. Logbook, St. Andrew's School, Enfield.
5. General Registry.
6. Kelly's Directories, 1899, 1903, 1907, 1909, 1915, 1918, 1922.
7. Obituary of Edward Dugdale, *Enfield Gazette*, 5 June 1936.
8. MTH, No. 2.
9. MTH, No. 14.
10. Letter from a contemporary, Violet Hilling.
11. St. Andrew's (Boys) School logbooks.
12. St. Andrew's School logbooks and P.O. Directories.
13. St. Andrew's School logbooks.
14. Personal information, J. E. Westaway.
15. Kate Hardy's postcard collection.
16. Florence Hardy to Rebekah Owen, 24 June 1917.
17. *Meyer's Observer and Local and General Advertiser*, Enfield.
18. Florence Hardy to Rebekah Owen, 1 March 1916.
19. Hardy to Edward Clodd, 22 July 1909, Ashley 5723, f. 6, British Library.
20. Macmillan archive, British Library.
21. Various letters to Rebekah Owen.
22. Hardy to Elspeth Grahame, 31 August 1907, Bodleian Misc. MSS.
23. See poem *On the Departure Platform*.
24. Florence Dugdale to Edward Clodd, 11 November 1910, reveals his name.
25. Obituary, *Lancet*, 8 June 1912, *Who Was Who*.
26. Florence Hardy to Rebekah Owen, 3 and 17 December 1915.
27. Emma Hardy to Rebekah Owen, 27 December 1899.
28. Hardy to Macmillan, 8 July 1907, Macmillan archive, British Library.
29. Florence Hardy to Rebekah Owen, 26 October 1916.
30. Hardy to Archibald Marshall, 9 July 1907.
31. Personal information.
32. Florence Hardy to Rebekah Owen, 22 November 1915.
33. Reginald Smith to Hardy, 22 September 1907, DCM.
34. C. J. Weber and C. C. Weber (eds.), *Thomas Hardy's Correspondence*.
35. Netta Syrett, *The Sheltering Tree*, 194.
36. Cf. Hardy's poems *Her Initials* and *At the Pyramid of Cestius*.

37. See below, p. 146.
38. MS. notes by Mrs. Healis, Colby College Library.
39. J.-E. Blanche, *Mes Modèles*, 85 (trans. Jo Manton).
40. Winifred Fortescue, *There's Rosemary . . . There's Rue*, 110.
41. In a letter to the author.
42. Bailey, 22.
43. V. Meynell (ed.), *Friends of a Lifetime*, 304.
44. Hardy to Clarendon Press, 19 January 1907, Bodleian Eng. lett. E i.
45. Hardy to Clarendon Press, 1907–1908, Bodleian Eng. lett. E i.
46. See the poems *Had You Wept* and *After the Visit* (to F.E.D.).
47. "Perhaps apocryphal though "symbolically true".
48. Gosse to Hardy, 4 March 1908.
49. Quoted LTH, 341.
50. LTH, 336.
51. Hardy to Edward Clodd, 29 October 1909, Ashley 5723, f. 9, British Library.

11: FLORENCE AND EMMA AND THOMAS, pp. 137–148

1. Hardy to Edward Clodd, 22 and 28 July, 30 August, 3 November 1909; LTH, 349, Kate Hardy's postcard collection; Hardy to Edward Clodd, October 1911, May 1912.
2. Hardy to Edward Clodd, Ashley 5768 f. 44, 5723 f. 6, 5768 f. 45, A3350 p. 132, f. 67, British Library.
3. LTH, 346, 347.
4. Hardy to Edware Clodd, 13 July 1909, Ashley 5723, f. 4, British Library.
5. Hardy to Edmund Gosse, 14 July 1909.
6. Hardy to Edward Clodd, 1 May 1909, Ashley 5768, f. 43.
7. See above, p. 82.
8. Typescript of *The Later Years* (Mrs. Hardy's copy), DCM.
9. Wrongly named "Trevett" in MTH, No. 65.
10. Wrongly named "Griffiths", ibid.
11. *"Dearest Emmie"*, 68, wrongly assumes her to be Florence Dugdale.
12. I. C. Willis to Evelyn Hardy, 1961. I am greatly indebted to Evelyn Hardy for this information.
13. W. R. Rutland, *Thomas Hardy* (O.M. Series), 110.
14. Emma Hardy to Rebekah Owen, 14 February and 24 April 1899; 26 December 1906.
15. Emma Hardy to Rebekah Owen, 26 December 1906.
16. Emma Hardy to Rebekah Owen, 7 November 1907.
17. Emma Hardy to Rebekah Owen, 13 May 1908.
18. *"Dearest Emmie"*, 72–82.
19. Mrs. Watts Dunton to Emma Hardy, January 1909, Miriam Lutcher Stark Library, University of Texas, and DCC.
20. See above, p. 119.
21. Personal information, Norman Atkins.
22. Emma Hardy to Rebekah Owen, 20 May 1908.
23. Ethel M. Richardson, "Recollections of Thomas Hardy, O.M. (1910–1928)", *St. Katherine's College Magazine* (1961), 26.
24. Emma Hardy to Alda, Lady Hoare, 20 April 1910.
25. LTH, 350.
26. DCM.
27. LTH, 350.
28. W. F. Oakeshot, *The Times Saturday Review*, 19 February 1977.
29. Florence Dugdale to Edward Clodd, 11 November 1910.
30. ibid.
31. DCM.
32. V. H. Collins to C. J. Weber, 13 September 1943.
33. Florence Dugdale to Edward Clodd, 9 November 1910.
34. Kate Hardy's postcard collection, Eton School Library.
35. ORFW, 147.

36. Florence Dugdale to Edward Clodd, 2 February 1911.
37. Purdy, 285–286.
38. ORFW, 146.
39. According to Florence's sisters. Purdy, 314.
40. Hardy to Edward Clodd, 17 June 1910, Brotherton Library.
41. Purdy, 314.
42. DCM.
43. Florence Dugdale to Emma Hardy, 22 August 1910, DCM.
44. Reprinted MTH, No. 29.
45. Henry Gifford, "Thomas Hardy and Emma", *Essays and Studies*, N.S. XIX (1966), **114.**
46. "I was Emma Lavinia's personal maid", *Hardy Year Book* No. 4.
47. A. M. Ashdown, *A Complete System of Nursing* (1917), 195–196.
48. Emma Hardy to the Rev. R. G. Bartelot, Colby College Library.
49. ORFW, 153.
50. Beinecke Library, Yale University.
51. D. F. Barber (ed.), *Concerning Thomas Hardy*, 77.

12: A SATIRE OF CIRCUMSTANCE, pp. 149–163

1. Florence Dugdale to Edward Clodd, 16 January 1913.
2. Florence Dugdale to Edward Clodd, 21 August 1913.
3. Florence Dugdale to Edward Clodd, 30 January 1913.
4. "I Was Emma Lavinia's personal maid". *Thomas Hardy Year Book*, No. 4.
5. Florence Dugdale to Edward Clodd, 7 March 1913.
6. Florence Dugdale to Edward Clodd, 30 January 1913.
7. Florence Hardy to Edward Clodd, 7 March 1913.
8. Florence Hardy to Edward Clodd, 30 January 1913.
9. Florence Hardy to Edward Clodd, 7 March 1913.
10. Charles Moule to Emma Hardy, DCM.
11. Florence Hardy to Edward Clodd, 30 January 1913.
12. ORFW, 154.
13. Richard Hunter, *Psychiatry for the Poor*, 191.
14. Emma Hardy to Rebekah Owen, 19 February 1897.
15. *The Master Christian* (1900), 89.
16. F. R. Leavis, "Hardy the Poet", *The Southern Review*, Summer 1940.
17. DCM.
18. Florence Hardy to Howard Bliss, 9 March 1936, Princeton University Library.
19. Mistranscribed "T. C. Dugdale" in Purdy, 246.
20. Florence Dugdale to Edward Clodd, 11 March 1913.
21. ibid.
22. ibid.
23. See SREH, *passim*.
24. Florence Hardy to Rebekah Owen, 20 March 1914.
25. Florence Hardy to Louisa Yearsley, 10 April 1923.
26. LTH.
27. DCM, H. 1975. 316.22.
28. Mary Hardy to Thomas Hardy, June 1913, DCM.
29. All quotations are from the *English Review* version.
30. By Bailey, 307–308.
31. Florence Hardy to Alda, Lady Hoare, 9 April 1914.
32. Florence Hardy to Alda, Lady Hoare, 22 July 1914.
33. Florence Hardy to Rebekah Owen, 9 February 1914.
34. Florence Hardy to Rebekah Owen, 15 December 1915.
35. Florence Dugdale to Edward Clodd, 11 November 1911.
36. P.C.C. Wills, Somerset House. Obituary, *British Medical Journal*, June 1912.
37. Personal information.
38. Florence Hardy to Alda, Lady Hoare, 9 December 1914.

39. Florence Hardy to Alda, Lady Hoare, 7 April 1914.
40. Florence Dugdale to Rebekah Owen, 31 December 1913.
41. Florence Hardy to Rebekah Owen, 10 February 1914.
42. Florence Dugdale to Edward Clodd, 1 January 1914.
43. Florence Hardy to Rebekah Owen, 9 February 1914.
44. St. Andrew's School logbook.
45. Hardy to Alda, Lady Hoare, 13 February 1914.
46. F. Mabel Robinson to Hardy, 12 February 1914, DCM.
47. Hardy to Alda, Lady Hoare, 13 February 1914.
48. Florence Hardy to Rebekah Owen, 13 February 1914.
49. Hardy to Frederic Harrison, 17 February 1914, Miriam Lutcher Stark Library, University of Texas.
50. Florence Hardy to Alda, Lady Hoare, 5 April 1914.
51. Florence Hardy to Rebekah Owen, 1 June 1914.
52. Florence Hardy to Alda, Lady Hoare, 22 and 26 July 1914.
53. Florence Hardy to Rebekah Owen, 5 September 1914.
54. From "A Poet".
55. Purdy, 172.
56. Hardy to Gosse, 16 April 1918.

13: DEATHS AND VISIONS, pp. 164–176

1. Florence Hardy to Rebekah Owen, 17 October 1914.
2. Anne [Thackeray] Ritchie to Hardy, 24 July [1917].
3. Florence Hardy to Alda, Lady Hoare, 29 November 1914.
4. Florence Hardy to Alda, Lady Hoare, 6 December 1914.
5. Florence Hardy to Alda, Lady Hoare, 27 January 1915.
6. Florence Hardy to Alda, Lady Hoare, 7 January 1922.
7. Florence Hardy to Alda, Lady Hoare, 23 March 1915.
8. Hardy to Alfred Pope, 28 May 1915, quoted in *Concerning Thomas Hardy*, 144.
9. Florence Hardy to Rebekah Owen, 30 December 1915.
10. Florence Hardy to Rebekah Owen, 1 October 1915.
11. ibid.
12. Florence Hardy to Rebekah Owen, 23 June 1915.
13. ibid.
14. Florence Hardy to Rebekah Owen, 17 July 1915.
15. Florence Hardy to Rebekah Owen, 23 June 1915.
16. Florence Hardy to Rebekah Owen, 4 March 1917.
17. Florence Hardy to Rebekah Owen, 5 May 1915.
18. Florence Hardy to Rebekah Owen, 17 July 1915.
19. ibid.
20. Florence Hardy to Rebekah Owen, 22 September 1916.
21. Florence Hardy to Alda, Lady Hoare, 24 August 1915.
22. Hardy later said "he would have welcomed a child" in 1914, but there is no evidence he "hoped" for one. The provision for one in his 1922 will is a legal formality; in 1923 the idea "fills him with horror". Add. MSS. 58498, British Library.
23. Puddletown registers, General Registry.
24. Kate Hardy's postcard collection, Eton School Library.
25. Florence Hardy to Rebekah Owen, 1 December 1914.
26. Florence Hardy to Alda, Lady Hoare, 6 February 1916.
27. Death certificate, General Registry.
28. Admons. P.C.C., Somerset House.
29. Florence Hardy to Rebekah Owen, 30 December 1915.
30. Mary Hardy to Augustus Hardy, March 1912, in the possession of James Gibson.
31. Kate Hardy's postcard collection, Eton School Library.
32. LTH, 371 and 430.
33. Florence Hardy to Alda, Lady Hoare, 20 May 1917.
34. Florence Hardy to Alda, Lady Hoare, 26 December 1917.

35. Florence Hardy to Rebekah Owen, 13 December 1916.
36. Florence Hardy to Rebekah Owen, 18 January 1916.
37. Sassoon to Sydney Cockerell, 14 October 1940.
38. Florence Hardy to Rebekah Owen, January 1916.
39. Florence Hardy to Rebekah Owen, 22 October 1916.
40. Florence Hardy to Rebekah Owen, 14 December 1916.
41. Mrs. Healis, MS. notes on Florence's letters, Colby College Library.
42. Edward Clodd to J. H. Bulloch, 14 January 1928, Miriam Lutcher Stark Library, University of Texas.
43. Florence Hardy to Rebekah Owen, 26 October 1916.
44. Florence Hardy to Rebekah Owen, 15 May 1916.
45. Florence Hardy to Rebekah Owen, 5 June 1916.
46. Florence Hardy to Rebekah Owen, 4 March 1917.
47. Florence Hardy to Rebekah Owen, 5 May 1916.
48. Florence Hardy to Alda, Lady Hoare, 5 September 1916.
49. Florence Hardy to Rebekah Owen, 5 June 1916.
50. Florence Hardy to Rebekah Owen, 3 December 1916.
51. Purdy, 187.
52. H. V. Marrot (ed.), *The Life and Letters of John Galsworthy*, 750–753.
53. Florence Hardy to Alda, Lady Hoare, 6 August 1915; List of titles, Hardy's copy of *Collected Poems* (1923), DCM.
54. Purdy, 208.

14: LATE AND EARLY, pp. 177–190

1. Notably J. C. Squire and Edward Shanks.
2. Hardy to Gosse, 18 February 1918, Ashley MS. A. 858, British Library.
3. Hardy to Sir George Douglas, 12 December 1915, Royal Library of Scotland.
4. E. Clodd, *Memories*, 34.
5. Kate Hardy's Diary, DCL.
6. Receipt, Lock Collection, DCL.
7. DCM.
8. Bodleian, 28001, d. 533.
9. Florence Hardy to Louisa Yearsley, 10 June 1917.
10. Florence Hardy to Louisa Yearsley, May 1917.
11. Florence Hardy to Louisa Yearsley, 17 June 1917.
12. ibid.
13. Florence Hardy to Louisa Yearsley, August 1917.
14. ibid.
15. Florence Hardy to Louisa Yearsley, 17 June 1917.
16. Florence Hardy to Rebekah Owen, 28 August 1917.
17. Purdy, 266.
18. Florence Hardy to Howard Bliss, 10 January 1931, Princeton University Library.
19. J. I. M. Stewart, *Thomas Hardy*, Chapter 1.
20. LTH, 229.
21. Lock Collection, DCL.
22. LTH, 21.
23. Florence Hardy to Rebekah Owen, 24 June 1917.
24. Florence Hardy to Rebekah Owen, 28 August 1917.
25. Florence Hardy to Louisa Yearsley, July 1918.
26. Florence Hardy to Louisa Yearsley, August 1919.
27. Florence Hardy to St. John Ervine, 8 August 1921, Miriam Lutcher Stark Library, University of Texas.
28. Florence Hardy to Paul Lemperly, 19 March 1919, Colby College Library.
29. Kate Hardy's Diary.
30. Florence Hardy to Rebekah Owen, 4 August 1920. Hardy still used a hip-bath.
31. Florence Hardy to Louisa Yearsley, 7 July 1920.
32. Florence Hardy to Louisa Yearsley, 1 June 1920.

33. Purdy, 287–288.
34. Florence Hardy to Louisa Yearsley, 16 May 1920.
35. ibid., 10 November 1918.
36. H. M. Marrot (ed.), *Life and Letters of John Galsworthy*, 416.
37. LTH, 400.
38. Florence Hardy to Rebekah Owen, 8 July 1917.
39. Florence Hardy to Paul Lemperly, 28 October 1918.
40. LTH, 402.
41. Florence Hardy to Siegfried Sassoon, 9 February 1922.
42. ibid.
43. Florence Hardy to Paul Lemperly, 13 May 1922.
44. August 1910, DCM.
45. DCM, for the whole correspondence and Hardy's notes.
46. DCM.
47. LTH, 415.
48. Florence Hardy to Paul Lemperly, 5 December 1922.
49. D. Mackail, *The Story of J. M. Barrie*, 555.
50. "A Jingle on the Times", December 1914.
51. Florence Hardy to Louisa Yearsley, 27 February 1920.

15: A HUMAN SHOW, pp. 191–202

1. V. Meynell (ed.), *Friends of a Lifetime*, 306.
2. H. V. Marrot (ed.), *Life and Letters of John Galsworthy*, 507.
3. Florence Hardy to Louisa Yearsley, 16 May 1920.
4. Florence Hardy to Rebekah Owen, 15 October 1920.
5. LTH, 422–423.
6. L. Abercrombie, "Mr Hardy's Play", *Nation and Athenaeum*, XXXIV, 29 December 1923.
7. Florence Hardy to Louisa Yearsley, 21 December 1923.
8. Literary Notebook II, DCM.
9. Florence Hardy to Alda, Lady Hoare, 21 June 1921.
10. Florence Hardy to Paul Lemperly, 2 August 1923.
11. Kate Hardy's Diary.
12. Purdy, 349–350.
13. Florence Hardy to Louisa Yearsley, undated, c. 1923.
14. V. Meynell (ed.), *Friends of a Lifetime*, 300.
15. Florence Hardy to Louisa Yearsley, 19 June 1921.
16. Kate Hardy's Diary, DCL.
17. Florence Hardy to Louisa Yearsley, 17 September 1922.
18. ibid., 30 September 1920.
19. Florence Hardy to Rebekah Owen, 29 October 1922.
20. Hardy to Macleod Yearsley, 7 June 1923.
21. Florence Hardy to Louisa Yearsley, 21 December 1923.
22. Kate Hardy's Diary.
23. MTH, No. 17.
24. Kate Hardy's Diary.
25. Florence Hardy to Louisa Yearsley, 30 December 1920.
26. Florence Hardy to Gertrude Bugler, 13 June 1922, in the possession of Mrs. Bugler.
27. Florence Hardy to Louisa Yearsley, 20 June 1924.
28. ibid.
29. Florence Hardy to Rebekah Owen, 24 November 1924.
30. Personal information, Gertrude Bugler.
31. MTH, No. 1.
32. Wilfred Blunt, *Cockerell*, 214–216.
33. Florence Hardy to Rebekah Owen, 16 February 1925.
34. MTH, No. 2.
35. Florence Hardy to Paul Lemperly, 25 March 1925.

36. Purdy, 265.
37. LTH, 419.
38. Purdy, 247.
39. "Two Innovators", *Saturday Review*, CXL, 19 December 1925.

16: WINTER'S LAST WORD, pp. 203-214

1. Kate Hardy's Diary.
2. V. Meynell (ed.), *Friends of a Lifetime*, 293.
3. Harold Owen and John Bell (eds.), *Letters of Wilfred Owen*, 505.
4. S. Jackson, *The Sassoons*, 179.
5. Florence Hardy to Louisa Yearsley, n.d., c. 1925.
6. R. Graves, *Goodbye to All That*, 268-272.
7. Florence Hardy to Siegfried Sassoon, 17 December 1924.
8. Virginia Woolf, *A Writer's Diary*, 89-94.
9. C. Tolchard (ed.), *Letters to Clifford Tolchard from John Cowper Powys*, 29.
10. Gosse to Hardy, 9 November 1927.
11. V. Meynell (ed.), *Friends of a Lifetime*, 309-310.
12. ibid., 301.
13. MTH, no. 25.
14. LTH, 440.
15. E. Margaret Lane, *Edgar A. Lane, Musician*, 17.
16. Desmond Hawkins, "Concerning Agnes", *Encounter*, February 1977.
17. V. Meynell (ed.), *Friends of a Lifetime*, 314.
18. Purdy, 257, says, "It is a woman addressed", but gives no authority.
19. See above, pp. 156-7.
20. Florence Hardy's Diary, DCM.
21. ibid.
22. ibid.
23. Florence Hardy to Siegfried Sassoon, 4 January 1928.
24. Orel, 233-235
25. Kate Hardy's Diary.
26. Florence Hardy to Siegfried Sassoon, 13 March 1928.
27. W. Blunt, *Cockerell*, 184.
28. ibid., 218.
29. V. Meynell (ed.), *Friends of a Lifetime*, 315.
30. Kate Hardy's Diary, 315.
31. Florence Hardy to R. A. Scott-James, 9 May 1930, Miriam Lutcher Stark Library, University of Texas.
32. Dean of Westminster to the Rev. R. G. Bartelot, 17 January 1928.
33. W. Blunt, *Cockerell*, 219.
34. ibid., 220.
35. Florence Hardy to Colonel Weber, churchwarden of Stinsford, 11 November 1930, DCRO.
36. Florence Hardy to Paul Lemperly, 28 December 1928.
37. DCM.
38. Mrs. Thomas Hardy, obituary, *Enfield Gazette*.
39. Florence Hardy to Siegried Sassoon, 24 February and 13 March 1928.
40. ibid., 8 November 1933.
41. Florence Hardy to Paul Lemperly, 7 March 1937.
42. General Registry, deaths.
43. Florence Hardy to Paul Lemperly, 7 April 1935.
44. Information, John Antell.
45. Kate Hardy's Diary.

List of Sources

A. MANUSCRIPT

Berkshire County Record Office. Berkshire parish records, Quarter Sessions, etc.
Bodleian Library. Letters of Emma Hardy and Thomas Hardy to Mrs. Kenneth Grahame.
British Library. Letters of Thomas Hardy to Edward Clodd and Edmund Gosse. Macmillan Archive. Stopes Archive.
Brotherton Library. Letters of Florence Hardy to Edward Clodd. Letters of Thomas Hardy to Clodd and Gosse.
Bugler, Gertrude. Letters, etc.
Colby College, Waterville, Maine. Special Collections. Letters. Emma Hardy to the Revd. Richard Bartelot and to Rebekah Owen. Letters of Florence Hardy to Paul Lemperly and Rebekah Owen.
Dorset County Library. Lock Collection. Kate Hardy's Diary.
Dorset County Museum. Hardy Collection. Letters, etc.
Dorset County Record Office. Dorset Parish registers, etc.
School Library, Eton College. Letters. Florence Hardy to Siegfried Sassoon and Louisa Yearsley. Letter of Thomas Hardy to Macleod Yearsley.
Portsmouth City Library. Census. St. Paul's parish.
Probate of Wills, Public Record Office and Somerset House.
Potts, Mrs. Elizabeth. Letter. Thomas Hardy to Archibald Marshall.
Registers of Births, Marriages, and Deaths. General Registry.
St. Andrew's School (Boys), Enfield. Log Books.
Voremberg, Mrs. R. P. MSS. of the Revd. Richard Bartelot.
Warneford Hospital. Case Books.
Wiltshire County Record Office. Letters. Emma Hardy to Alda, Lady Hoare. Florence Hardy to Alda, Lady Hoare.

B. TYPESCRIPT

Hardy, F. E., "Notes of Thomas Hardy's Life . . . (taken down in conversations, etc.)". Dorset County Museum.
Sampson, Edward, "Thomas Hardy—Justice of the Peace".

C. PUBLISHED

Atherton, G., *Adventures of a Novelist*, New York, 1932.
Bailey, J. O., *The Poetry of Thomas Hardy: A Handbook and Commentary*, Chapel Hill, 1970.
Barber, D. F. (ed.), *Concerning Thomas Hardy*, London, 1968.
Beatty, C. J. P. (ed.), *The Architectural Notebook of Thomas Hardy*, Dorchester, 1966.
Björk, Lennart A. (ed.), *The Literary Notes of Thomas Hardy*, 2 vols., Gothenburg, 1974.
Blanche, J.-E., *Mes Modèles*, Paris, 1928.
Blunt, Wilfred, *Cockerell*, London, 1964.
Brooks, Jean R., *Thomas Hardy: The Poetic Structure*, London, 1971.
Brown, Douglas, *Thomas Hardy*, London, 1961.
Chadwick, Owen, *The Victorian Church*, 2 vols., London, 1970.
Clark, G. S. R. Kitson, *The Making of Victorian England*, Oxford. 1960.
Clemens, Cyril, "My Chat with Thomas Hardy", *Dalhousie Review*, April 1943.
Clodd, E., *Memories*, London, 1916.
Colby Library Quarterly, *A Descriptive Catalogue . . . of the Works of Thomas Hardy*, Waterville, Maine, 1940.
Collins, V. H., *Talks with Thomas Hardy*, New York, 1928.
Compton-Rickett, A., *I Look Back: Memories of Fifty Years*, London, 1933.

Cox, J. S. (gen. ed.), *Materials . . . for a Life of Thomas Hardy*, 72 vols., St. Peter Port, Guernsey, 1962–.

(ed.), *The Thomas Hardy Year Book*, 1970–.

Deacon, Lois and Coleman, Terry, *Providence and Mr. Hardy*, London, 1966.

Dolman, Frederick, "An Evening with Thomas Hardy", *Young Man*, VIII, March 1894, 74–9.

Ellis, S. M., "Some Personal Recollections of Thomas Hardy", *Fortnightly Review*, N. S. CXXIII, March 1928, 393–406.

Felkin, Elliott, "Days with Thomas Hardy: from a 1918–1919 diary", *Encounter*, XVIII, April 1962, 27–33.

Flower, Newman, *Just As It Happened*, New York, 1950.

"Walks and Talks with Thomas Hardy", *The Countryman*, XXXIV, Winter 1966, 193–5.

Ford, F. Madox, *Mightier than the Sword*, London, 1938.

Gerber, H. E. and Davis, W. E. (eds.), *Thomas Hardy: An Annotated Bibliography of Writings about Him*, Northern Illinois, 1973.

Gifford, Henry, "Thomas Hardy and Emma", *Essays and Studies*, N. S. XIX (1966), 106–121.

Grosskurth, P., *John Addington Symonds*, London, 1964.

Grove, Agnes, *The Social Fetich*, London, 1907.

Guerard, Albert J., *Thomas Hardy, The Novels and Stories*, Oxford, 1959.

Haggard, H. Rider, *Rural England*, 2 vols., London, 1902.

Halliday, F. E., *Thomas Hardy: His Life and Work*, Bath, 1972.

Hardy, Evelyn, "Hardy and the Phrenologist", *John O'London's Weekly*, 26 February 1954.

"Some Unpublished Poems by Thomas Hardy", *London Magazine*, III (1956), 28–39.

Thomas Hardy: A Critical Biography, London, 1954.

"An Unpublished Poem by Thomas Hardy", *Times Literary Supplement*, 2 June 1966; and Robert Gittings (eds.), *Some Recollections by Emma Hardy*, Oxford, 1961; and F. B. Pinion (eds.), *One Rare Fair Woman: Letters of Thomas Hardy to Florence Henniker*, London, 1973.

Hardy, Florence E., *The Early Life of Thomas Hardy: 1840–1891*, London, 1928.

The Later Years of Thomas Hardy: 1892–1928, London, 1930.

The Life of Thomas Hardy: 1840–1928, London, 1962. (*The Life* is a one-volume publication of *The Early Life* and *The Later Years*. All, except the last few years, was really written by Hardy himself.)

Hardy, Thomas, "Death of Miss Mary Hardy", *Dorset County Chronicle*, 2 December 1915.

Hawkins, Desmond, *Thomas Hardy*, Newton Abbot, 1976.

Hickson, E. Cathcart, *The Versification of Thomas Hardy*, Pennsylvania, 1931.

Holland, Clive, "My Walks and Talks in Wessex with Thomas Hardy", *John O'London's Weekly*, 30 March 1951.

Howe, Irving, *Thomas Hardy*, London, 1967.

Hunter, R. and Macalpine, I., *Psychiatry for the Poor*, London, 1974.

Hynes, Samuel, *The Pattern of Hardy's Poetry*, Chapel Hill, 1961.

Jones, Bernard (ed.), *The Poems of William Barnes*, 2 vols., Fontwell, 1963.

Kay-Robinson, Denys, *Hardy's Wessex Re-Appraised*, Newton Abbot, 1972.

Kerr, Barbara, *Bound to the Soil: A Social History of Dorset*, repr. Wakefield, 1975.

Kingsgate, J., "*Tess* and Thomas Hardy, New Facts about his Life in London", *Graphic*, CXII, 5 September 1925.

Lane, E. Margaret, *Edgar Lane, Musician*, Dorchester, 1976.

Lewis, R. W. M., *The Family of Moule of Melksham, Fordington, and Melbourne*, privately printed (1938).

Maitland, F. W., *The Life and Letters of Leslie Stephen*, London, 1906.

Marrot, H. V. (ed.), *Life and Letters of John Galsworthy*, London, 1935.

Meynell, Viola (ed.), *Friends of a Lifetime: Letters to Sydney Cockerell*, London, 1940.

Miller, J. Hillis, *Thomas Hardy: Distance and Desire*, Cambridge, Mass., 1970.

Millgate, Michael, *Thomas Hardy, His Career as a Novelist*, Bodley Head, 1971.

Morgan, Charles, *The House of Macmillan*, London, 1943.
Morrell, Ray, *Thomas Hardy, The Will and the Way*, Kuala Lumpur, 1943.
Moule, H. C. G., *Memories of a Vicarage*, 1913.
Nevinson, H. W., *Thomas Hardy*, London, 1941.
Newman, J. and Pevsner, N., *The Buildings of Dorset*, London, 1972.
Orel, Harold (ed.), *Thomas Hardy's Personal Writings*, Kansas, 1966.
Owen, H. and Bell, J., *Letters of Wilfred Owen*, Oxford, 1967.
Phelps, W. L., *Autobiography and Letters*, Oxford, 1939.
Pike, E. Royston, *Human Documents of the Victorian Golden Age*, London, 1969.
Pinion, F. B., *A Hardy Companion*, London, 1968.
Purdy, R. L., *Thomas Hardy: A Bibliographical Study*, Oxford, 1954, repr. 1968.
    "The authorship of Hardy's Biography", TLS, 30 December 1960.
Reports of the British and Foreign School Society.
Rutland, W. R., *Thomas Hardy: A Study of his Writings and their Background*, Oxford,
    1938, New York, 1962.
    Thomas Hardy, London, 1938.
St. Helier, *Memories of 50 Years*, London, 1909.
Scott, Harold, *The Early Doors*, London, 1946.
Smith, S. Nowell (ed.), *Letters to Macmillan*, London, 1967.
Smith, W. Sylvester, *The London Heretics, 1870–1914*, London, 1967.
Southerington, F. R., *Hardy's Vision of Man*, London, 1971.
Stewart, J. I. M., *Thomas Hardy*, London, 1971.
Webb, A. P., *A Bibliography of the Works of Thomas Hardy*, London, 1916.
Weber, Carl J., *Hardy of Wessex*, London, 1940; rev. and repr. 1965.
    (ed.), *"Dearest Emmie"*, London, 1953.
    (ed.), *Hardy at Colby*, Waterville, Maine, 1936; *Hardy and the Lady from Madison
    Square*, Waterville, Maine, 1952.
    (ed.), *The Letters of Thomas Hardy*, Waterville, Maine, 1954.
Webster, H. C., *On a Darkling Plain: The Art and Thought of Thomas Hardy*, Chicago,
    1947.
Williams, Merryn, *Thomas Hardy and Rural England*, London, 1972.
Wreden, W. P., *Books from the Library of Thomas Hardy*, New York, 1938.
Wright, W. F., *The Shaping of "The Dynasts"*. Nebraska, 1967.

D. MAGAZINES, NEWSPAPERS, PERIODICALS
Academy
Athenaeum
Cornhill Magazine
Daily News
Daily Telegraph
Dorset County Chronicle
Dorset Evening Echo
Encounter
Enfield Gazette
Gentleman's Magazine
Illustrated London News
Saturday Review
Spectator
The Sphere
Times Literary Supplement

ACKNOWLEDGEMENT OF QUOTATIONS

Extracts from the novels of Thomas Hardy and from *The Complete Poems of Thomas
Hardy*, The New Wessex Edition, edited by James Gibson, 1976, and *The Dynasts*,
and quotations from *The Life of Thomas Hardy* by Florence Hardy are reprinted by
permission of the Trustees of the Estate of the late Miss E. A. Dugdale; Macmillan,
London and Basingstoke; and the Macmillan Company of Canada Limited.

Index